Wordsworth: A Poet's History

Wordsworth:
A Poet's History

Keith Hanley
Professor of English Literature
Lancaster University

palgrave

First published 2001 by
PALGRAVE
Houndmills, Basingstoke, Hampshire RG21 6XS and
175 Fifth Avenue, New York, N.Y. 10010
Companies and representatives throughout the world

PALGRAVE is the new global academic imprint of
St. Martin's Press LLC Scholarly and Reference Division and
Palgrave Publishers Ltd (formerly Macmillan Press Ltd).

ISBN 0–333–91883–5

This book is printed on paper suitable for recycling and
made from fully managed and sustained forest sources.

A catalogue record for this book is available
from the British Library.

Library of Congress Cataloging-in-Publication Data
Hanley, Keith.
    Wordsworth : a poet's history / Keith Hanley.
        p. cm.
    Includes bibliographical references and index.
    ISBN 0–333–91883–5
    1. Wordsworth, William, 1770–1850—Knowledge—History. 2.
Literature and history—Great Britain—History—19th century. 3. France-
-History—Revolution, 1789–1799—Influence. 4. Wordsworth, William,
1770–1850—Psychology. 5. Poetry—Psychological aspects. 6.
Psychology in literature. 7. Patriotism in literature. 8. History in literature.
I. Title.
    PR5892.H5 H36 2000
    821'.7—dc21
                                                        00–041496

10   9   8   7   6   5   4   3   2   1
10 09 08 07 06 05 04 03 02 01

Printed and bound in Great Britain by
Antony Rowe Ltd, Chippenham, Wiltshire

In memory of
Emma Hanley

Relating simply as my wish hath been
A poet's history

Wordsworth, *The Prelude*

No, life as the eternal continuing of mind and wit does not represent itself to us as a vision of savage greatness and ruthless beauty; we who are set apart and different do not conceive it as, like us, unusual; it is the normal, respectable, and admirable that is the kingdom of our longing: life, in all its seductive banality! That man is far from being an artist, my dear, whose last and deepest enthusiasm is the raffiné, the eccentric and satanic; who does not know the longing for the innocent, the simple, and the living, for a little friendship, devotion, familiar human happiness – the gnawing, surreptitious hankering, Lisabeta, for the bliss of the commonplace.

Thomas Mann, *Tonio Kröger*

Contents

List of Illustrations

List of Abbreviations

For works referred to throughout

BL	*Biographia Literaria*, ed. James Englell and W. Jackson Bate (1984), vol. 7 of *The Collected Works of Samuel Taylor Coleridge*, gen. ed. Kathleen Coburn, Bollingen Series LXXV (London and Princeton, 1969–).
CLL	*Lectures 1808–1819: On Literature*, ed. R. A. Foakes, 2 vols (1987); vol. 5 of the *Collected Works of Samuel Taylor Coleridge*.
DQ	*The Complete Works of Thomas De Quincey*, 3rd edn, ed. David Masson, 16 vols (Edinburgh, 1862–71).
H	*The Complete Works of William Hazlitt*, ed. P. P. Howe, 21 vols (London, 1930–4).
HCRBW	*Henry Crabb Robinson on Books and Their Writers*, ed. Edith J. Morley, 3 vols (London, 1938).
LSTC	*Collected Letters of Samuel Taylor Coleridge*, ed. Earl Leslie Griggs, 6 vols (Oxford and New York, 1956–71).
Memoirs	Christopher Wordsworth, *Memoirs of William Wordsworth*, 2 vols (London, 1851).
Prel	*The Prelude: 1799, 1805, 1850*, ed. Jonathan Wordsworth, M. H. Abrams and Stephen Gill (New York, 1979).
Prose	*The Prose Works of William Wordsworth*, ed. W. J. B. Owen and Jane Worthington Smyser, 3 vols (Oxford, 1974).
PSTC	*The Complete Poetical Works of Samuel Taylor Coleridge*, ed. Ernest Hartley Coleridge, 2 vols (Oxford, 1912).
PW	*The Poetical Works of William Wordsworth*, ed. Ernest de Selincourt and Helen Darbishire, 5 vols (Oxford, 1940–9).
S	*Shakespeare's Dramatic Works; with explanatory notes. A new edition*, ed. S. Ayscough, 3 vols (Dublin, 1790). The copy of vols I and II, bound together, at the Wordsworth Library, Grasmere.
TT	*Table Talk*, ed. Carl Woodring, 2 vols (London and Princeton, 1990); vol. 14 of *The Collected Works of Samuel Taylor Coleridge*.
WL	*The Letters of William and Dorothy Wordsworth*, 2nd edn, gen. ed. Alan G. Hill, 8 vols (Oxford, 1967–93), comprising:

The Early Years, 1787–1805, rev. Chester L. Shaver (1967);
The Middle Years, Pt 1: 1806–1811, rev. Mary Moorman
(1969); *The Middle Years, Pt 2: 1812–20*, rev. Mary Moorman
and Alan G. Hill (1970); *The Later Years, Pt 1: 1821–1828*,
rev. Alan G. Hill (1978); *The Later Years, Pt 2: 1829–1834*,
rev. Alan G. Hill (1979); *The Later Years, Pt 3: 1835–1839*,
rev. Alan G. Hill (1982); *The Later Years, Pt 4: 1840–1853*,
rev. Alan G. Hill (1988); *A Supplement of New Letters*, rev.
Alan G. Hill (1993).

Acknowledgements

Readers of this book may hardly be surprised to learn that it is primarily indebted to my mother. I still hear many passages of English poetry, and especially Wordsworth, which she had by heart, in her rapt voice. Much of the time it has taken I owe to the understanding of my wife, Jadzia, and my children, Timothy and Kitty.

Foremost among those others without whom it could not have been written is Jonathan Wordsworth, not only because of his scholarly and critical example since the days when I attended his unforgettable seminars, assisted by Mary Jacobus, at Oxford, but also for many acts of imaginative generosity over the years. Though he will be anxious not to have influenced my theorizing, I hope he will not disown the contours of a reading that I at least believe in many ways proceeds from his teachings.

When some of the ideas behind this work were gestating through the 1980s, I attended several Wordsworth Summer Schools at Grasmere, where I enjoyed and greatly profited from the company, among others, of Jonathan Bate, Tony Brinkley, Peter Larkin, Tom McFarland, Lucy Newlyn, Nick Roe, Nicky Trott and Duncan Wu. My particular interest in Lacan was deepened by attending the Lacan Seminars organized by the French Department of Manchester University in the mid-1980s, and in the mid-1990s by the discussions I had with John Peacock and Douglas Fraser in the Manchester Centre for Freudian Analysis cartel. My colleagues in the Wordsworth Centre at Lancaster University, Tony Pinkney and Fred Botting, have never failed in their support, and I warmly thank and acknowledge the intellectual stimulus that I gained from the late John Stachniewski and Raman Selden, from Chris Baldick and, most especially, Richard Wilson.

For various acts of help and encouragement I am grateful to the following friends and colleagues: David Carroll, Bill Galperin, Stephen Gill, Roger Holdsworth, Ken Johnston, Greg Kucich, Kevin McLaughlin, Vince Newey, Bernard and Heather O'Donoghue, Peter Swaab, Dick Watson and Michael Wheeler. Jeff Cowton, Librarian of the Wordsworth Library, Grasmere, generously shared his knowledge of Wordsworth's reading with me. Lynne Pearce commented usefully on Chapter 2 and David Carroll on Chapter 5, while Tony Brinkley, whose engagement with my work on Wordsworth has been a long-standing stimulus, has read and reacted to the whole manuscript with characteristic warmth and sensitive insight. Yet, for all the above advantages, I alone, of course, am responsible for the present book.

St Deiniol's Library, Hawarden, granted me a Residential Scholarship, partially supported from the Canon Symonds Fund, to pursue my research on the later Wordsworth in 1994. Some ideas that inform the introduction were broached in a guest paper, 'Wordsworth's Revolution in Poetic Language', for the bicentenary issue of *Romanticism on the Net*, 9, edited by Nicola Trott and Seamus Perry in February 1998; a version of Chapter 1 appeared in the journal *News from Nowhere: Theory and Politics of Romanticism*, edited by Tony Pinkney, Keith Hanley and Fred Botting (Keele, 1995); some material included in Chapter 2 was delivered in a panel on 'Feminists Reading Wordsworth' organized by Laura Haigwood for the Toronto Modern Language Association convention in 1993 and part was also given in a paper read at the British Association for Romantic Studies conference organized by Viv Jones and John Whale at Leeds in 1997; part of Chapter 3 was published in *Wordsworth in Context*, a special issue of the *Bucknell Review*, edited by Pauline Fletcher and John Murphy (Lewisburg, 1992), and is included here with the publisher's permission; some of the ideas from which Chapter 4 developed were shared at a staff seminar I was invited to give in the English Department at Leicester University and were delivered in a paper at the Interdisciplinary Nineteenth-Century Studies conference at the College of William and Mary, Williamsburg, in 1994; and Chapter 5 grew out of lectures I delivered on 'The Electrification of Great Britain' at the invitations of Amitava Roy of the Rabindra Bharati University, Calcutta, and of Martin Zerlang of the Centre for Urbanity and Aesthetics, Copenhagen, in 1995, before they were gathered into a shorter written version published in *Mortal Pages, Literary Lives: Studies in Nineteenth-Century Autobiography*, edited by Vincent Newey and Philip Shaw (Aldershot, 1996), which is included here with permission of Scolar/ Ashgate Press.

I should like to thank the Trustees of Dove Cottage, Grasmere, for permission to quote from manuscript inscriptions made in Wordsworth's copy of Shakespeare's *Dramatic Works* (1790). Figures 1, 2 and 11 are reproduced with permission of the Musée du Louvre, Paris; Figures 5 and 6 by courtesy of Dove Cottage, the Wordsworth Trust, Grasmere; and Figure 10 with permission of the British Museum.

K. H.
The Wordsworth Centre, Lancaster

Introduction: The Secret Histories of 'Wordsworth'

Secret Agents

> *Knowing that Nature never did betray*
> Wordsworth, 'Tintern Abbey'

This book might loosely be seen in the light of current attempts to uncover yet again a clandestine and even scandalous seam in Wordsworth's life and works. Past skeletons – an illegitimate child and desertion (since Legouis's and Harper's investigations), incest (boosted notably by F. W. Bateson), and betrayal, both personal (for those who take Coleridge's part) and political (Browning's 'The Lost Leader' made the liberal case enduringly) – have of course long been familiar presences, but Kenneth Johnston's recent biography, *The Hidden Wordsworth: Poet, Lover, Rebel, Spy*, has reviewed every trace of these and other dark secrets with relentless curiosity, exhuming in the process what may be further ignominy as well as the average sensuality of our 'one human heart'[1] that Wordsworth tends to have neglected, or concealed. Johnston's rigorous researches have prompted him to pursue a host of speculations as to what he sees, or thinks he sees, was really going on behind the poems, but the shadowy details and occasionally shady motivations of lover, rebel and spy do not of themselves begin to account for the operations of poetic composition. The *poet* lies hidden still.

Yet there seem to be undeniable connections to be made with an obscurer, darker side. If a retired captain of a small trading vessel turned amateur sleuth, such as the narrator of 'The Thorn', had taken a ham-fisted interest in the serial deaths and disasters of a large contingent of the Wordsworth entourage over the years, he could hardly have failed to conclude who had stood to gain the most. Such a mind

1

might well cleave obtusely to the nursing of the dying Raisley Calvert (resulting in a £900 bequest), or perhaps to the disappearance of the rival for Mary Wordsworth's affections, Wordsworth's brother John, who went down on *The Earl of Abergavenny*, and most obviously to the poet's scary concern for the protective removal of so many young women and children from the violating 'touch of earthly years' ('A Slumber Did My Spirit Seal', 4). However open to comic distortion, the pattern of capitalizing on and finding a kind of empowerment in the losses of those around him remains suggestive. Each poem in the first edition of *Lyrical Ballads* is, as Charles Burney first observed with only slight exaggeration, 'a tale of woe',[2] and so are 'The Ruined Cottage' and Books VII and VIII of *The Excursion*, 'The Churchyard Among the Mountains', which John Constable complained to his wife are 'sad melancholy stories, and as I think only serve to harry you up without a purpose, it is bad taste' (see Harris, 385). 'Only' certainly sounds unfair, but some resentment is understandable in readers who are presented with painful experiences while finding the consolatory framework either inadequate or incomprehensible, as Wordsworth's would-be disciple, John Wilson, felt about 'The Idiot Boy' while pointing out the tie between perverse taste and immorality: 'The inability to receive pleasure from descriptions such as that of *The Idiot Boy* is, I am convinced, founded upon established feelings of human nature, and the principle of it constitutes, as I daresay you recollect, the leading feature of Smith's theory of moral sentiments' (see Elsie Smith, 57). T. S. Eliot's distinction between 'the man who suffers and the mind which creates' – one that has to be collapsed in the 'perfect...artist' – may seem unusually irrelevant to the eccentric sang-froid of a poet whose principal *alter ego*, the Pedlar / Wanderer's strange power depended on his being able to 'afford to suffer / With them whom he saw suffer',[3] and who grimly acknowledged the affinity of his methods of analysis with acts of killing and sacrilege, describing himself as

> A happy man, and therefore bold to look
> On painful things – slow, somewhat, too and stern
> In temperament – I took the knife in hand,
> And, stopping not at parts less sensitive,
> Endeavoured with my best of skill to probe
> The living body of society
> Even to the heart. I pushed without remorse
> My speculations forward, yea, set foot
> On Nature's holiest places.[4]

Wordsworth's literary stature, his standing apart from and above mere sympathy, is founded on this impersonality which might be thought to enable a more comprehensive vision, a positioning in part outside the standard exchange and circulation of human interactions. A biographical crux was the death of his three-year-old daughter, Catherine, in 1812. While De Quincey reacted with extravagant demonstrations of grief, Wordsworth 'sustained the shock', as his sister-in-law, Susanna, reported, with 'dignified, yet acute sensibility', and a rare 'constitutional philosophy' which pervaded the whole family. (See Overton and Elizabeth Wordsworth, 9). It is precisely the role specified by Coleridge for the Recluse, 'the great philosophical poet' of the age, whom he willed Wordsworth to become: 'it seems to me that he ought never to have abandoned the contemplative position which is peculiarly – perhaps I might say exclusively – fitted for him. His proper title is *Spectator ab extra.*'[5] Yet Coleridge was deeply ambivalent about the peculiar talent for converting suffering into strength which he knew Wordsworth possessed but which he himself found unlikeable: 'Although Wordsworth and Goethe are not much alike, to be sure, upon the whole; yet they have this peculiarity of utter non-sympathy with the subjects of their poetry. They are always, both of them, spectators *ab extra*, – feeling *for*, but never *with*, their characters' (*TT* II 200). Nonetheless, he censured Wordsworth for failing to achieve the uncompromising detachment required in the only part of the grand work which he did complete, *The Excursion*: 'Can dialogues in verse be defended? . . . I have no admiration for the practice of ventriloquizing through another man's mouth' (*TT* I 307). Wordsworth himself, who notoriously failed to deliver the project, came to emphasize that his kind of creative security was more domesticated than aloof when he coupled Coleridge's lack of his own kind of contentedness to the latter's failure as a poet: 'Poor dear Coleridge's constant infelicity . . . prevented him from being the poet that Nature had given him the power to be. He had always too much personal and domestic discontent to paint the sorrows of mankind. He could not afford to suffer with those whom he saw suffer.'[6]

For Ruskin, too, in *Modern Painters* Wordsworth's power of controlling while expressing strong feelings is impressive, though it falls short of Dante's supreme quality of equanimity: 'Therefore the high creative poet might even be thought, to a great extent, impassive . . . receiving indeed all feelings to the full, but having a great centre of reflexion and knowledge in which he stands serene, and watches the feeling, as it were, from afar off.'[7] Indeed, Ruskin ended up by ridiculing Wordsworth for the absurd parochialism that insisted on deriving its pretended overview from the local and private.[8] Wordsworth's limitation, it was suggested, came from his inability to appreciate the disjuncture between the narrow range of his informing experience and the cultural languages which he could not make it convincingly match. In the event, there was to be no authoritative 'system of philosophy' for Wordsworth of the kind that Coleridge claimed they had 'agreed on' and on the strength of which the Recluse was to 'assume the station of a man in repose, whose mind was made up' in order to reveal 'a redemptive process in operation – showing how this Idea reconciled all the anomalies, and how it promised future glory and restoration' (*TT* I 307–8).[9] Though the Wordsworthian imagination did find expression in the myth of the 'happy fall' throughout *The Prelude*, together with the narrative of political 'restoration' after the French Revolution, the underlying paradigm of fulfilment through loss and conflict remains more preoccupied with achieving its distinctive claim to such resonances than in articulating any culminating and original vehicle of its own, a Divine Comedy or Paradise Lost and Regained. All the shifts and instabilities of Wordsworth's world-view, however, are guided by an irreducible kernel of power and conviction. At various times, of course, he espouses contradictory political positionings across the spectrum from left to right, and affirms a set of varying religious creeds swerving from semi-atheism to Anglo-Catholicism. They are all to a large extent provisional instruments of 'something far more deeply interfused' ('Tintern Abbey', 97), and, like the message which he sends to cheer 'the most unhappy Man of Men', the imprisoned Haitian freedom fighter, they mark the radically unspecifiable promptings of an 'unconquerable mind', its 'exultations, agonies, / And love' ('To Toussaint L'Ouverture', 13–14), that under changing conditions can and do become formulated in disconcertingly diverse terms.

Patently, the deeper agenda of Wordsworth's apparent detachment, which tended to filter his whole-hearted engagement in the instinctive emotions of others and which resulted in some ideological slipperiness, what Coleridge called his 'malice prepense' (*Crabb Robinson's Diary* I 159), represented an alternative preoccupation that was bent on the production of poetic language. David Bromwich, in his *Disowned By Memory: Wordsworth's Poetry of the 1790s*, is more interested than Johnston in the constructive occlusions of Wordsworth's revolutionary crimes accomplished by, as he writes in the introduction, 'a criminal seeking expiation' (1) (Haydon's 'The Brigand' portrait faces the title page), though he too dwells on a poet who is 'a good deal like' his 'murderous men', and does not flinch from painting an unusually 'disagreeable'

(126) image of, for example, a terrorist (in *The Borderers*) and a wife and child deserter (in 'Tintern Abbey'). I am, however, encouraged by Bromwich's understanding of Wordsworth's motivating sense of transgression in viewing the poetry, however indirectly the result of guilt and sorrow it may be, as in effect the record of the exertion of an unusual kind of control rather than simple evasion, or the machinations of concealment or denial. Yet something *has* undoubtedly gone missing within the process of creation. Matthew Arnold famously found the poetry deficient in tragic awareness: 'But Wordsworth's eyes avert their ken / From half of human fate',[10] and one recurrent reaction to the later poems especially has been that of David Masson, writing four months after the poet's death, who found them sadly lacking in 'energy, fire, impulse, intensity, passion' (386).[11] They are the work of a writer who remained characteristically resistant to 'that dark side of nature which is recognized in theological doctrines of corruption, or in the scientific theories about the fierce struggle for existence' that Leslie Stephen felt the want of, and such comments are part of an entrenched tradition of response that regards the absences described as odd and distinctive, in the way Arnold again celebrated on Wordsworth's death in the 'Memorial Verses': 'The cloud of mortal destiny, / Others will front it fearlessly – / But who, like him, will put it by?' (68–70)

It is on the veiled operations of this *putting by* that the present book reflects. The phrase recalls Wordsworth's effort to summon up the unexpected 'Soul's immensity' (110) of the child in the Intimations Ode: 'Thou, over whom thy Immortality / Broods like the Day, a Master o'er a Slave, / A Presence which is not to be put by' (119–21). In the transmission, that which cannot be put by is able to put by that which threatens to subdue it: in Wordsworth's poem, 'The Clouds that gather round the setting sun' (196). Arnold stresses an effortless and somehow blessedly pre-programmed power of rendering the menace irrelevant, recalling the inbuilt, redemptive scheme for *The Recluse*, but the power Wordsworth describes is more unopposable, and demands continuity by versatility. Its mastery is sustained by consciously switching from the 'time when' (1) of a state that preceded his entering cultural being, 'the primal sympathy' (182), to the retention of 'What was so fugitive' (133), the insistence that it 'must ever be' (183) within the 'habitual sway' (192) of what 'the philosophic mind' has slowly concluded from 'the soothing thoughts that spring / Out of human suffering' (184–5). The claim is for more than simply getting used to the facts of loss and death: it is also for the cultural work which they enable of making something valuable out of them.

Wordsworth's *putting by* is both passive and active. It started to realize itself in poetry as a state providentially given, emerging from 'conversation' poems in which the effect was brought about by a mute other, like the 'secret ministry' of Coleridge's frost at midnight, silently and inexorably working towards its own enunciation and the achieved rigidity of completion, 'Quietly shining to the quiet Moon'.[12] But it ended up having to negotiate its social and cultural representation, and crucial to this transition was the exemplary control of mediation itself, which revealed itself in the course of composing his account of crossing the Alps in Book VI of *The Prelude*, when he came up against his own theory of the poetic imagination:

> Imagination! – lifting up itself
> Before the eye and progress of my song
> Like an unfathered vapour, here that power,
> In all the might of its endowments, came
> Athwart me. I was lost as in a cloud,
> Halted without a struggle to break through,
> And now, recovering, to my soul I say
> 'I recognise thy glory'.
>
> (525–32)

The recognition involved is of the power to effect the conversion of a past 'glory' ('Intimations', 5) into poetic language, of the necessity of its loss within the creative design that is thereby able to obscure it once more 'in the access of joy / Which hides it like the overflowing Nile' (547–8).[13] Brought to fuller consciousness here, 'blest in thoughts / That are their own perfection and reward' (545–6), was the immanent self-reflexivity in all the poetry related to *The Prelude*: the realization that it was always fundamentally about its own genesis. And yet that renewed celebration of restored glory was also to pass away.

Overall, Wordsworth's career was characterized by an increasing will to conform, to assume the orthodox and conventional in thought and expression. It was the extension of his consistently extraordinary concern to appear ordinary, constraining 'the startling yet undramatic... originality' of Geoffrey Hartman's 'unremarkable Wordsworth'.[14] His passion to be acknowledged as an exceptionally representative figure, 'a man speaking to men'[15] about 'nothing more than what we are' ('Prospectus' to *The Recluse*, 59) and 'differing in kind from other men, but only in degree' (Preface to *Lyrical Ballads*, I 142), comes close to the motivation of all his schemes. Every poem by Wordsworth sets out to resolve, or at least bears the traces of, a related inner history, whose quietly regulating influence transforms very different landscapes and weathers through a series of religious and political changes – changes which turn out in effect to be subsidiary to its radical purpose of communal representation.[16] In the Preface to *Lyrical Ballads*, Wordsworth theorized a common language as the aim of modern poetry: 'But Poets do not write for Poets alone, but for men...the Poet...must express himself as other men express themselves' (I 143). Yet, as Coleridge observed of Wordsworth's stylistic signature in Chapter 20 of *Biographia Literaria*, the trial led inevitably to linguistic idiosyncrasy: 'To me it will always remain a singular and noticeable fact; that a theory which would establish this *lingua communis*, not only as the best, but as the only commendable style, should have proceeded from a poet, whose diction, next to that of Shakespeare and Milton, appears to me of all others the most *individualized* and characteristic' (*BL* II 99). The paradox sprang from Wordsworth's singular self-consciousness in his relation to language. Coleridge's comments on *An Evening Walk* and *Descriptive Sketches* show, perhaps with gathered hindsight, that he had understood some of the difference Wordsworth registered from the start: 'seldom, if ever, was the emergence of an original poetic genius above the literary horizon more evidently announced', even in the 'harshness and acerbity' of the style of the second poem (*BL* I 77). Most obviously that difference produced the take-it-or-leave-it experimentation with 'the language of conversation in the middle and lower classes of society' that led to readers' 'feelings of strangeness and aukwardness' (Advertisement to *Lyrical Ballads*, I 116), but Wordsworth also had another underlying conviction that 'the Poet's art' was 'a homage paid...to the grand elementary principle of pleasure, by which he knows, and feels, and lives, and moves', and he significantly defended metre as the epitome of poetic pleasure in representing 'the sense of difficulty overcome' (Preface to *Lyrical Ballads* I 140, 150). Wordsworth became increasingly self-aware about his own peculiar strength having to do with his difficulty in finding satisfactory expression, as in *The Prelude* he described 'The glory of [his] youth' (III 171) being 'far hidden from the reach of words' (185): 'Points have we all of us within our souls / Where all stand single; this I feel, and make / Breathings for incommunicable powers' (186–8). Yet, as a poet, Wordsworth was compelled to overcome as well as scrutinize his predicament.

   Coleridge had wanted the 'principles' of his Recluse 'made up' so as to empower the originality of the language in which they were to be communicated. But Wordsworth's characteristic problem with language was preoccupied rather with the *making up* of his mind, though that concern was in some measure resolved by the upshot of another, parallel history – his urgent experience of personal and political loss and failure in the course of the French Revolution – which had begun to activate the paradigm of restoration through poetic language, from the mid 1790s onwards. Writing through the history of the revolution operated as an enabling resistance for the articulation of the full scheme of imaginative power and was brought conclusively to consciousness in Books X and XI of *The Prelude*, 'Residence in France and the French Revolution' and 'Imagination, How Impaired and Restored'. As long as these secret histories of language and events were intertwined in this way (while, that is, Wordsworth's struggle for self-expression and political representation were coterminous), his individualizing relation to language itself remained immanent in the poetry. But once the historical error and personal transgression of revolution had been effectively contained within his evolving poetic language, the more prosaic passage into social and cultural influence began to preside. When as a result of realizing this symmetry *The Prelude* was finished, and Wordsworth's mind was 'made up' for making an assured public intervention in the *Recluse* project, his poetic language more and more became a professional discourse operating within the web of cultural empowerments. The history of his poetry's private genesis was effaced in the way some remarks of Coleridge to Lady Beaumont describe:

> As proofs meet me in every part of the Excursion, that the Poet's genius has not flagged, I have sometimes fancied that having by the conjoint operation of his own experiences, feelings, and reason *himself* convinced *himself* of Truths, which the generality of persons have either taken for granted from their Infancy, or at least adopted early in life, he has attached all their own depth and weight to doctrines and words, which come almost as Truisms or Common-place to others.   (*LSTC* IV 564)

Coleridge's insight, which might equally apply to the cognate structure of Wordsworthian bathos in the ballads, points up the continuities between the separate histories of Wordsworth's private relation to poetic language and the social discourse of writing poetry that do or do not appear to inform his poetry at different times, and that, though they are indeed distinct, do have their secrecy of motivation in common – psychological and discursive – to obfuscate the shift in predominance from one to another. What was so regularly received as the puzzling inconsequentiality of poems like 'Simon Lee' or 'We Are Seven', for example, had an intimate significance for the poet that was still imbricated with the discourses of state and national church in the later poetry. Those discourses found representation in his poetry after *The Prelude* with what *for him* was the hidden power of their passage through *The Prelude* to both linguistic and discursive restoration.

Wordsworth's efforts at consistency were awesome, and they dictated an 'obsessive'[17] urge to revise his poetry that was interested, impossibly, in substituting a completeness of expression for the lost questing after poetic language that had animated his former compositions. The route for this alternative quest was laid out in 'Ode to Duty', where Wordsworth spelled out his need for a 'Stern Lawgiver' (49): 'I supplicate for thy controul; / . . . / My hopes no more must change their name, / I long for a repose which ever is the same' (35, 39–40). Though the submission to moral discourse marked an enormous achievement in self-regulation and communal responsibility, it did not help him to achieve an original poetic language. Rather, it tended to deny precisely that risky engagement with failing and transgression which had generated his distinctive kind of poetic power, and his inability successfully to effect the transition from a restlessly self-reflexive language to one of explicit declaration, according to the Coleridgean recipe, 'prepared to deliver upon authority a system of philosophy' (*TT* I 307), brought about the dilemma that resulted in his failure to produce *The Recluse*.

Wordsworth was to write four poems towards Coleridge's project, but the only sustained attempt on it was the extended fragment of Book I of *The Recluse*, 'Home at Grasmere', where he muses on the enigmatic connection between his individual gift and his desire to communicate it:

> Of ill-advised Ambition and of Pride
> I would stand clear, yet unto me I feel
> That an internal brightness is vouchsafed
> That must not die, that must not pass away.
> Why does this inward lustre fondly seek
> And gladly blend with outward fellowship?
> Why do *they* shine around me whom I love?
> Why do they teach me whom I thus revere?
> Strange question, yet it answers not itself.
> (673–81)

His most private feelings could be declared most effectively within the restricted circle of those who would reliably share them, like his 'Strange fits of passion': 'And I will dare to tell, / But in the Lover's ear alone, / What once to me befell' (2–4). This is the community of feeling addressed above all in the Poems on the Naming of Places, where a private family code is invented – 'Emma's Dell', 'Joanna's Rock', 'Mary's Nook', and so on – whose meaning largely depends on its exclusivity, but when Wordsworth solicited the same response outside the field of assured reciprocity, which could be safely extended, for example, to his young devotee, John Wilson, whom he praised for having gratifyingly 'entered into the spirit' (*WL* I 353) of his poetry, he was liable to be met with incomprehension. He was particularly stung by the waywardness of one of the inner circle, Sara Hutchinson, who could not gather the significance of 'Resolution and Independence': 'everything is tedious when one does not read with the feelings of the Author' (*WL* I 367). But in order to fulfil the demands of *The Recluse* he realized that he had to bridge isolation and a broad cultural reception: he had both to accept the solitariness of a singular gift *and* determine to create a medium through which it could be transmitted:

> Possessions have I that are solely mine,
> Something within which yet is shared by none,
> Not even the nearest to me and most dear,
> Something which power and effort may impart.
> I would impart it, I would spread it wide,
> Immortal in the world which is to come.
>
> (686–91)

Yet this ambition was never to be actualized. Once the difficulties with communicating which constituted his originality were more or less removed by his espousal of languages of power, his writing for those who had formerly recognized his gift was in danger of descending into unredeemed banality.

If Johnston is right, and Wordsworth's turning of political coats did result in what has been presented as the latest scandal about 'the hidden poet' – his possible recruitment in the later 1790s for an espionage network run by the Duke of Portland, Home Secretary under Pitt – it would be most revealing of his writing to enquire finally what would really have been in it, apart from nearly £100, for the poet whose vicar attested to his striking 'willingness to discuss all subjects on first principles',[18] who claimed plausibly to his former co-revolutionary, James Losh, '*you* have been deluded by *Places* and *Persons*, while I have stuck to *Principles*' (*WL* IV 97), and whom his collaborator, Coleridge, chose to epitomize by his 'Unity of Interest, & that Homogeneity of character which is the natural consequence of it' (*LSTC* II 1033). Throughout all his switchings of allegiance, whether or not Wordsworth was a spy, the secret agents that turned Wordsworth from side to side represented the community he was continuingly trying to define in order to join, from the time he began to outline a considered position for his proposed political journalism to William Matthews: 'There is a further duty incumbent upon every enlightened friend of mankind; he should let slip no opportunity of explaining and enforcing those general principles of the social order which are applicable to all times and all places' (see Roe, 278). If that elusive community had formerly seemed to be revolutionary France and was then becoming a plausible if idealized construction of Great Britain, from Wordsworth's viewpoint they were at different times the social and political expressions of those same founding relations with the outer world on which his problematic acquisition of language had been, after resistance, happily negotiated. The 'natural consequence' of this constancy was both spontaneous and highly regulated, a character interested above all in homogenizing both modes:

> Yet not the less would I throughout
> Still act according to the voice
> Of my own wish; and feel past doubt
> That my submissiveness was choice.
> ('Ode to Duty', 41–4)

Reviewing his engagement in the Anglo-French radical tradition in *The Prelude*, he tells how he had come to feel

> betrayed
> By present objects, and by reasonings false
> From the beginning, inasmuch as drawn
> Out of a heart which had been turned aside
> From Nature by external accidents.
> (X 882–6)

The sign for the desired continuity was always 'nature', preceding language and then constructed within the cultural domain in literary and social discourses of inevitable power. As Wordsworth, who as one of the 'Prophets of Nature' offered *The Prelude* as a work of social 'redemption' (XIII 442, 441), assured his sister about his past and her future, 'Nature never did betray / The heart that loved her' ('Tintern Abbey', 123–4).

The present study is an attempt to decipher and regain the pattern of secret histories that produced the specific language of Wordsworth's poems at different times and their cultural and social effects, or 'Wordsworth'. Accordingly it is rooted in the literary textuality of the poems which are quoted, and requoted, throughout. My readings are informed by the shapings of some Marxist and Freudian analyses of the ideological unconscious and the personalizing work of sublimation and transference that have been tracked in several preceding works, though the leading frames in my narration of the poet's psychobiography and its historical contextualization are taken from structuralist and poststructuralist theory.[19] In particular, the book relies on and intends marginally to contribute to both theories of the psychonanalysis of language after Lacan and of discursive formation derived from Foucault in proposing shifting connections between both the singularity and the historical representativeness of 'Wordsworth'.[20] But because my engagement with these cultural theorists aims at more than application and hopes to interest general readers and critics of Romanticism, I explain my own understanding of their terms and ideas and the ways I have found they elucidate Wordsworth's textuality as I go along. In the course of Wordsworth's long and posthumous career, the secret agencies were at times interwoven and at times unravelled into three separate histories, though I argue that the first predominated throughout.

The Case History: 'Wordsworth' the Poem

> *A certificate tells me that I was born. But I repudiate this certificate. For I am not a poet, but a poem. A poem that is being written, even if it looks like a subject.*
>
> Lacan, Preface to *Four Fundamental Concepts*

In the opening two chapters, I re-examine issues embedded in the psychoanalytic tradition of Wordsworth criticism in the light of Lacanian reframings. Richard Onorato's classic Freudian reading viewed Wordsworth as 'fixated to a trauma, obsessed by a vital relationship with Nature which has come to stand unconsciously for the lost mother' (64), who died when Wordsworth was seven years old, and Barbara Schapiro's Kleinian critique argued that rather than seeking to recapture the lost mother, the resolution of an earlier infantile trauma lay rather in the attempt 'to fortify the self in relation to her' (see Hanley, 1995, 214), emphasizing the destructive and aggressive feelings towards the parent imagos from which the need to make reparation comes. Strands of these psychoanalytic schemas of restitution and restoration extend into my application of Lacan's retelling of the Oedipus story in terms of the infant's language acquisition to Wordsworth's primary case history, as indeed they extend into Lacanian theory itself.

According to the later psycholinguistic narrative, the trauma of mother-separation at Wordsworth's mother's death may be viewed as only the first, though most formative of a series of traumas that in effect rehearsed the primary trauma of his entry into the 'symbolic order' of language and culture in infancy.[21] If the original sin was the appropriation of the phallus of language, the seizing of the 'word of the father', then the memory of the disruption and renunciation of the bond with the mother that it also entailed was crucially reawakened by the subsequent literal loss of the mother which, because it so rudely reminded him of the shock of self-division, thereafter complicated his relation to the passage into language that had already taken place some six years previously. From that time on, Wordsworth became interested in so regulating his relation to language that he could both reaccentuate his original attachment to the mother and yet be saved from foreclosure, the failure of subjectivity that denying his subsequent identification with the father would bring about. This silent insistency is the theme of Chapter 1, 'The Spectral Mother'.

The subject position which was repeatedly called upon to sustain the equilibrium of these conflicted interests dates back to what Lacan calls the 'mirror stage', when from the age of six to eighteen months what is to become the subject, which was previously pure unrestrained life instinct, begins to form as the 'imaginary ego' becomes a self-awareness produced as a mirror image. The imaginary ego is represented either by a literal reflection or by the so-called '"specular" recognition of its existence as a "you" by the attending parents',[22] when, in a moment of jubilant self-recognition, the infant has gone beyond the simple reflection of the mother's gaze to identify with an image of its bodily wholeness. In this way the illusion is produced of a unified ego that continues as an ideal throughout life and that informs the life-long quest of the ego to provide the subject with a sense of permanence and stability.

Proceeding from the imaginary order of the mirror stage will come the birth of the subject with the acquisition of language and the passage into the symbolic order, or the domain of the father. Though the imaginary ego initiates that series of dialectical identifications that will eventually constitute the subject of language, it nevertheless precedes the entry into language, the moment of primary repression, which will inaugurate the speaking subject and split it forever from the unconscious subject. A successful Oedipal resolution, involving the taking possession of the phallus of language, admits the child into the symbolic order of language and cultural practice. The subject so inscribed, however, will always seek, impossibly, to heal its symbolic castration and to replenish the lack of the undifferentiated fullness that preceded the mirror stage which, from within the symbolic system, Lacan can only call 'the real'.

In denying the loss of the original object of his desire – the mother – Wordsworth is also necessarily interested in denying the ambiguous *désir de la mère*, which entails the simultaneous desire to have been the object of the mother's desire. The metaphorical substitution for this desire, which takes the form of the phallus of language, implies an acknowledgement of the specific loss of the mother which his own re-experience made him particularly unwilling to accept. Though the dyadic structure of the imaginary has already introduced an image of self-alienation, it nevertheless precedes an inscription in the domain that is boundaried by the *nom du père* (the name and the prohibitive '*non*' of the father, since it and '*nom*' are homonyms in French), and so can operate in an illusory way as a metonymic substitution for a retained maternal relation, that hangs back from an inscription in the symbolic order, even after it has in fact entered upon it. The steady recall of the mirror stage over time is immanent in Wordsworth's fascination with images of perfect reflection in which the structure of the imaginary ego as the first other, but not yet completely divided subject is represented. He, for example, came to feel most at home enclosed in the Vale of Grasmere, which, with its mountains duplicated in the lake, presented him with the constant image of the imaginary order, where the infant confuses image and reality in the way Wordsworth describes in 'Home at Grasmere': 'all along the shore / The boundary lost, the line invisible / That parts the image from reality' (575–7).[23]

It was the arrest of the mirror stage, its representation of the border between uninterrupted being and the intimation of irreversible self-alienation, that recurrently insisted through Wordworth's various experience of fragmentation. The infant's dawning vision of the world could be recalled as a configuration extending out from its own image into the circumambient space, simulating a pleasurable sensation of 'spreading', of unopposed and potentially universal oneness, that even harked back to his pre-imaginary condition: 'a sense sublime / Of something far more deeply interfused, / Whose dwelling is the light of setting suns, / And the round ocean, and the living air, / And the blue sky, and in the mind of man' ('Tintern Abbey', 96–100). On the other hand, it carried also the inescapable awareness of another, decentred subjectivity, beyond the fringes of the consciousness-perception system, and disconcertingly occupying 'the place of the Other' and of the Other's desire which was not subject to the agency of the ego and existed only as represented in language. An inkling of such a topography was aroused particularly in moments of physical disorientation, when habitual positioning was upset by exceptional shifts of perspective, as in the course of unusual physical activities described in *The Prelude*, like rowing, rock-climbing, or speed-skating: 'while the distant hills / Into the tumult sent an alien sound / Of melancholy, not unnoticed' (I 469–71).

The crucial reaffirmation of the imaginary is conveyed in the heightened awareness of the 'Blessed the infant babe' passage from the 1799 and subsequent *Preludes* which approaches the clarity of theory. It describes the role of a prelinguistic mother–infant bond in the primary self-recognition of the baby, 'who, when his soul / Claims manifest kindred with an earthly soul, / Doth gather passion from his mother's eye' (*1799*, Pt II 271–3), and the related perception of *gestalts* in first experiencing the outer world:

> hence his mind,
> Even in the first trial of its powers,
> Is prompt and watchful, eager to combine
> In one appearance all the elements
> And parts of the same object, else detached
> And loth to coalesce.
>
> (275–80)

The infant, 'Subjected to the discipline of love' (281), is seen as enlarging its relation with the mother as the foundation of all its relations with objects of observation: 'his mind spreads, / Tenacious of the forms which it receives' (283–4). A maternal presence umbilically invests the phenomenalism from which all coherent knowledge appears to proceed:

> In one beloved presence – nay and more,
> In that most apprehensive habitude
> And those sensations which have been derived
> From this beloved presence – there exists
> A virtue which irradiates and exalts
> All objects through all intercourse of sense.
> No outcast he, bewildered and depressed;

> Along his infant veins are interfused
> The gravitation and the filial bond
> Of Nature that connect him with the world.
>
> (285–94)

Because the reflective relation breaks down the division between self and other, the locus of agency is problematized, and its operations are felt to correspond with those it sees happening everywhere:

> Emphatically such a being lives,
> An inmate of this active universe.
>
> . . .
>
> his mind,
> Even as an agent of the one great mind,
> Creates, creator and receiver both,
> Working but in alliance with the works
> Which it beholds.
>
> (295–6, 301–5)

Wordsworth understands that the subject position he is describing is unusually powerful in his own case, and I am arguing that it had indeed been reinforced by returning at his urgent need, first when his mother died in childhood. When Wordsworth came to write this passage, however, he considered it explicitly as represented by poetry:

> Such, verily, is the first
> Poetic spirit of our human life –
> By uniform control of after years
> In most abated and suppressed, in some
> Through every change of growth or of decay
> Preeminent till death.
>
> (305–10)

The attractiveness of literary representations of a longed-for undivision of subjectivity had formatively appeared in his boyhood reading. It offered an uncensored economy of wish-fulfilment that apparently elided Oedipal conflict, even to seeming virtually unmediated. The inner eye/I, for example (a homonymous slide that would always tend to sustain the imaginary quality of the visible world, bringing the objects of sight into relation with a recessive subjectivity), invested all its dealings with an imperturbable 'ideal grace' (V 479) that derived from the

kind of literary fantasy evoked in the *Prelude* description of the body of
the schoolmaster, drowned in Esthwaite soon after Wordsworth first
moved to Hawkshead:

> no vulgar fear,
> Young as I was, a child not nine years old,
> Possessed me, for my inner eye had seen
> Such sights before among the shining streams
> Of Fairyland, the forests of romance.
>
> (473–7)

In the same book, Wordsworth hints at how in his irksomely dependent and dispossessed childhood he was able to deny the socially constructed self he resented by authorizing an alternative self-assertiveness
in fairy-tale fantasies of invulnerability, revenge, and the redistribution
of wealth to which he felt entitled:

> Oh, give us once again the wishing-cap
> Of Fortunatus, and the invisible coat
> Of Jack the Giant-killer, Robin Hood,
> And Sabra in the forest with St. George!
> The child whose love is here, at least doth reap
> One precious gain – that he forgets himself.
>
> (364–9)

Jack the Giant-Killer – the Oedipal rebel – is a critical identification. In
Book VII of *The Prelude* he is struck by the word 'invisible', used in a
pantomime at Sadler's Wells, which he sees as an example of compliant
credulity, 'How willingly we travel, and how far' (301). What is being
accepted is a willing complicity in the deeper Oedipal plot of a representation that denies while it declares its hostile presence:

> To have, for instance, brought upon the scene
> The champion, Jack the Giant-killer: lo,
> He dons his coat of darkness, on the stage
> Walks, and atchieves his wonders, from the eye
> Of living mortal safe...
>   ...
> How is it wrought? – his garb is black, the word
> INVISIBLE flames forth upon his chest.
>
> (302–6, 309–10)

After his mother's death, the next serious trauma came with that of his father when Wordsworth was thirteen. Though it was an event steeped in Oedipal guilt, it nonetheless resulted in an obscure empowering as a consequence of the domain of the father having for many years been subdued by the predominating relation with the mother. The literal loss of his father, while it led him to acknowledge and feel remorse over a contest for power in his paternal identification, nonetheless enabled him to celebrate an indirect licensing that alleviated his guilt regarding the earlier infantile breach of the maternal relation in acquiring the word of the father. In Chapter 2, 'The Elided Father', I examine Wordsworth's account of his father's death and its involvement in the initiation into poethood in 'The Vale of Esthwaite', the fragmentary juvenile poem that he had drafted by the time he left school in 1787. That work is itself the uneasy product of his struggle to represent the maternal relation within the domain of the father, his mother tongue, a compromise he found especially feasible within the feminized registers of contemporary poetry, featuring the sensibility and sentimental melancholy which his educational father-figures at Hawkshead Grammar School had encouraged him to emulate in early youth.

Throughout his life and writing Wordsworth asserted that 'Still glides the Stream, and shall for ever glide' ('After-Thought', *The River Duddon*, 5) and that he derived 'Strength from what remains behind' ('Immortality Ode', 181), from the years stretching out of his infancy up to the repositioning in his eighth year. Speculations about this period depend heavily on his own accounts, written between his late twenties and early thirties, at a time when later insistencies of the imaginary order in response to the trauma of his revolutionary experiences had led to his invention of the Wordsworthian myth of childhood that could be insulated within maturity, and even ambiguously prolonged into fathering the man. The crucial re-insistence came with the call simultaneously to write 'the FIRST GENUINE PHILOSOPHIC POEM' (*BL* II 156) *and* to contain the trauma of his revolutionary self-knowledge – that is, both to confront and to play down his linguistic self-consciousness. In these years, the axis with the remote foundation of his overdetermined subjectivity was strongly reactivated:

> A tranquilllizing spirit presses now
> On my corporeal frame, so wide appears
> The vacancy between me and those days,
> Which yet have such self-presence in my mind
> That sometimes when I think of them I seem

Two consciousnesses – conscious of myself,
And of some other being.

(*Prel* II 27–33)

Because it was repeatedly probed in this way, in order to protract it, the exact borderland of Wordsworth's passage into subjectivity is fudged. When, for example, he writes in *The Prelude* of the 'isthmus which we cross / In progress from our native continent / To earth and human life', he is no longer referring to early childhood but to the period of his early youth which is still considered a 'tract' of that 'same isthmus' (V, 560–2), though it is a time when 'words themselves / Move us with conscious pleasure' (568). Still, when that condition had been revolutionized, he looked back for assured continuity to the exceptional positioning which his orphanings had confirmed – that first represented as the Pedlar's childhood and adolescence which he himself owns in *The Prelude*: 'I had a world about me – 'twas my own, / I made it; for it only lived to me, / And to the God who looked into my mind' (III 142–4), and that of the 'under-soul' (540) which had accompanied him from the Lakes to Cambridge, however temporarily 'Hushed' (539).

Yet this protective shell also impeded the self-expression that Wordsworth increasingly craved in adolescence. Its narcissism harboured the seeds of frustrating intensity that could not completely deliver itself into otherness. Lacan writes of the mirror stage as the source of the ego's power as well as its coherence. For Lacan, the narcissistic formation of the ideal ego has to lead into the symbolic function of organizing relations with the world outside according to the ego-ideal.[24] But Wordsworth describes this mounting will to educe a purely visual syntax as having become desperate and restrictive:

I had an eye
Which in my strongest workings evermore
Was looking for the shades of difference
As they lie hid in all exterior forms,
Near or remote, minute or vast – an eye
Which from a stone, a tree, a withered leaf,
To the broad ocean and the azure heavens
Spangled with kindred multitudes of stars,
Could find no surface where its power might sleep,
Which spake perpetual logic to my soul,
And by an unrelenting agency

Did bind my feelings even as in a chain.

(Prel III 156–67)

It is the same condition in which he first visited the banks of the Wye, when he was still driven by evasion, 'more like a man / Flying from something that he dreads, than one / Who sought the thing he loved' ('Tintern Abbey', 71–3), and natural sights:

> Their colours and their forms, were then to [him]
> An appetite: a feeling and a love,
> That had no need of a remoter charm,
> By thought supplied, or any interest
> Unborrowed from the eye.
>
> (80–4)

Wordsworth never did break from the structure of self-reflection, though the captivation it implied was clearly dangerous for an intending professional who could not remain 'A *silent* Poet' ('When, to the attractions of the busy world', 80) as he described his brother John. The fragmentary draft (intended for *The Prelude* but included finally in Book IX of *The Excursion*), 'Whether the whistling kite', contains his most fixated reduplication: the 'snow-white ram' with its reflection of 'Another and the same' (*Prel*, 506: 19–20). Metonymically, it is a startling image of maternalized virility, and the mesmerizing moderation of power is sustained throughout. The 'mountain's voice' (7) is, after all, that of a bleating lamb, and it is where 'A mountain torrent...was becalmed' (16) that, he writes,

> at a glance I saw
> A two-fold image; on the grassy bank
> A snow-white ram and in the peaceful flood
> Another and the same. Most beautiful
> The breathing creature was, as beautiful
> Beneath him with his shadowy counterpart;
> Each had his glowing mountains, each his sky,
> And each seemed centre of his own fair world.
>
> (17–24)

The fragment ends with a restrained impulse to disrupt the fixation: 'A stray temptation seized me to dissolve / The vision, but I could not, and the stone / Snatched up for that intent dropped from my hand' (25–7). The moment is paradigmatic of Wordsworth's predicament, on the cusp of the heterogeneity of subjectification in language but held back from passage. It indicates the irksomeness for the choosing subject of a position in which, as Lacan says, 'his mother is constantly on his back,' because 'there is no possibility of lack'[25] without which the child will never accept his submission to linguistic substitution. Yet the alternative choice was painfully retraumatizing, especially when Coleridge's summons repeatedly came for him to make a notable entry into the cultural domain.[26] The most successful outlet from his struggle to find a compromise expression in 'nature and the language of the sense' ('Tintern Abbey', 109) was to be the self-referential language of *The Prelude*, the poem that began 'was it for this . . . ?' and proceeded to establish the emphatic imaginary register of the poetic discourse of 'Wordsworth' as constituting itself by constantly problematizing and locating its own origins and authority. In the 1802 Preface to *Lyrical Ballads*, Wordsworth could already reaffirm that the poet 'considers man and nature as essentially adapted to each other, and the mind of man as naturally the mirror of the fairest and most interesting qualities of nature' (I 140); but in the course of completing *The Prelude* it was to become more apparent how that correspondence itself represented the foundational self-reflexivity within his poetry that became fully articulated in the language of the Simplon Pass in Book VI ('like workings of one mind, the feature / Of the same face', 568–9) and the description of the imaginative 'power' (84) displayed in the panorama beheld on the Ascent of Snowdon in Book XIII:

> a genuine counterpart
> And brother of the glorious faculty
> Which higher minds bear with them as their own.
> . . .
> They from their native selves can send abroad
> Like transformation, for themselves create
> A like existence, and, when'er it is
> Created for them, catch it by an instinct.
> (88–96)

Though the structure of this creative agency is primarily visually based, it becomes sublated as the imaginary register of language after subjectification – one that in Wordsworth's case is peculiarly insistent. The fate of the 'lonely pair / Of milk-white Swans' (238–9) who have gone from the lake in 'Home at Grasmere' is exemplary. They offer reduplications of Wordsworth's symbiotic reduplication of the mother–infant dyad in his and Dorothy's return to childhood:

> to us
> They were more dear than may be well believed,
> Not only for their beauty, and their still
> And placid way of life and constant love
> Inseparable, not for these alone,
> But that their state so much resembled ours.
>
> (247–52)

Their disappearance from the vale, with its premonitions of mortality, can only be borne by converting the suspicion of violation – Wordsworth knows they might well have been shot – into the redeeming 'voice' of a 'presiding Spirit' (274–5), which insists on some deeper ecological discourse in which the food chain figures conjecturally to reinstate the religious register of blessedness that the Wordsworths need to represent the survival of their own past despite loss and change:

> Ah no, the Stream
> Is flowing, and will never cease to flow,
> And I shall float upon that Stream again.
> By such forgetfulness the Soul becomes,
> Words cannot say, how beautiful.
>
> (294–8)

The words deny themseves, yet they are inevitably caught up in the power of representation. All language is materially pluralized, and even poetic language in the ways Bakhtin influentially demonstrated is made up of different special languages.[27] It is also a discursive medium in Foucault's analysis of the representation and dissemination of power which may be expected to look for its reflection in congruent special languages and social discourses. Recurrently, Wordsworth's own language starts off from childishly plangent *whys* that frequently, however, are actually addressed to children: ' "And tell me, had you rather be," / I said and held him by the arm, / "At Kilve's smooth shore by the green sea, / Or here at Liswyn farm?" ' ('Anecdote for Fathers', 29–32), and ' "How many are you then," said I, / "If they two are in Heaven?" ' ('We Are Seven', 61–2); or to those for whom 'nourishment' also seemed as if it 'came unsought' (*Prel*, II 7): ' "How is it that you live, and what is it you do?" ' ('Resolution and Independence', 126). The assurance he was demanding was radically for the kind of social definition that could speak from special positions that were relatively unself-conscious, yet still within present recall and so not unconscious, like the voice of the Derwent he tries to summon to begin writing *The Prelude*: 'was it for this / That one, the fairest of all rivers, loved / To blend his murmurs with my nurses's song, / And . . . sent a voice / To intertwine my dreams?' (MS fragment in *Prel*). Wordsworth did indeed find this *additional* interest in the languages and discourses that his poetry represents. He discovered it, for example, in the kind of languages that in the Preface to *Lyrical Ballads* he describes his poetry as comprising: philosophical associationism with its empiricist terminology of 'impulse' and 'influx' in the pre-1802 works, stressing the principle of balancing pleasure and pain rather than an autonomously active subject, and the timeless languages of permanence, arising from customarily 'repeated experience and regular feelings' (*Prose* I 124) and from the traditionalism impacted in abstract moralism and classicism, to which he became increasingly drawn as expressions of order and fixity. Similarly, the discourses of Tory rural politics and the Church of England represented the social effectivity of unbroken organicism and an influential counter to the competitive subject of industrial capitalism.

Yet all these discourses of literature, politics and religion are, according to Foucault's argument, subservient to the historically master discourse of 'Discipline', by which power constituted itself in the institutions of the post-revolutionary society.[28] The techniques of surveillance that were representatively codified for the regime of Bentham's model prison, the Panopticon, where prisoners occupy cells surrounding the central gaze of an invigilator, are conceived as exerting imaginary control. Some of the founding texts of structuralism, such as Lacan's 'The Mirror Stage' and Foucault's *Discipline and Punish*, are so resonant with Wordsworth's writing precisely because they highlight the fascination with homologies in which Wordsworth is exceptionally interested. Frederic Jameson has pointed out the general relation between New Historicism and the stucturalist 'method of homology',[29] but it may be argued that post-revolutionary discipline is distinctively *homologizing*, in that its regulatory apparatus may be historicized as having been generated precisely by the shock of massive social upheavals. If discipline can be viewed in this way as enforcing the realization of the homological principle, it is easy to appreciate how congenially it might appear to Wordsworth in particular to be doing the work of an unusually strengthened imaginary insistence, making him, as Hazlitt wrote, 'a pure emanation of the Spirit of the Age' (*H* XI 86). That is part of the recognition of the Pedlar's painfully slow 'meditation' (524) at the end of 'The Ruined Cottage' on the acceptance of the necessity of the disappearance of the state of being that precedes and is confronted by alienation: 'what we feel of sorrow and despair / From ruin and from change, and all the grief / The passing shews of being leave behind' (520–2), in order to begin to choose to become a subject that can participate in social discourses – and in discourses that are after all defined by the same structure of relation to the past ('I well remember...', 513) as had obtained in the blessed past: 'She sleeps in the calm earth, and peace is here' (512). What was being produced with increasing consciousness was a disciplinary social reality that, as Wordsworth realized in his remarkably prescient account of Lacanian 'separation' in 'Ode to Duty', in his case might conform to his rejection of erratic renaming – 'My hopes no more must change their name' – and to his controlling the free play of the linguistic unconscious by constantly requiring reflexivity. It represents an underlining of the structure of 'forced choice'[30] in separation that Lacan views as informing the child's acceptance of his submission to alienation in language, in that the child is acquiescing in his subjectification and thereby refusing to refuse it: 'Yet not the less would I throughout / Still act according to the voice / Of my own wish; and feel past doubt / That my submissiveness was choice.'

In Chapter 1 I trace a moment in early childhood when Wordsworth's mother formatively drew his attention to a practice of ecclesiastical discipline that may have been more vividly recalled in response to her loss and other subsequent traumas. I see it as the origin of the penitential scheme of his poetry whereby an act of (radically Oedipal) transgression results in a successful inscription in the maternally endorsed 'law of the father'. (This deflection of retribution by internalization was to be the plot of Wordsworth's early works, *The Borderers* and 'Adventures on Salisbury Plain', and that which he proposed for 'The Ancient Mariner', whereby 'some crime [was] to be committed', bringing about 'spectral persecution'.)[31] Crucial to the founding incident of ritual humiliation is the splitting of the mother figure into both a transgressive woman caught in adultery and the upholder of moral law, so that she reveals herself as a divided subject who can nevertheless reconstitute her unmarred presence within the domain of the father. Wordsworth's personal assent to the scheme of maternalized discipline leads him into its internalization in forms of self-sacrifice, constantly presided over by the dispersed figuration for the controlling relation, the Woman in White, who is spotted as a spectral presence within all the condign literary registers and discursive practices.

'Wordsworth' as History

> *From the idea that the self is not given to us, I think that there is*
> *only one practical consequence: we have to create ourselves as a work*
> *of art.*
>
> Foucault, 'On the genealogy of ethics: an overview of
> work in progress'

The second secret history is that of the post-revolutionary reaction which is so closely plaited with Wordsworth's own case history because, as it finds covert representation within the same poetic language, its traces often appear to make it identical with that other history. For this self-fashioning, the history and the historian are as one. While there is a given coincidence between Wordsworth's originary trauma of language acquisition and his personal engagements with the period trauma of the French Revolution, leading to blockage or fixation, for Wordsworth in particular to resolve that later reawakening the historical experience had to be accommodated within the fuller paradigm of restoration. What made that sought-after scheme so marvellously restitutive of the imaginary order for Wordsworth was that it could be seen to be actually unfolding in the political evolution of Great Britain during and following the Napoleonic Wars.

Chapter 3, 'Describing the Revolution', traces the way in which Wordsworth's representation of revolutionary discourse came to absorb the shock of the 1789 French model of the overthrow of governing power into that of the British constitutional settlement of 1689, the Glorious Revolution, which was founded on the etymological idea of a single complete rotation to contain the course of deviation and return. The vicious circularity of the latter diehard version is the theme of Hazlitt's 1823 essay for *The Liberal*, 'Arguing in a Circle', which finds wheels within wheels and plays on the figure to try to appropriate it for democratic dispute rather than the hierarchization which he comes round to denouncing in the European nations he sees as the heirs of Burke. He ends with an arraignment of the 'turn-coats' (*H* XIX 277) and 'deserters' of the '*Lake School*' (276) as the present opponents of reform. And yet for Wordsworth this political narrative was peculiarly one of personal consistency. The circularity of a relation to power that returns to a form of sovereignty redefined and secured in response to a compromise with rebellion – the template of the outcome of the English Revolution – manifestly provided a historiographical re-enactment of the resolution of Wordsworth's primary linguistic trauma. Overall, the misrecognition of his subjectivity in the early phases of the French Revolution progressively corrected itself by surveying a sequence of political revisions, through philanthropism, republicanism, nationalism, and constitutional monarchism – from Rousseau to Burke[32] – in order to negotiate his steady reflection in changing languages of power.

Everywhere, Wordsworth's gaze is rewarded with a sympathetic cosmography, whether it is the 'Lines, circles, mounts, a mystery of shapes . . . By which the Druids covertly expressed / Their knowledge of the heavens, and imaged forth / The constellations' on Salisbury Plain (*Prel*, XII 340, 345–7), or a 'sense sublime' which dwells in 'the round ocean, and the living air . . . A motion and a spirit , that . . . rolls through all things' ('Tintern Abbey', 96, 99, 103), or the consolatory symmetry of Lucy's fate, 'Rolled round in earth's diurnal course' ('A Slumber Did My Spirit Seal', 7). Similarly, there is a subtly constraining geometry of release and control that circumscribes his chosen 'Home at Grasmere', 'Within the bounds of this huge Concave' (42), where the birds 'wheel' (289) and loop:

> Behold them, how they shape
> Orb after orb their course still round and round
> Above the area of the lake, their own
> Adopted region, girding it about
> In wanton repetition, yet therewith
> With that huge circle evermore renewed:
> Hundreds of curves and circlets high and low,
> Backwards and forwards, progress intricate,
> As if one spirit was in all and swayed
> Their indefatigable flight.
>
> (292–301)

Political power is legitimized by maintaining radial connections between a centre of origin, the Wordsworth circle at Grasmere, and its expanding circumference, as from 'the imperial station' ('View from the Top of Black Comb', 13) of the summit of the mountain on the tip of Cumberland from which 'the amplest range / Of unobstructed prospect may be seen / That British ground commands' (3–5) the eye strains to take in the most distant panorama and is then instructed 'Look homeward now!':

> In depth, in height, in circuit, how serene
> That spectacle, how pure! – Of Nature's works,

In earth, and air, and earth-embracing sea,
A revelation infinite it seems;
Display august of man's inheritance,
Of Britain's calm felicity and power!

(28–34)

All Wordsworth's excursions likewise lead back home, like *the* Excursion, or like the schoolboy outing to Furness Abbey described in *The Prelude* that was out of bounds but effectively contained by the ruin's admonitory 'repose and quietness' (II 121), and which was reinvoked when the news that '*Robespierre was dead*' (X 535) and the Jacobin terror passed temporarily convinced Wordsworth that the true revolution was back on course and 'The mighty renovation would proceed' (556):

Thus, interrupted by uneasy bursts
Of exultation, I pursued my way
Along the very shore which I had skimmed
In former times, when, spurring from the Vale
Of Nightshade, and St Mary's mouldering fane,
And the stone abbot, after circuit made
In wantonness of heart, a joyous crew
Of schoolboys, hastening to their distant home,
Along the margin of the moonlight sea,
We beat with thundering hoofs the level sand.

(557–66)

The structural outline of Wordsworth's personal and post-revolutionary history is transparent in all these circular motions and curvings back.

The bridge between his case history and political trajectory is further accented by the work of those historians of the semiotics of the French Revolution (including Stephen Blakemore and François Furet) who approach it as a 'linguistic event', making it exceptionally packed with the knowledge of subjectification that he precisely wished to ignore. They have argued that the crisis of political representation formulated by Rousseau's 'social contract' invoked a neologizing tendency as the basis of a new nation. Lynn Hunt and Mona Ozouf describe the underlying manoeuvre as 'a transference of sacrality' (Hunt, 23) in which 'charisma came most concretely to be located in words' (26), and see it portrayed most strikingly by 'The ritual oaths of loyalty taken around a liberty tree or sworn *en masse* during many revolutionary festivals [which] commemorated and re-created the moment of social contract' (27). For

Wordsworth in particular, the great national Fête de la Federation in which he participated a year after the fall of the Bastille on 14 July 1790 became the epitomizing practice for nationalist discourses which underwent serial revision, notably in the lyrics of 1802, from when it became naturalized into alternative *British* festivities. In order to negotiate that metamorphosis, Wordsworth had to temper the revolutionary potential of popular communities confronted in the Bakhtinian *carnivalesque* of the lyrical ballads and St Batholomew's Fair in London, as construed in Book VII of *The Prelude*. Instead, he constructed a counter-discourse of the imaginary community of Grasmere Fair as his version of the nation.

The progression of Wordsworth's nationalist discourses is in effect a reversal in political terms, and the place where that turn most characteristically does and does not occur – where one predominating order of continuity deletes another of discontinuity – is his description of his Parisian experiences over almost six weeks on his way back to England in October 1792, which is centred on his account of the recent storming of the Tuileries palace and subsequent September massacres in 'The Square of the Carrousel' in Book X of *The Prelude*, with the imminent regicide to come. Here it was that his faith in the British constitution, with the superimposition of the Glorious for the French Revolution, came full circle. Chapter 4, 'Changing Spots', scrutinizes this historical 'spot of time' which represents the structure of Wordsworth's political conversion. It takes the form of an elaborated investigation of the complex Oedipal plot that is involved in the subtle pledging of Wordsworth's allegiance to constitutional monarchism in this text, around which revolve several spheres of intertextuality. A key intertext for fixing Wordsworth's reflections on the French Revolution turns out to be *Hamlet*, which had formerly attended the Oedipalism of Wordsworth's becoming an author in 'The Vale of Esthwaite' and now recurs to organize a network of other Shakespearean allusions. Shakespeare, rather than Milton, whom Coleridge regarded as Wordsworth's great English exemplar as a 'great philosophical Poet' (1835, II 69), emerges as the literary antecedent whose capacious textuality could fully enable the conflicted narrative of transgression and its vindication that Wordsworth needed for the representation of *his* revolution.

Wordsworth was effectively gaining his desired poetic discourse through a strifeless emulation of Shakespearean textuality in a manoeuvre that was itself homologous with the confessional acknowledgment of his implication in historical insurrection that had turned into a realization of the paradigm of (post-revolutionary) restoration. The pivotal text that merges into Wordsworth's is recoverable from Acts III and IV of *The Second Part of King Henry IV*, with the filial rebellion of the Prince resolved in the ultimately patriotic career of Henry V, by allusion to the whole history of the *Henriad*. Thereby an outer framing by English national history is also accomplished.

Finally, investigating the distinctive character of Wordsworth's Oedipal plot, which ultimately derives from language trauma, I contrast Lacan's seminar on Poe's *The Purloined Letter*, which famously reveals the free play of the intersubjective unconscious that slips beneath the circulation of signifiers, with another kind of crime narrated in Conan Doyle's 'The Beryl Coronet' from *The Adventures of Sherlock Holmes*. I read the latter tale as a structural reduction of *2 Henry IV* which points up the crucial Wordsworthian dilemma over language acquisition that *for him* governs the prior terms of all signification. In Conan Doyle's and Shakespeare's histories, as well as in Wordsworth's scene of Parisian Terror, an 'upbraiding silence' represents an act of transgression that cannot be articulated because it cannot be denied until it becomes recognized as after all bespeaking an enactment of restoration.

The History of 'Wordsworth'

> *every great poet...before he can be thoroughly enjoyed, has to call forth and communicate power...Genius is the introduction of a new element into the intellectual universe...Therefore to create taste is to call forth and bestow power, of which knowledge is the effect.*
> 'Essay, Supplementary to the Preface', 1815

As an agent of acculturation to British nationalism, 'Wordsworth', the *oeuvre*, became arguably the most influential literary discourse in the nineteenth century. It actively constructed the naturalization of shock as *the* typifying aesthetic project of shielding the British subject from the century's catastrophic rifts in social organization. It withstood, that is, the modernist reception of the terrifying exhilarations of social dislocations resulting from the French Revolution and the impact of industrialization, the *shock of the new*, while it more or less finessed the necessary guilt of military imperialism. Wordsworth, who wished 'either to be considered as a Teacher, or as nothing' (*WL* II 195) and dedicated his verse 'to Nature's self / And things that teach as Nature teaches' (*Prel* V 230–1), ends *The Prelude* by adjuring Coleridge:

> what we have loved
> Others will love, and we may teach them how:
> Instruct them how the mind of man becomes
> A thousand times more beautiful than the earth
> On which he dwells, above the frame of things
> (Which, mid all revolutions in the hopes
> And fears of men, doth still remain unchanged).
>
> (XIII 444–50)

The dissemination of Wordsworthianism accordingly provided a language for educational, cultural and political discourses which operated to have a pre-established 'structure of feeling'[33] promulgated anew by 'United helpers' and 'joint labourers in the work . . . / Of . . . redemption, surely yet to come' (438–41) as the foundation of a new post-revolutionary society.

In Chapter 5, 'The Shock of the Old', I follow the continuous trajectory of the restoration paradigm of 'Wordsworth' into cultural reaction. The last major trauma, occasioned by the ecclesiastical and political discourses of Benthamite reform in the later 1820s and 1830s, revealed a disjuncture between the nation that had been coming into actuality and that which Wordsworth had imagined. The post-revolutionary disciplinary regime and organic traditionalism that had formerly occupied his construction of 'nature' uncontroversially now became quarrelsome bedfellows, precipitating a crisis which brought about Wordsworth's interventionist reinscription of church and state in Catholic and feudal discourses. But without national institutions in which Wordsworth could any longer easily recognize or renegotiate his self-reflection, he could only resort to half-gestures towards what remained foreign Roman traditions, or strident defence of pre-Reform practices, or absolutist abstractions of Law and Order issued from an endangered mindset. In short, he found himself effectively in the same often baffling predicament of having to try to translate the 'Wordsworth' of his earlier poetry into a new cultural effectivity within the very different and changing Victorian nation. Even Gerard Manley Hopkins, who still felt himself empowered by Wordsworth's spiritual vision in the 1880s, had to look back to the Intimations Ode for what he described as an electric shock whose 'tremble' was still 'spreading' in his day. Hopkins viewed Wordsworth's poetic responsiveness as highly individual but contagious – that of a seer. For Hopkins the ambivalent metaphor of the electric shock registered both his own contemporary fear of revolution (focused on agitation for Home Rule) and the consequent transmission of a counter-linguistic dynamism of a kind of poetic language that wonderfully by-passes such resistances as it is propelled through 'the growing mind of the English speaking world'. Throughout the chapter, I follow this period metaphor in the works of a series of writers to characterize their various engagements with 'Wordsworth'.

Though Hopkins describes 'Wordsworth' specifically as the exporting of Christian imperialism, the religious discursivity may obviously be placed as incidental to the more generalized programme of cultural dominion as it has been reconstructed in the teaching of Shakespeare and Milton in India by Gauri Viswanathan. Hopkins's reference to India needing 'a continual supply' of high quality English literature takes its place in the British construction of the English-speaking imperial subject from Thomas Macaulay's Indian Education Minute of 1835 – 'the great object of the British Government ought to be the promotion of European literature and science among the natives of India' (see Trevelyan, 292) – to George Orwell's proposed agenda for English poetry in the BBC's broadcasting to post-independence India, and beyond. But the question remains – however it may risk clouding the post-colonialist sense of purpose – whether the particular impact of 'Wordsworth' is not due to its *also* operating at levels that may be felt to be more or less pre-discursive and that derive from primary engagements with language itself, even though it can of course never evade its various discursive appropriations. That complication might, indeed, make it a particularly insidious instrument of indoctrination, though it can also serve to problematize and expose the provisionality of its discursive affinities: '*was* it for this...?'[34] In the final chapter, I touch on these considerations by presenting a curiously stratified document I came across in the Regenstein Library, Chicago, the Wordsworth Centenary Number of *The Government College Miscellany, Mangalore*, the Republic of Indian Union (1951), as one (arguably) not unrepresentatively conflicted post-colonial response to the trauma of independence, leading to 'separation', in the Lacanian sense of the alienated subject's attempt to come to terms with the various forces outside itself that have brought about its social being ('the Other's desire'), resulting in loss turning to self-affirmation, autonomy gaining 'Strength from what remains behind'.

Though the imaginary ego seeks out elective representation, it may or may not find it, or it may find that what had once seemed beautifully congruent becomes distorted and alienating, so that its insistence becomes more urgently available for new and different discursive participation. The history of 'Wordsworth', its cultural recension, is the continuing appeal to the scheme within the poetic textuality for post-traumatic discursive reflexivity, following the shock of non-recognition. It is definable in part by contrast with the Marxist construction of revolution which proceeds from that which punctuates modern French history and has sometimes produced the aesthetic characterized in Walter Benjamin's essay 'On Some Motifs in Baudelaire', where the dislocating material shocks of modern urban experience generate a battery of artistic creativity powered by 'a reservoir of electric energy'. From the intertextualities of *The Recluse* and *Frankenstein* I recover a debate between Wordsworth's imaginative procedure and the begetting of Benjamin's industrialized automata which, lacking the maternal relation, are operated by power that does not bestow coherence. For the transmission of 'Wordsworth', however, through a reflective intertextuality that organizes divergent discursive engagements in the writing of his followers, I turn to George Eliot's observations on originality as the conversion of pre-existing languages into new forms of nurture. In this way, the earlier poetic textuality of 'Wordsworth' provided the cue for reconfronting the disturbances of social reform in her later novels while emerging with very different discursive commitments from those of the late Wordsworth himself. In particular, I examine how some of her later novels are arranged around the profitable but anti-triumphalist assimilation of shocks, and the way in which the intertextuality with 'Wordsworth' frames and supports her related realization of several kinds of disappointment in *Middlemarch*.

Wordsworth was notoriously unable to write his epochal masterpiece, *The Recluse*, so that it remained a set of unwieldy fragments, like Casaubon's project for *The Key to All Mythologies*. In the end, Eliot achieved her *magnum opus* in *Middlemarch* itself, but only by accepting it as a history of compromise and failure. In that way, she succeeds whereas proverbially Casaubon falls short in his great work, and in that respect he reiterates Wordsworth's own failure for most of his career consciously to acknowledge the impossibility of realizing his ambition: in his case of finding full self-representation in the word of the father. Instead, Wordsworth had already revealed the secret histories of this alternatively empowering deficiency as the imaginary pre-subject of *The Prelude*.

1
The Spectral Mother

'Pater semper incertus est, sed mater certissima'
Quoted by Freud in 'Family Romances'

The Woman in White

The most vivid of Wordsworth's recollections of his mother from the Cockermouth days, before she died when he was seven, are included in his 'Autobiographical Memoranda', dictated at Rydal Mount in 1847:

> I remember my mother only in some few situations, one of which was her pinning a nosegay to my breast when I was going to say the catechism in the church, as was customary before Easter. I remember also telling her on one week day that I had been at church, for our school stood by the churchyard, and we had frequent opportunities of seeing what was going on there. The occasion was, a woman doing penance in the church in a white sheet. My mother commended my having been present, expressing a hope that I should remember the circumstance for the rest of my life. 'But,' said I, 'Mama, they did not give me a penny, as I had been told they would.' 'Oh,' said she, recanting her praises, 'if that was your motive, you were very properly disappointed.' (*Memoirs* I 9)

This second event – the woman doing penance in a white sheet – which took place in the parish church some time before the death of Wordsworth's mother in 1778 was extraordinary.

Cases of public penance, nearly always for breaches of the seventh commandment, had long been rare enough to attract particular attention in the press. *Fogg's Weekly Journal*, for example, gives an account in

1733: 'On Sunday last a Woman did Penance in the Parish Church of St. Bride's, by standing in a white Sheet, with a Wand in her Hand, on a Stool in the middle Isle during the time of Divine Service for Adultery and Fornication, and having a Bastard Child in the Absence of her Husband.'[1] The church historian who provides the above instance is right in disputing the statement of another, who writes that 'Stephen Hales, the famous physiologist and chaplain to the prince afterwards King George the Third [who] died in 1761 . . . is said to have been the last of the clergy who made his female parishioners do penance.' (ibid., 104) But he himself is able to refer specifically to only four other examples of this form of 'Discipline and Penance' up to 1813, including Wordsworth's account: two in Durham and North Yorkshire in 1770 (the year of Wordsworth's birth), and one recorded by Augustus J. C. Hare, a member of the influential Anglican clan, in describing his grandmother, Mrs Hare-Naylor's life at Hurstmonceaux in the early 1800s. This last is recorded in a Proustian sketch from Hare's *Memorials of a Quiet Life* (1872–6):

> Mrs Hare-Naylor's life at Hurstmonceaux must have astonished her rustic neighbours, and still more her neighbours in her own rank of life . . . Not only, when within the house, was she always occupied in the deep study of Greek authors, but during her walks in the park and shrubberies she was always seen dressed in white, and she was always accompanied by a beautiful tame white doe, which used to walk by her side, even when she went to church. Her foreign life led her to regard Sunday merely as a fête day, and she used frequently to scandalize the church-going population by sitting at a window looking out upon the road, working at her tambour-frame, when they were going to church. Her impetuosity in liking and disliking often led her to make friends with persons beneath her, or to take them into her service when they were of a character which rendered her notice exceedingly undesirable. The two women she took most notice of in the parish were the last persons who ever did public penance at Hurstmonceaux, having both to stand in a white sheet in the church-yard for their 'Various offspring,' so that people said, 'There are Mrs Hare-Naylor's friends doing penance.' And it was long remembered with amusement that when one of her maids was afterwards found to have misbehaved herself, she said, 'Poor thing, she cannot help it; I really believe it must be *something in the air!*'   (I 142–3)

Hare's grandmother appears outlandishly exempted from the moral regime to which her scandalous acquaintances are subjected. Though in her attire she doubles the other transgressive mothers, she does so with a difference. *Her* white dress is exempt from institutionalization and affirms her odd social and cultural apartness that, in its premonition of Emily in Wordsworth's *White Doe of Rylstone*, lays claim through an alternative spirit of forgiveness to symbolic spotlessness and the innocence of 'nature' (*'something in the air!'*). The split between these different Women in White serves to point up the critical split within Wordsworth's own mother, and her implication in the penitential figure of his reminiscence. While the church's white tunic marks the imposed acceptance of penitence as an authoritative restitution of innocence, Wordsworth's mother's emancipation from a sexual association with the woman – that of all mothers for their sons – relies on her acceptance of the scheme and her further effort for its social habituation, redirecting her son's desire for herself into a field of desire not of his or her making. In the case of Wordsworth's mother, what absolves her (and his) fall into knowledge is the instruction in a penitential discourse of self-discipline that she is actively inaugurating for her son.

Wordsworth's woman in white represented a crucial subjection of the body, whereby his (good) mother introduced her son (according to Lacan) to the name of the father, and the logic of the paternal law. His early childhood was invested with a strict sense of moral prohibition: in old age he claimed to remember having had an early premonition of evil at the age of four, when he had quaked in bed, though his mother in his most individualized analysis of her in *The Prelude* is seen as imbuing him with the sense that it came with her milk. He writes that she

> had virtual faith that He
> Who fills the mother's breast with innocent milk
> Doth also for our nobler part provide,
> Under His great correction and controul,
> As innocent instincts, and as innocent food.
>
> (V 271–5)

This mother, 'the heart / And hinge of all our loves' (257–8), who had 'a grace / Of modest meekness' (287–8) and whose words as recalled by Wordsworth may carry a softening humour ('very properly disappointed'), was nonetheless concerned to impart that fundamental regime of 'correction and controul'. She 'commended my having been present, expressing a hope that I should remember the circumstance for the rest of my life', as Wordsworth in fact did, so that the injunction to remember the woman in white makes memory itself a penitential rite, converting difference and change into a structure of pious constancy. It is obviously appropriate that the accompanying recollection should have been one of her proudly preparing him for being catechized, as he was again to recall in his sonnet, 'Catechising', from the sequence *Ecclesiastical Sonnets*:

> From Little down to Least, in due degree,
> Around the Pastor, each in new-wrought vest,
> Each with a vernal posy at his breast,
> We stood, a trembling, earnest Company!
> With low soft murmur, like a distant bee,
> Some spake, by thought-perplexing fears betrayed;
> And some a bold unerring answer made:
> How fluttered then thy anxious heart for me,
> Belovèd Mother! Thou whose happy hand
> Had bound the flowers I wore, with faithful tie:
> Sweet flowers! at whose inaudible command
> Her countenance, phantom-like, doth reappear.
>
> (XXII 1–12)

His mother's spectral surveillance pins down signifieds that she helps happily naturalize ('With low soft murmur, like a distant bee'), binding flowers into ritual expression ('with a faithful tie'), and mediating an authorization that remains a *silent* corroboration within the word of the father – issuing an 'inaudible command'. It was to be Wordsworth's abiding way of keeping mum.

The unfolding story of a mother's mute religious teaching organizes *The White Doe of Rylstone*, completed in 1808 and published in 1815, into an historical allegory of the workings of Wordsworthian discipline. His chief source, Thomas Dunham Whitaker's *History and Antiquities of the Deanery of Craven* (1805), offered deeply familiar resonances of penitence and female suffering by commenting that the doe's 'weekly pilgrimage from [Rylstone] over the fells' to join the service at Bolton Abbey 'awakens the fancy. Shall we say that the soul of one of the Nortons had taken up its abode in that animal, and was condemned to do penance, for his transgressions against "the lords' deere" among their ashes? But for such a spirit the Wild Stag would have been a fitter vehicle. Was it not then some beautiful and injured female, whose name and history are forgotten?'[2] 'The milk-white Doe' (205, 974), that Wordsworth derives from Whitaker, is closely associated with Emily Norton's vision of the 'Spirit of maternal love' (1048) and the figure 'who with mild looks and language mild / Instructed here her darling Child, / While yet a prattler on the knee' (1039–41), so that the animal becomes the embodiment of the Protestant religious discourse she had then imparted of 'The faith reformed and purified'. But Wordsworth's own creation of Emily herself, whose grave mound is separated from the others in 'A penitential loneliness' (177), is made to bear the history of religious strife in the penally enforced conformism of the Reformation, and onto her is displaced a rite of acquiescent suffering which issues in the vindication of a non-triumphalist Elizabethan settlement tradition of Anglican quietism. (Her association with Elizabeth is overt: 'Behold her, like a virgin Queen', 1590). In short, the doe becomes the phallus of the national religious tradition whose sectarian conflicts have become internalized and controlled by Emily, the offspring of a mixed marriage of Protestant mother and Catholic father. Her brother Francis is engaged in the same conflicted transmission of family pieties. A Protestant sympathizer who will not entirely oppose his father's law, he can neither join with nor detach himself from the insurrection to which his father is dedicated, and accompanies his father and brothers on their campaign unarmed. As the people of York cry when the others are to be executed: '" . . . he the worst defied / " For the sake of natural Piety; / "He rose not in this quarrel, he / " His Father and his Brothers wooed, / "Both for their own and Country's good, / " To rest in peace . . . ' (1245–50). Francis had his own inward struggle to subdue an inchoate Oedipalism ('"Might ever son *command* a sire, / The act were justified today"', 455–6), and later to accept his father's dying injunction, which brings about his own death, to uphold the rival phallus, the Catholic banner embroidered by Emily with the cross and wounds of Christ, and bear it back to Bolton Abbey. In the end, though the banner (which inscribes the potential split of their religious loyalty from the maternal national religion) has to be relinquished, it has been borne by Francis in such a way as to have it stand for the more powerful maternal revision, whereby violent opposition has been disciplined into the demure inexorability of a prevalent discourse figured by the returning doe.

'Penance', according to Robert Phillimore, the most notable of all authorities on English canon law, quoting previous authorities,

> is said to be an ecclesiastical punishment used in the discipline of the church, which effects the body of the penitent; by which he is obliged to give a public satisfaction to the church for the scandal he has given by his evil example. So in the primitive times they were to give testimonies of their reformation, before they were re-admitted

to partake of the mysteries of the church. In the case of incest, or incontinency, the sinner is usually enjoined to do a public penance in the cathedral or parish church, or public market, barelegged and bareheaded, in a white sheet, and to make an open confession of his crime in a prescribed form of words; which is augmented or moderated according to the quality of the fault, and the discretion of the judge.   (II 1367–8)

Primitively, it had been a corporal punishment, that was accompanied by 'thrusting [the culprit] into a monastery, branding, fustigation [i.e. beating], and imprisonment' (Burn, III 103). But by Wordsworth's day, demonstrating some of the force of Foucault's leading argument in *Discipline and Punish* – that with the Enlightenment penal authority switched its attention from the body to the mind of the criminal – its physically punitive function had become practically outmoded, and where it had anomalously survived, as at Hurstmonceaux, it seems to have become something of an ineffective customary practice that was more or less consciously dying out. With the passage of time, the sentence was to become a metaphor for unspecific communal censure. In 1854, for example, a squib in *Punch* entitled 'The Abundant Harvest' pretends to record that 'a miller and a baker . . . were compelled to stand in the middle aisle during the service, dressed in a white sheet in penitence for the price of bread, seeing that wheat had been so abundant' (XXVII, 15). What Wordsworth's woman in white represented in the 1770s, however, was more of an historical cusp, a provincialism that still provided an exceptional spectacular exhibition of ritual humiliation and purification and that retained a striking visual effect, though by then it could easily find a place also on the classroom syllabus as a lesson for the admonishment of young pupils in the disciplinary moral regime his mother was reinforcing. What Wordsworth had witnessed, and what his mother had ministered to, was the passage of staged institutional violence into the invisible moral regime of 'nature'.

Discipline, normalization of power (or 'nature'), is, of course, Urizenic. Wordsworth's trembling company of schoolchildren awaiting interrogation, 'From Little down to Least, in due degree, / Around the Pastor, each in new-wrought vest', links unwittingly with Blake's charity orphans in the 'innocent' version of 'Holy Thursday', 'walking two & two in red & blue & green', 'these flowers of London town; / Seated in companies they sit with radiance all their own'.[3] There is the same impression of regimentation in Blake's song (in the word 'companies'), and the contrivance of a ceremony in which the law is imposed by domesticated instruments (white wands) of institutional authority to achieve an impression of natural ineluctability: 'Grey headed beadles walk before with wands as white as snow, / Till into the high dome of Paul's they like Thames waters flow' (3–4). In Blake's analysis, the 'lambs' (7) are being trained in the process of self-sacrifice, whereby their subservience serves to constitute the economic and religious discourses of charity, which occludes the injustices of social and economic division by using its victims to represent its illusory magnanimity.

In Wordsworth's autobiographical anecdote a similar move is made by his mother, who sacrifices one version of herself, the sexually transgressive penitent, as the defining Foucauldian other of the moral regime of the law, and thereby constitutes her own dominating presence within the disciplinary discourses she is endorsing. In this way, the Lacanian good mother courts resemblance to the abusive Blakean institution, concealing her self-interested enforcement of a perhaps precocious alienation in her son. But Wordsworth's interest in recuperating his mother's interest in a penitential figure stands out by implying added and more than commonly complicated investments in the mechanics of disciplinary discourse. After her death, her pointing to an image of guilt relieved by suffering and representing the acceptance of punishment as the necessary origin of empowerment by the disciplinary regime became more impressive for Wordsworth's own privately intensified predisposition to evade Oedipal struggle. Because he had additional, already formed motives for making his relation to the mother abhor the realization of sexual difference in favour of facilitating an untroubled reconciliation with the father, his mother's lesson was unusually benign for him.

This early experience of conversion, from transgression into piety, is both preformative and exemplary of the personal history that can be recovered from the key discourses into which Wordsworth's poetry enters at several different stages throughout his career. In Lacanian terms, it rehearses the primary inception of his subjectivity through a fall into language which would be redeemed through language and culture itself. Throughout his adolescence, he was to remember the lesson of penitence by courting self-chastisement, whether at the hands of his domestic disciplinarians, especially his uncle Kit Cookson: 'But possibly, from some want of judgement in punishments inflicted, I had become perverse and obstinate in defying chastisement, and rather proud of it than otherwise' (*Memoirs* I 9); or in welcoming divine vengeance after Wordsworth had seemed obscurely to conspire in his father's death, as is revealed by the horse-waiting episode in Book XI of *The Prelude*: 'The event, / With all the sorrow which it brought, appeared / A chastisement … And I do not doubt … The workings of my spirit thence are brought' (367–9, 384, 388). Later, in 'Ode to Duty', with its definitive statement of the completion of his moral regeneration, he celebrated his subjection as a 'Bondman' (64) in 'The spirit of self-sacrifice' (62). All such self-characterizing regulations are transformations of what the woman in white represents and the effect of remembering her. In Book IX of *The Prelude*, for example, he recounts a fascinated recognition of the female figure in Charles Le Brun's *Repentant Magdalene* (Figure 1) which, following the fall of the Bastille, had pleasurably distracted his gaze from the unresolved signs of revolution when he was in Paris in 1791. Having picked up a stone from the prison's ruins as a 'relick' (66), he writes that it

> Less moved me, gave me less delight, than did
> A single picture merely, hunted out
> Among other sights, the Magdalene of le Brun,
> A beauty exquisitely wrought – fair face
> And rueful, with its ever-flowing tears.
>
> (75–80)

In redefining his particular engagement in the disorders of those years long after he had distanced himself from their aftermath, this memory of penitent transgression helps to relocate the principal focus of his own inscription in revolutionary violence as one that had always, more or less, been subject to discipline.[4]

Something similar, though more complex, happened figurally in the course of the revisions Wordsworth made to the 1802 sonnet, 'The Banished Negroes', which describes a female 'fellow-Passenger'[5] on a Channel crossing who was a casualty of a racist decree that 'effectively forbade all people of color from entering the continental territories of France' (Page, 69). Beyond the racially constructed exoticism of the black woman in the first published version of 1803 – 'gaudy in array, / A negro woman, like a Lady gay' (2–3) – lies a silenced and subdued vitality:

> Yet silent as a woman fearing blame;
> Dejected, downcast, meek, and more than tame:
> She sate, from notice turning not away,
> But on our proffer'd kindness still did lay
> A weight of languid speech, or at the same
> Was silent, motionless in eyes and face.
>
> (4–9)

Figure 1 Charles Le Brun, *Sainte Madeleine repentante renonce a toutes les vanités de la vie* (c. 1656–7)

By the final version of 1845, however, when the political topicality of Napoleon's ordinance and its rejection of former revolutionary values are no longer pressing, the woman's subjection has become assertive rather than passive:

> Yet still her eyes retained their tropic fire,
> That burning independent of the mind,
> Joined with the lustre of her rich attire,
> To mock the Outcast.
>
> (*PW* III 113–14)

On review, an inner division has clarified itself that rejects her earlier aspect of rejection ('To mock the Outcast'), and it is signalled by her latest clothing: her 'gaudy . . . array' has been altered to show her now as 'spotless in array, – / A white-robed Negro' (2–3). Judith Page suggests that the white robe may have derived from another female portrait in the Louvre, Marie-Guillermine Benoist's *Portrait of a Negress* (Figure 2), and it would be easy to suppose that the attractions of the 'negress's' dishabille have become assimilated in the 'lustre' of her 'spotless' dress in order both to regulate Wordsworth's own response and to do some justice to her separate condition by converting it from one of uncontested victimhood. Different kinds of transgression are redeemed in that spotlessness, which, while it certainly fails to represent the autonomy of the woman's blackness, seeks rather to join with it in a shared Christian protest for tolerance: 'O ye Heavens, be kind! / And feel, thou Earth, for this afflicted Race!' (13–14).

In fact, all Wordsworth's key relations with women, with Dorothy Wordsworth and his wife for example, and even his daughter Dora, are governed by the structure of memory fixed by the prevailing relation with the mother as the return of the knowledge of trespass transmuted into acceptance of the law: 'emotion recollected in tranquility' (Preface to *Lyrical Ballads*, I 148). In his poem to Dora, beginning '*A little onward lend thy guiding hand*', composed in 1816, Wordsworth wishes still to conduct his eleven-year-old daughter's moral instruction, though he is aware also of the possibility of his approaching dependency, signalled by the opening quotation from *Samson Agonistes* and his own fear of blindness. Dora's coming power is in part sexual – his fantasy of dependency is enabled also by observing her increasing maturity – and its implications for Wordsworth have been spelled out by Geoffrey Hartman, who sees his fatherly attentions as 'displacements' amounting to 'an elaborate disguise of the incest wish' (1987, 110). Perhaps

Figure 2 Marie-Guillermine Benoist, *Portrait d'une négresse* (1800)

Wordsworth's invitation to Dora, 'From thy orisons / Come forth' (20–1), and his stated aim 'to curb / Thy nymph-like step swift-bounding o'er the lawn, / Along the loose rocks, or the slippery verge / Of foaming torrents' (17–20) echo Hamlet's greeting to Ophelia, 'Nymph, in thy orisons / Be all my sins remember'd.'[6] Certainly, following Hamlet's suppression of his own sexuality, Wordsworth is about to say 'Get thee to a nunn'ry' (120) to Dora, who is seen as promising him a reciprocal programme of spiritual control, 'To calm the affections, elevate the soul, / And consecrate our lives to truth and love.' (56–7) The path along which Wordsworth needs to guide Dora to the recognition of her own growing influence on himself leads inevitably to seeing her invested with the habitual garb of moral discipline:

> But we such schools
> Of reverential awe will chiefly seek
> In the still summer noon, while beams of light,
> Reposing here, and in the aisles beyond
> Traceably gliding through the dusk, recall
> To mind the living presences of nuns;
> A gentle, pensive, white-robed sisterhood,
> Whose saintly radiance mitigates the gloom
> Of those terrestrial fabrics, where they serve,
> To Christ, the Sun of righteousness, espoused.
>
> (39–48)

After their friendship had cooled, Coleridge found it hard to accept the oddly balanced make-up of this Wordsworthian desire, claiming that Wordsworth was

> by nature incapable of being in Love, tho' no man more tenderly attached – hence he ridicules the existence of any other passion, than a compound of Lust with esteem and Friendship, confined to one Object – first by accidents of Association, and permanently, by the force of habit and sense of Duty . . . but still it is not *Love*, and there is such a passion as Love – which is no more a compound, than Oxygen. (See Byatt, 43)

Instead, he characterized Wordworth's feelings in terms of those of 'a man of sensibility . . . towards his wife with her baby at her breast' (*TT* I 206). De Quincey concurs: 'never could [Wordsworth], in any emphatic sense, have been a lover' (*DQ* II 188). Certainly, Wordsworth was not interested in removing a garment that, while it hid sexual difference, also affirmed his disciplinary language of 'nature', as Percy Shelley's caricature of him depicts:

> But from the first 'twas Peter's drift
> To be a kind of moral eunuch,
> He touched the hem of Nature's shift,

Felt faint – and never dared uplift
The closest, all-concealing tunic.[7]

The kind of satisfaction that Wordsworth sought instead is transparent in, for example, 'The Mad Mother', a poem that dramatizes the latent conflict between a mother's various family ties, to husband and child, and which I read as being as much engaged in disregarding her sexual craving as in stirring a different, compensatory response to it in her sucking babe: '"Thy father cares not for my breast, / 'Tis thine, sweet baby, there to rest; / 'Tis all thine own!"' (61–3).[8]

'The ghosts of dead mothers' (J. M. Barrie)

Wordsworth did not really see the importance of the woman in white – he was only in it for the money – until his mother drew his lasting attention to her, because, in the interplay of power between them, her adjuration was felt to be particularly necessary *for him*. Another recollection from one of his mother's friends shows her consciousness of his unusually forceful personality: 'the only one of her five children about whose future life she was anxious, was William; and he, she said, would be remarkable either for good or for evil' (*Memoirs* I 9). The figure, and the lesson that she imparted, became established as one of the very few precious memories he had retained of his mother after her early death at the age of thirty. Thereafter, the woman became an unforgettable presence that was to help shape his future history.

Despite her disciplinary import – and the white dress is, of course, the uniform of institutionalization – there is something uncanny about the woman, something threatening before she facilitates naturalization at every major juncture in his life and career. She reoccurs as a monitory spectral figure throughout Wordsworth's works, on the boundary between the literal and the figural, mysteriously deflecting and transforming the power of the father, and modifying the story of Oedipal origin. Because her apparition is fraught with the anxiety of first loss, she returns uncertainly and unexpectedly, before being welcomed in the place of the father for having so helpfully replaced his function and screened its violent implications.

Traces of the dispersed figuration can be 'busted'. Following his mother's death, Wordsworth was sent away to school at Hawkshead, in the Vale of Esthwaite. No less than most rural communities, Hawkshead has its local wraiths, such as the 'tall, white-robed female', which by local report was often seen to '[walk] regularly on the road between

Belmount avenue and Hawkshead Hall, or in Scarhouse Lane.' (Cowper, 327) Such apparitions are so commonplace as to be expected. The author of the *History of Hawkshead* records a late example of 'the oldest inhabitant of Satterthwaite . . . [who] . . . when working at Hawkshead, as a lad, about 1825, . . . was riding in a cart from Hawkshead Hall towards Gallow-barrow, when he saw a tall female figure, dressed well but old-fashionedly, suddenly leave the highway and rapidly ascend into the air, finally disappearing from sight' (328). This was the local atmosphere in which Wordsworth moved and was of course spooked during those formative experiences of his childhood in that and other Lake District vales recounted in Books I and II of *The Prelude*. There, gigantic and blanched forms are described as pursuing his guilty retreat when, in the fantasy that is the aftermath of his stealing the shepherd's skiff,

> no familiar shapes
> Of hourly objects, images of trees,
> Of sea and sky, no colours of green fields,
> But huge and mighty forms that do not live
> Like living men moved slowly through my mind
> By day, and were the trouble of my dreams.
>
> (I 422–6)

He experienced the same form of moral terror when, in that paradigmatic Oedipal act, 'the bird / Which was the captive of another's toils / became my prey' (326–8):

> I heard among the solitary hills
> Low breathings coming after me, and sounds
> Of undistinguishable motion, steps
> Almost as silent as the turf they trod.
>
> (329–32)

Wordsworth seems in these and similar episodes to have been haunted by a disturbed recollection that the confessional act of memory itself somehow resolves. Though the past event seemed to be threatening punishment, at the time of writing about it Wordsworth can recoup the obscure fascinations of his fear as being after all the *sine qua non* of a formative lesson he still needs to heed.

The vale was steeped in much more horrific historical crime. In the Penrith Beacon episode in Book XI of *The Prelude*, the story of the Hawkshead poisoner, Thomas Lancaster, who killed eight people with white arsenic and who was hanged in 1672 in Colthouse meadows – adjacent to the house where Wordsworth boarded during his schooldays – becomes confused with that of the later Penrith robber-murderer, Thomas Nicholson. Wordsworth evokes their composite crime when he describes his having become lost near the Penrith Beacon as a five-year-old:

> I . . . at length
> Came to a bottom where in former times
> A murderer had been hung in iron chains.
> The gibbet-mast was mouldered down, the bones
> And iron case were gone, but on the turf
> Hard by, soon after that fell deed was wrought,
> Some unknown hand had carv'd the murderer's name.
> . . .
> Faltering, and ignorant where I was, at length
> I chanced to espy those characters inscribed
> On the green sod.
>
> (287–301)

The victims of the calculated Hawkshead murder, which was described by a contemporary as 'the most horrid act that hath been heard of in this countrey' (225), were the murderer's wife and her family, and several neighbours who survived were also intended to die. Though this hanging was the last recorded use of the gibbet in the Hawkshead Parish Register, the stump of the gallows-post remained until about 1860, and the local writer of a common-place book 'records [at so late a date] the popular dread of approaching the site even by daylight' (44). The place where the murderer was hung up in chains at Pool Stang was known as Gibbet Moss, and, according to the local historian, Henry Swainson Cowper, it was 'thoroughly haunted' (ibid.).

Another local historian records that the other hanging of Nicholson 'for the murder of Thomas Parker, a butcher, of Langwathby' was the occasion when 'The ghastly spectacle [of the gibbet] was witnessed for the last time in Penrith, in 1767': 'The body of the murderer hung exposed until nothing but the skeleton remained. One stormy night, the gibbet, which stood near Nancy Dobson's stone, where the murder was committed, was blown down, and some of the inhabitants of Eden-hall gathered the bones together, and wrappng them in a winnowing sheet, buried them' (Bulmer, 622). Both these notorious sentences were therefore among the last local manifestations of a penal code that specialized in the display of punishment exacted as the price of transgression.

The communal memory that Wordsworth inherited had passed into a bogeyman tradition of admonitory dread through which spectacular retribution had become replaced by spectral discipline.

In the Gothic nightmares of 'The Vale of Esthwaite', Wordsworth shows how the Hawkshead victim may have taken the shape of a 'wan' woman, clad 'in silken vest' and holding a taper, passing along 'aisles' to deliver her threatening disclosure of the iron case and gallows-chains:

> Now did I love the dismal gloom
> Of haunted Castle's pannel'd room
>   . . .
> When as I heard a rustling sound
> My haggard eyes would turn around,
> Which strait a female form survey'd
> Tall, and in silken vest array'd.
> Her face of wan and ashy hue
> And in one hand a taper blue;
> Fix'd at the door she seem'd to stand
> And beckoning slowly wav'd her hand.
>   . . .
> Through aisles that shuddered as we pass'd
> By doors [?] flapping [?] the blast
> And green damp windings dark and steep,
> She brought me to a dungeon deep,
> Then stopp'd, and thrice her head she shook,
> More pale and ghastly seem'd her look.
> [   ] shew'd
> An iron coffer mark'd with blood.
>   . . .
> With arms in horror spread around
> I mov'd – a form unseen I found
> Twist round my hand an icy chain
> And drag me to the spot again.

(240–67)

The woman compels Wordsworth back to 'the spot', forcing him to fix his gaze on the scene where violent crime and capital execution have become confused. It was in order to describe another specific childhood trauma that had happened during his mother's lifetime and in her home town of Penrith – of being lost and looking for guidance – together with that of his father's death that Wordsworth invented, in the two-part

Prelude of 1799, the expression 'spots of time' (Pt. I, 288), and by then he had become more conscious over time of the empowerment involved in resorting to these ambivalent configurations of violence: 'Life with me, / As far as memory can look back, is full / Of this beneficent influence' (XI 276–8). In the Penrith occurrence, he recognizes a crucial formation in what to others might simply have been the 'ordinary sight' (308) of what he feels to be an oppressed but strangely forceful female:

> forthwith I left the spot,
> And, reascending the bare common, saw
> A naked pool that lay beneath the hills,
> The beacon on the summit, and more near,
> A girl who bore a pitcher on her head
> And seemed with difficult steps to force her way
> Against the blowing wind.
>
> (301–7)

A bleached supernaturalism surrounding a suffering woman features again, partially a spectre of the Hawkshead murder victim who had entered the composite *after* his mother's death:

> I should need
> Colours and words that are unknown to man
> To paint the visionary dreariness
> Which, while I looked all round for my lost guide,
> Did at that time invest the naked pool,
> The beacon on the lonely eminence,
> The woman, and her garments vexed and tossed
> By the strong wind.
>
> (308–15)

There is a burdened ambiguity about the figure, distressed but unyielding, as about the letters written on the grass that Wordsworth writes are the initials of the killer, though they were in fact those of the Penrith victim. If the encounter reveals the originary violence of the alphabet – of language itself [9] – in an episode generally about unwilling autonomy, the figure demonstrates a difficult but unstoppable way forward. Though, disturbingly, the Hawkshead woman had been the object of male violence, haunting the locality of the gallows, as an unquiet revenant she is also the forceful subject of the legal retribution which the Penrith community insists on recording. Besides being a site of transgression (including the Oedipal attractions of her bodily shape, revealed by the blustering wind: see 'And, when against the wind she strains / Oh might I kiss the mountain rains / That sparkle on her cheek', 'Louisa', 10–12), she is also the embodiment of a hard-won inscription in the law, through which Wordsworth's own subject, instructed by the maternal presence, had survived a series of traumas.

A fine figurative ectoplasm extends throughout much of the writing, in which the sense of the numinous that is attached to evanescent vision, especially through mists and vaporous veils, typically emerges as having come to possess and inspirit some appropriate language. Accordingly, Mary Wordsworth is 'A lovely Apparition' (3) in 'She was a Phantom of delight' whose liminality – 'A Traveller betwixt life and death' (24) – and whose regulated passion offer such a stable mirroring of what makes Wordsworth himself tick ('And now I see with eye serene / The very pulse of the machine', 21–2) that she conforms flawlessly to the requirements of his ideal ego: 'A perfect Woman; nobly planned, / To warn, to comfort, and command; / And yet a Spirit still...' (27–9). After death, the child-woman Lucy lingers transparently in the landscape to awaken a pantheistic theology rather than simply disintegrate into material things. It is the unearthliness of these female figures which enables them to organize their lives against the grain of public events. In *The White Doe of Rylstone*, Emily, though her life is largely determined by the bloody Rising of the North, is nevertheless 'consecrated' (591, 999) to overcoming her historical context with a spirit of purged protestantism, embodied in the doe's returning 'like a gliding Ghost' (1902).

With time, the phantoms grow closer to institutionalization and are by no means exorcized by the turn to orthodoxy, but increasingly invoke the ecclesiastical overtones of their Cockermouth source. Passing into a settled discourse, their survival becomes less precarious. As Wordsworth writes in Book IV of *The Prelude*, the whole Vale of Esthwaite had always been presided over by the church: 'I saw the snow-white church upon its hill / Sit like a thronèd lady, sending out / A gracious look all over its domain' (13–15). All those dying or bereaved mothers who process through Wordsworth's work become increasingly explicit representations of redemptive promise. Such is the assurance eventually offered (in 1845) by the revised fate of Margaret in 'The Ruined Cottage' (who 'learned, with soul / Fixed on the Cross, that consolation springs, / From sources deeper than the deepest pain, / For the meek Sufferer' – *The Excursion* I 936–9); by Lady Alice De Romilly, who founded Bolton Priory, parts of Carlisle Cathedral and Crosthwaite Parish Church, Keswick, as lasting memorials of her drowned son in 'The Force of Prayer' (1815);

and by the mother in 'The Widow on Windermere Side' (?1837), who
envisions her transfigured son, 'His raiment of angelic white, and lo! /
His very feet bright as the dazzling snow' (18–19). This crazy widow's
moving restitution, 'passing through strange sufferings towards the tomb'
(36), is among the most evolved of Wordsworth's mothers' in making
explicit his understanding of spiritual vision as the story of maternal
reunion:

> Oft, when light breaks through clouds or waving trees,
> With outspread arms and fallen upon her knees
> The Mother hails in her descending Son
> An Angel, and in earthly ecstasies
> Her own angelic glory seems begun.
>
> (38–42)

In 'Ode to Duty' the disembodied figure reappears as an abstraction.
Her most manifest function is laid bare in allegorizing Wordsworth's own
submission to moral discipline, personified as Pallas (offspring of power
and wisdom), and the taper held by the Cockermouth penitent has
become a phallic rod, the attribute of a commanding female voice:

> Stern Daughter of the Voice of God!
> O Duty! if that name thou love
> Who art a light to guide, a rod
> To check the erring, and reprove;
> Thou, who art victory and law
> When empty terrors overawe;
> From vain temptations dost set free;
> And calm'st the weary strife of frail humanity!
>
> (1–8)

The same moral structure was to be readily politicized, especially in the
veiling of power and violence. By 'Ode, 1814', actually written in 1816
to commemorate the final overthrow of Napoleon at Waterloo, Wordsworth beholds a domesticated British version of a French revolutionary
festival in terms of defensive nationalism. He personally 'took an active
part in [the] patriotic celebration' of Waterloo, ascending Skiddaw to
attend the 'scene of festivity' round Southey's bonfire, which the second
stanza probably recalls, as British triumphalism is legitimized in images
that ritually reinstate a united, undifferentiated imaginary family, where
the mother is nowhere and everywhere:

> And lo! with crimson banners proudly streaming,
> And upright weapons innocently gleaming,
> Along the surface of a spacious plain
> Advance in order the redoubted Bands,
> And there receive green chaplets from the hands
>   Of a fair female train –
>   Maids and matrons, dight
>   In robes of dazzling white;
> While from the crowd bursts forth a rapturous noise
>   By the cloud-capt hills retorted;
>   And a throng of rosy boys
>   In loose fashion tell their joys;
> And grey-haired sires, on staffs supported,
> Look round, and by their smiling seem to say,
> 'Thus strives a grateful Country to display
> The mighty debt which nothing can repay!'
>
>   (53–68)

To the caricaturist, James Gillray, and Percy Shelley who both parodied this kind of display in their prints and satires (notably in the mock triumphalism of the latter's own pageant poem, 'The Mask of Anarchy'), it represents the hypocritical façade of institutional power. But Wordsworth's inner history welcomes a necessary and benign construction of national power in deeply familiar forms. A military discourse is feminized as he sees the innocent 'upright weapons', familiarly dis- and re-empowered, decked by admiring women in white. The regalia seems inseparable from the natural scene, and the staff-supported images of aged power recall Burke's representation of the emasculated paternalism that generates Britain's gentle might in *Reflections on the Revolution in France*.[10] In Wordsworth's poem, a debt has been incurred to those whose deaths have protected the nation from further violence, including of course the knowledge of its own inner discords. Their suffering has legitimized the British war effort, making it an unquestionable good by constituting the enemy as the source of a different, unsanctionable violence. So, in the companion 'Ode 1815', Wordsworth could in the original versions hail the beneficence of what he calls the 'pure intent' of British 'Carnage':

> But Thy [Almighty God's] most dreaded instrument
> In working out a pure intent,
> Is Man – arrayed for mutual slaughter,

– Yea, Carnage is thy daughter!

(106–9)

As with Pallas, that other 'Stern Daughter', so with Wordsworth's Valkyrie: the deflection of filiation to the daughter side-steps the issue of Oedipal rivalry while it confirms the seamless passage of authority.

Mummies

Terry Castle has historicized the turn to the spectral, with the result that Wordsworth's familiars may be placed in a more general context. Writing of what she terms 'the spectralization of the other' in the later eighteenth century, she claims that, in 'the moment of romantic self-absorption', '[t]he corporeality of the other' was 'reduced to a phantom – a purely mental effect', and that a 'new obsession with the internalized images of other people' (237) was produced. Castle contends that the Radcliffean hero or heroine in particular is 'haunted' (234) by this impression, but the effect is also pervasive in Wordsworth's writing. It belongs, for example, to the fantastic quality that Coleridge describes as having 'above all' struck him in Wordsworth's early writing: 'the original gift of spreading the tone, the *atmosphere*, and with it the depth and height of the ideal world around forms, incidents, and situations, of which, for the common view, custom had bedimmed all the lustre, had dried up the sparkle and the dew drops' (*BL* I 80). Such 'a feeling analogous to the supernatural' in 'things of every day' (*BL* II 7) was, by agreement, to invest Wordsworth's contributions to *Lyrical Ballads*.

The form it takes in *The Mysteries of Udolpho* (1794) is to produce a mirroring or blurring of characters into each other, and, with reference to Piaget and Eve Kosofsky Sedgwick, Castle psychologizes the spectral by suggesting that 'the Gothic and romance in particular, atavistically dramatize the primal stage in human awareness' (240). She then proceeds to define the historicity of this reversion more particularly by adopting the argument of Philippe Ariès's *L'Homme devant la mort* (1977) which enables her to see the Radcliffean ambience 'as an aspect of a much larger cognitive revolution in western culture' consequent on the alienation occasioned by 'Changing affectional patterns, the breakdown of communal social life, and the increasingly individualistic and secular nature of modern experience' (242). The 'new spiritualization of human experience' from that time, it is proposed, was involved in 'hiding or denying the physical signs of mortality and decay', leading, for example, to an urgently emotional attachment to 'The cosmetic preservation of the corpse: the arts of embalming and even mummification (one thinks of Bentham's corpse) became common practices among all but the very lowest classes' (ibid.).

Some recurrent figurations in Wordsworth's poetry can be reviewed in the light of these insights that the literary registers indicated enable the replay of the primary stages of subjectification, prior to the exposure to full indivdualization, with its attendant awareness of fatality, which, socially and historically, the mortuary arts were aimed to arrest. It was the early loss of Wordsworth's mother which had fixed what remained of her immovably in his recollection. If her death had reawakened the primary disjunction of language acquisition in infancy, it was also to have the effect of helping to seal that continuing split by interesting him in *preserving* their special relation, lifted from historical time by her absence, within the domain of the father. For Wordsworth, memory and memorialization work endlessly to repeat, or freeze, this determining relation from the emergent subject's earliest organization.

A case in point is that of Betsy Lewes, the notorious mistress of Wordsworth's father's employer, Sir James ('Wicked Jimmy') Lowther, first Earl of Lonsdale. Contemporary accounts describe Lonsdale's 'distraction' and refusal to accept her death, after their many years of companionship, in 1797: 'Lord L's lady died last Tuesday 3 weeks and she remains in the house and the coffin not closed. The effect of a corpse in so putrid a state is seriously alarming to all in the house' (Owen, 294). He was to delay her burial for seven weeks. De Quincey's sentimentalized version in his memoir of Wordsworth recounts some interesting details, which were probably the theme of widespread gossip, about the 'fine young woman, of humble parentage' whom Lonsdale

> persuaded to leave her father, and put herself under his protection. Whilst yet young and beautiful, she died: Lord Lonsdale's sorrow was profound; he could not bear the thought of a final parting from the face which had become so familiar to his heart: he caused her to be enbalmed; a glass was placed over her features; and at intervals, when his thoughts reverted to her memory, he found a consolation (or perhaps a luxurious irritation) of his sorrow, in visiting this sad memorial of his former happiness.   (*DQ* II 154)

This scandal must have been well-known to Wordsworth, and it is possible that the preserved body in question, as a site of transgression, remorse and strange survival, lies buried in the network of associations around the prostitute's 'lovely boy' (396) in Book VII of *The Prelude*, whom

Wordsworth saw in a London theatre and described as 'embalmed / By nature' (400–1), escaping the reality of death and decomposition. What individualizes Wordsworth's fascination with this state of immutability in Book VII is its functioning as a moral preservative. The preoccupation that surfaces from his London reminiscences at this point in the poem is that of sexual transgression, and it is effectively curbed, even as it is acknowledged, by being broached through descriptions of mothers and their illegitimate offspring. Indeed, his attitude to London, in the description which found its way into Book VIII, is one directed by a mother-figure from whom he is keen to learn a guiding lesson: 'Preceptress stern, that didst instruct me next, / London, to thee I willingly return' (678–9). As his contemplations develop in Book VII, the child ceases to be a sign of debauchery and becomes rather an affirmation of the mother's resilient influence, so that her lapse becomes part of a larger moral prospect. For as long as the boy could be imagined as 'embalmed', he would never emerge from that stage at which the issues of sexuality and precarious individuality would arise:

> through some special privilege
> Stopped at the growth he had – destined to live,
> To be, to have been, come, and go, a child
> And nothing more, no partner in the years
> That bear us forward to distress and guilt,
> Pain and abasement.
>
> (401–6)

In the end, however, the boy's likelier fate is compared unfavourably with the dead child of Mary Robinson, the so-called Maid of Buttermere, who was herself the victim of an infamous seduction: 'but he perhaps, / Mary, may now have lived till he could look / With envy on thy nameless babe that sleeps / Beside the mountain chapel undisturbed' (409–12). Like Betsy, who had ended up frequenting London theatres and pleasure gardens in Lonsdale's company,[11] Mary, a more modest Lake District belle, had been enticed from her lowly occupation as a waitress in her father's inn, but she had returned to '[live] in peace / Upon the spot where she was born and reared' (351–2), to follow, in effect, the path of Wordsworth's unchanging fantasy and become effectively embalmed in her past.

Wordsworth's mortuary attentions are directed to the maternal relation, in which mother and infant equally participate, but his concern for maintaining their union usually focuses on the autobiographical position of the mummified child, including Hartley Coleridge: 'Nature will either end thee quite; / Or... / Preserve for thee, by individual right, / A young lamb's heart among the full-grown flocks' ('To H.C. Six Years Old', 21–4), and Burns's dead son: 'For he is safe, a quiet bed / Hath early found among the dead, / Harboured where none can be misled, / Wronged, or distrest' ('At the Grave of Burns', 67–70). The extreme protectiveness that prefers death to corruption is not simple negation, but after all offers a translation of being into the law – the law of the unbroken maternal relation. On that basis alone will maturity be acceptable to Wordsworth, together with all its social and cultural activities. Even his own role as father is consequently dominated by the maternal relation, insisting on its founding lesson, as indeed are all the Wordsworthian family relations which are manoeuvred into the enactment of that supervisory influence, all the more ubiquitously displaced from its actual absence.

Nevertheless, the preoccupation with averting the child's degradation is intensified by a real anxiety over ensuring the lawful assumption of the name of the father. Wordsworth's pressing interest in absolving the stigma of illegitimacy is urged by his relation with the family member whose exposure to Wordsworthian influence was most precarious – his own love-child by Annette Vallon, Anne-Caroline Wordsworth. During the truce between France and England, in March 1802, he revisited his French attachments prior to his marriage with Mary Hutchinson, and in a sonnet written at that time describing his reunion with his other virtual family on the French coast near Calais, 'It is a beauteous evening, calm and free', he addresses this 'untouched' ten-year-old as one who, in enjoying a suspended and still unfallen condition, was in some way already in heaven:

> Dear Child! dear Girl! that walkest with me here,
> If thou appear untouched by solemn thought,
> Thy nature is not therefore less divine:
> Thou liest in Abraham's bosom all the year;
> And worshipp'st at the Temple's inner shrine,
> God being with thee when we know it not.
>
> (9–14)

The scriptural allusion is to the story of Lazarus and Dives in Luke 16: 19–31, where the beggar Lazarus is 'carried by the angels into Abraham's bosom' (22) while Dives remains on the other side of 'a great gulf [that had been] fixed: so that they who would pass from hence to you

cannot; neither can they pass to us, that would come from thence' (26).
Caroline is seen as similarly occupying a position enviably on the other
side of an untransgressable border, literally the war zone of the English
Channel, but more fundamentally, (and perhaps by added implication
to that other Lazarus of Bethany, whom in John 11: 11 Jesus awoke
from his 'sleep' of death), between being and non-being.

Until 1922, with the publication of Emile Legouis's *Wordsworth and
Annette Vallon*, Caroline did not exist in Wordsworth's official biography. His nephew, Bishop Christopher, had left the 'lapse' out of his
commissioned memoir in the belief that the dead poet would have considered the omission 'most conducive to the divine honour and good of
men's souls'.[12] In the above sonnet, Wordsworth had already safely
embalmed Caroline in the phrase 'Abraham's bosom', an Hebraism with
obvious motherly overtones in English, which prematurely conferred
on her eternal life with the blessed. The procedure is effectively one of
legitimization, as the daughter is brought into the lineage of maternal
discipline by converting her implication in transgression, through the
surveillance of her heavenly father ('with thee when we know it not'),
into a superior regime of chastened spectrality. The girl's imagined
death-in-life is represented as the promise of life after death by which
she is viewed as participating in the Christian discourse of spirituality.
In this way it is good that father and daughter should remain out of
touch, able to communicate only by letter, in order for them to be able
to meet and relate within a shared discursive existence. The issue (in
both senses) of bodily transgression is thereby hazed over: the girl has
hardly ever been conceived into any other reality, since her subjectivity
is held never simply to have entered into consciousness of a fallen
domain from which her parents' offence might be knowable. She is to be
acknowledged in that order of being only through an intersubjectivity
that is informed by the maternal relation.

Yet the apparent absentee from this family reunion is the real mother,
Annette, whose converting presence is, in fact, what pervades and
enables it, and in so doing she comes to fulfil *in propria persona* the teas-
ing aspiration displaced from her onto the figure of the deserted mother
throughout the earlier poetry. There the hint is always of seeking relief
from a history of shame or violation by the promise of some further
inner strength to be valued in the maternal relation itself: because it
seems to lie outside of cultural constructions, its potential rediscovery
within them makes its reappearance unexpectedly sustaining. Wordsworth's mad mothers, for example, mostly make a virtue of obsessive
behaviour resulting from their damaged pasts, which they will not

relinquish, and the refusal to let go itself affirms an insistence which heroically promises the object of their fixed attention, usually a baby, some kind of fulfilment, however brief. The puzzling grotesquerie of 'The Thorn' has to do with the irrepressible effect of the Gothic spectrality stirred by the hinted infanticide, with the baby's face in the pond and the moving moss, particularly in its appeal – in a way Wordsworth barely suggests – to his own formidable investment in and implicit expectation from any returning mother figure: 'I never heard of such as dare / Approach the spot when she is there' (98–9). Scrutinizing the mother relation for all-sufficiency involves the superfluity of the father, and so excuses his manifest absence, while his presence is nevertheless indirectly reconstituted within the mother's supervisory regime.

In reconstructing Wordsworth's (legal) case for his own defence on the charge of desertion, the complications of his own (psychological) case history should not be overlooked. As Judith Page has pointed out, Wordsworth 'experiences abandonment not just from the perspective of having abandoned Annette and Caroline, but, paradoxically, with an understanding of what it means to be left behind' (Page, 6). For the losses of both his own parents Wordsworth had preformulated strategies of compensation and replacement which he was now passing on in his turn. Some of the strain of his own nostalgia for the child's position, instead of having to convert it into the mature responsibilities of fatherhood, shows up in the lyrics of boyhood reminiscence of 1802. While Dorothy strengthens the presence of the maternal relation in several of them – 'Dead times revive in thee' ('To a Butterfly', ['Stay near me – do not take thy flight!'], 6) – it is one to which he can never simply resort, and by then he could ventriloquize it only by a childish falsetto:

> Oh! pleasant, pleasant were the days,
> The time, when, in our childish plays,
> My sister Emmeline and I
> Together chased the Butterfly!
> (10–13)

Still, the whole of Wordsworth's family romance is effectively regulated by the common solvent of the maternal relation, and the role of the daughter turns out to be crucial in enabling its social and cultural efficacy. In their path-finding essay collection, *Daughters and Fathers*, Betty Flowers and Lynda Boose strenuously unearthed this key but typically occluded father/daughter relation. Boose's individual chapter, 'The Father's House and the Daughter in It: the Structures of Western

Culture's Daughter–Father Relationship', argues that our 'culture has essentially been built upon the relationship it has seemed least eager to discuss – that between father and daughter' because 'the prohibition of incest is essentially a mechanism to control internal family sexuality so that outward exchanges can take place', and *'The* exchangeable figure is the daughter' (19–20). Yet, Boose argues, the daughter figure is specifically absent from the patriarchal narrative: in Freudian and Lacanian terms, it is the daughter who most conspicuously lacks the phallus. The daughter, then, by definition finds it most difficult to enter the cultural story: 'She essentially lacks parentage [writes Boose] . . . Unlike the son, she is the temporary sojourner within her family, destined to seek legitimation and name outside its boundaries' (21). Yet, since the middle-class family is a founding disciplinary discourse, it can also be seen that the daughter possesses an ultimate power of social control by her compliance, or otherwise, though her influence is only ever represented as an implicit endorsement either bestowed or withheld. The base story of Wordsworth's preservation of the maternal relation within the symbolic order accordingly merges with its imaginary duplication by daughterly acquiescence in the law of the father – a strifeless fantasy that obstructs currency with any other but a paternally approved name. It is not therefore surprising that Wordsworth, for whom the family was peculiarly as one, found it particularly hard to part with his daughters.

The theme of family reunions, hopelessly yearned for in 'The Ruined Cottage' and 'The Brothers', or apparently achieved in 'We Are Seven' and 'Home at Grasmere', is constant in his poetry, and it seems that to him, as an orphan, they could only ever be possible within the spectral domain, where they are always subject to regulation by maternal discipline. It is crucial for Wordsworth that these reunions should remain in a field of desire that renounces the return of the live body, because acceptance of its forfeiture insures all family members from the threat of individual cancellation by generating *in its place* a shared moral structure of self-denial and self-sacrifice. 'Laodamia', composed in 1814 and published the following year, is Wordsworth's most overt dramatization of the conditions of this definitive restraint with its insistence on spectrality. The story adopted is peripheral to the major events of the Trojan War, and, since it existed only in a series of sketchy accounts in classical writers, it allowed Wordsworth more easily to infuse it with his own preoccupations, as they grew and altered. According to Wordsworth, his poem was prompted by an image in Pliny's *Natural History* 'of the trees growing and withering' as they came within view of the site of contested power, the walls of Troy, that the mourned Greek hero, Protesilaus, had dedicated himself to help conquer, but by which in the event he had been killed:

> And ever, when such stature they had gained
> That Ilium's walls were subject to their view,
> The trees' tall summits withered at the sight;
> A constant interchange of growth and blight!
>
> (171–4)

The living trees keep growing out of the dead hero's tomb and so continue to bring the durability of his sacrifice to mind, but they are also expressive of his wife Laodamia's contradictory frustration with it, and the private loss it had entailed. Husband and wife participate jointly in the repeated mutilation, but the poem shows they have very different responses to the endless oscillation of life and death. In the end, the poem mounts a lesson on how the achievement of spectral discourses proceeds from the virtuous representation of loss that necessarily regulates all familial and social claims.

While Protesilaus received his death willingly as the assertion of an heroic patriotic register ('resolved / That, of a thousand vessels, mine should be / The foremost prow in pressing to the strand, – / Mine the first blood that tinged the Trojan sand', 123–6), Laodamia refuses to admit the necessity of his bodily extinction. The 'Spectre' of her husband, which 'is not sent to scare . . . or deceive' but 'to reward' her 'fidelity' (38–40), requires her to co-operate in the self-sacrificial gesture that welcomes the surrender of the body. He is led back by Mercury, who administers gentle spectral discipline: 'Mild Hermes spake – and touched her with his wand / That calms all fear' (19–20). Though according to the twelfth-century Homeric commentator, Eustathius of Constantinople, for example, Protesilaus himself was the prime mover behind the reunion, because owing to Aphrodite he continued to desire his wife even after his death, there is no question of Wordsworth's hero being unwillingly austere. But Laodamia, who, echoing the Latin poets' treatment (Catullus and Ovid in the *Heroides*), reveals a degree of physical desire that is rare in Wordsworth's published works ('"Give, on this well-known couch, one nuptial kiss / To me, this day, a second time thy bride!"', 63–4), is unable to compromise the nature of her own kind of desire ('"No Spectre greets me, – no vain Shadow this; / Come, blooming Hero, place thee by my side!"', 61–2). Through a series of revisions of the original 1815 version, Wordsworth sides increasingly with the demands of the husband's spectrality, which makes a virtue of inexorable loss.[13]

Writing to a nephew in 1830, Wordworth explains how in the 1827 edition he had felt impelled to insist on Laodamia's 'punishment' for '[disregarding] ... the exhortation'[14] of Protesilaus to '[raise] and [solemnise]' (144) her affections. He had by then decided that the most fitting destiny for her reprehensible longing for the restoration of the living body was to be found in Virgil's condemnation of the wife to a sorrowful region of perpetual unfulfilment, the 'Lugentes Campi', or 'mournful Fields' in Dryden's translation of the *Aeneid*: 'There *Laodamia*, with *Evadne*, moves: / Unhappy both, but loyal in their Loves' (VI 596, 606–7; *Works*). Though she had been doomed in the first two versions of 1815 and 1820 only to what one editor calls 'the serene region tenanted by happy Ghosts' (Hutchinson ed., 901), in 1827 Wordsworth decided to place her 'in a grosser clime, / Apart from happy Ghosts' (*PW* II 272), and then, (somewhat relenting in the versions from 1832 onwards), after an 'appointed time' (161) she was allowed to join those 'happy Ghosts' (162), who, like Wordsworth himself, were already able to appreciate the reward of an ability 'to control / Rebellious passion' (73–4).

Pervasively, though undisclosed, the story behind Protesilaus's demand for his wife's equal submission is that of Euripides' *Iphigenia in Aulis*, with its consummate portrayal of the father's demand for self-sacrifice. It is this subdued parallelism that complicates Protesilaus' relation to his wife with other domestic narratives. That the play is one of Wordsworth's sources is indicated by his 1815 note to the poem which acknowledges it for providing him with the detail of Protesilaus's taste for intellectual pastimes. Less explicitly, it also informed the poem's critique of Laodamia's behaviour. In Euripides, instead of the marriage (to Achilles) which she had expected, Iphigenia submissively surrenders herself as her father Agamemnon's offering to placate Artemis in fulfilment of the oracle's other prerequisite for the Greeks' taking Troy, following the sacrifice of Protesilaus:[15]

> My father, at thine hest I come,
> And for my country's sake my body give,
> And for all Hellas to be led of you
> Unto the Goddess' altar, willingly,
> And sacrificed, if this is Heaven's decree.[16]

The Cornell editor suggests that Protesilaus's later resolution not to be influenced by his memories of his home and his wife ('In soul I swept the indignity away') perhaps echoes Iphigenia's 'Lo, resolved I am to die; and fain I am that this be done / Gloriously – that I thrust ignoble craven thoughts away' (529). The plot of Euripides' dramatic sequel reveals how the daughter's self-sacrifice averts the cycle of Oedipal revenge. Iphigenia's willingness to accomplish the grander design earned her reprieve from Artemis, who substituted a hind as her victim and carried Iphigenia off to become her priestess, in which role she was able (according to the legend added by Euripides in *Iphigenia in Tauris*) to become instrumental in saving her brother, Oedipus, from himself being sacrificed. Laodamia, on the other hand, is increasingly condemned in Wordsworth's account for not living up to that kind of death.

The Wordsworthian family romance was calling on these intertextualities urgently at the time that 'Laodamia' was written. Haydon gives an account of Mary Wordsworth's persuading her husband in 1820 that Laodamia 'had *too lenient a fate* for loving her Husband so *absurdly* – at her petition he corrected the conclusion as it was first published'.[17] Mary, then, co-authored some of the poem's conclusions which found words for her desire, as Haydon describes: 'While Wordsworth repeated this in his chaunting tone, his wife sat by the Fire quite abstracted, moaning out the burthen of the line, like a distant echo. I never saw such a complete instance of devotion, of adoration' (ibid.). John Barrell, who quotes this passage, hears Mary's moans as those of 'a wife who ... punishes herself to spare her husband the guilt of punishing her, and who adores him at the cost of despising herself' (456). This is a challenging shift of perspective on the nature of Wordsworth's demands, but it only begins to realize the various complicities and empowerments involved. Mary was wilfully raising the poetic as well as the moral stakes by exacting full punishment. As Ernest de Selincourt notes, from 1815 to 1820 the poem was grouped with those '"founded on the affections", and according to Crabb Robinson ... was "not much esteemed" by [Wordsworth] as belonging to this "inferior" class' (*PW* II 519). Thereafter it was placed among the 'Poems of Imagination'. In sacrificing herself to Wordsworth's idealism with such a will Mary was investing herself in and with Wordsworth's whole cultural project and collaborating in the conversion of the domestic into what she perceived as Wordsworth's epic mission to refound the nation in his time in *The Recluse*. Besides, Mary had an added interest in exorcizing the historical appeals of simple affection from that other abandoned partner, Annette, who was again touching on their lives at this time. As the good wife, Mary assimilated with the moralizing mother to cast off the transgressive wife, and in so doing embodied what De Quincey calls a 'second self of the poet' (*DQ* II 133), insightfully echoing Wordsworth's own aspiration in 'Ode to Duty' to 'breed a second Will more wise' from 'Denial and restraint' (47).

The reapparition of Annette had been caused by the forthcoming marriage of Caroline. In Book II of the *Iliad*, Homer refers not only to Laodamia's passionate reaction to her husband's departure, but also to their half-completed house (a detail developed by Catullus) – hints that led other mythographers to infer that the couple were newly married.

During the summer months prior to the poem's composition, Caroline's wish to receive her father's blessing for her intended marriage was made known, and the ceremony (which was eventually delayed until March 1816) was originally to have occurred in the month that Wordsworth wrote this poem. Wordsworth allowed his womenfolk to negotiate his own position on the match, which ostensibly focused on financial anxieties, but the imaginative pact he had arranged for himself with his illegitimate daughter in 1802 now required subtle rehandling. Once more he needed to ensure a way of parting with his daughter, of giving her away, that would be grounded in a continuing maternal relation, and so it was that Laodamia's case also came gradually to figure the passage from daughter to wife, and from wife to daughter.

Wordsworth's comment that 'Laodamia' 'cost him more trouble than almost anything of equal length [he had] ever written' (*PW* II 519) relates particularly to these changes made to the penultimate stanza over a period of thirty years. The poem's textual history demonstrates what may easily be misconstrued as an increasing bias to severity, only unwillingly modified, with its formal revisions of the judgement imposed, ('Ah, judge her gently . . . yet without crime' 1815; 'By no weak pity . . . not without the crime', 1827; 'passion desperate to a crime', 1840; 'as for a wilful crime', 1845 etc.). However each alteration is read, a crucial turn to condemnation clearly occurred in the variant composed in 1820 and published in the 1827 edition which was never completely withdrawn, though Barrell's minute scrutiny of these inflections points out that they are involved in a counter-movement of compromise from 1832 onwards, when Laodamia's sentence is commuted to spending 'an "appointed time" apart from the happy shades in Elysium, with whom however she would eventually be reunited' (457).

Barrell concludes that the variations do not readily add up, and he sees in them 'a sequence of concessions and affirmations made in response to the declining authority of the poem's account of heroic masculinity', specifically of 'the classical republican version' (459) that he argues the poem had originally promoted. Though his argument is persuasive that the poem's masculinity was indeed reconstructed by the early Victorian readers whom he adduces – Mary Wordsworth (by the later 1820s), Sara Coleridge, William Hazlitt, and especially Benjamin

Robert Haydon and Thomas De Quincey – that reception should not obscure the recognition that for Wordsworth himself the poem continued to enforce a moral regime which from the beginning had been the result of a composite engendering. The founding image of Pliny's trees on the farther shore of the Hellespont, with their 'constant interchange of growth and blight', was evidently conflicted from the start, and, like the subsequent revisionary impulses, it never had supported either the husband's masculine or the wife's feminine responses to heroic death unproblematically. But the leading variation behind the poem's revisions is in fact its increasing admission of Christian discourse which, however much it may have provided a vehicle for more feminine sensibility, presented Wordsworth with a particularly challenging instance of the kind of quandary that beset all his revisions. What is radically at stake in the shift from the register of republican heroism is the avoidance of having to acknowledge the disruption of one form of representation by another, as a specifically Christian discursivity is shaded in, because that awareness would have aroused the primary trauma of language acquisition. The sequence of variants betrays the painful management of inflections to that end.

By the early 1830s Wordsworth had become more sensitive to criticism of his Christian orthodoxy than when he had resisted Walter Savage Landor's objection to confusing Christian and pagan world-views in referring to the 'second birth' as 'degraded by Conventiclers' (*WL* IV 244) in the first version of 1815. Consequently his move to a measure of clemency seems to have been made in response to the judgement of the Revd Julius Charles Hare, who interpreted Laodamia's evolved punishment as one of eternal damnation, though she was 'not a voluntary suicide' (216). The allegation had not preoccupied Wordsworth previously, since orthodoxy had not been a significant issue. In fact, Wordsworth's treatment has some traditional validity. Laodamia's fate does not feature widely in ancient mythography, but according to the tradition spread by the Roman fabulist, Hyginus, and Ovid, Laodamia *was* in fact a suicide, throwing herself into the fire in which her father had burned her cherished image of Protesilaus. The dominant presence of the Virgilian influence on the poem, however, suggests another resonance with Laodamia's ardours in the tempting distractions of Aeneas's 'wife', Dido. Certainly, in Book VI of the *Aeneid*, which is Wordsworth's main source, Laodamia inhabits that part of Hell in which Aeneas centrally re-encounters Dido. This is the region that becomes the second circle of Dante's Hell reserved for the punishment of carnal sinners, and though Dido had contrived her death as a mock sacrifice, she was, unlike Laodamia, an indisputable suicide, whose death is aimed to pursue Aeneas with irreconcilable recrimination: 'Her angry Ghost, arising from the Deep, / Shall haunt thee waking, and disturb thy Sleep!' (IV 558–9). The principal cause of the delayed embarrassment with the poem's ending, bound up in the always given struggle to discriminate an act of wilful self-destruction from one of unselfish self-sacrifice, was this allegation of a hint of heterodoxy at precisely the time when Wordsworth was urgently interested in finding powerful representation for his own critique of the reformed nation in the discourse of Christianity.

But the greatest test of Wordsworth's father/daughter relation was to come with the deferment of his consent to his legitimate daughter Dora's marriage to Edward Quillinan. Born in 1804, Dora lived within the extended Wordsworth family until the marriage her father had deeply opposed. The engagement was announced by Dora in 1838, but the ceremony was delayed for several causes until 1841. After six years she was to return home to be nursed in her final illness at Rydal Mount. A letter from Wordsworth dated '8 February [1838]' contains his own copy of his sonnet 'At Dover' ('From the Pier's head long time and with encrease'), and at the bottom he added: 'Suggested by a passage in your journal, and sent as a peace-offering, at your dear Mother's request' (*WL* VIII 239). The journal referred to dates back to the summer of 1828, when Dora had taken a trip to the Continent with her father and Coleridge, and it is filled with lively descriptions of places and incidents. But Dora was at that later time visiting 'at Dover', and Wordsworth's maternally promoted wish to be at peace with his daughter goes back farther in memory to his 1802 stay at the channel ports and his formative meeting there with Caroline. Arriving back on the English coast he had then written two previous Dover sonnets to register a deepened sense of harmony, which his re-established nationalism drew from the temporary lull in the war, and which he represented in an ethereal cameo of Kent – cricket and the white cliffs: 'those boys who in yon meadow-ground / In white-sleeved shirts are playing; and the roar / Of waves breaking on the chalky shore; – / All, all are English' ('Composed in the Valley near Dover, on the Day of the Landing', 3–5). Now, in the late sonnet, he recalls the sacred quiet of the 1802 French ambience by being puzzled that the town seems 'Hushed to a depth of more than sabbath peace': 'What love of order guards their strange release / From noise and bustle? Or are both but flown / Soon to return? (4–7). What does, inexorably, return instead through the father's tortured domestic supervision of his delicate daughter's health and spiritual well-being is the might of the discourse of Christian moralism ('God's eternal word'), subjugating ('overpowering') in order to liberate the body ('set free / Thy sense'). And the costly reward of surviving annulled transgression – life in death – is a kind of death in life:

> Then Ocean cried, 'I drown
> Each petty turmoil; let thy wonder cease:
> My overpowering murmurs have set free
> Thy sense from pressure of life's hourly din,
> As the dread voice that speaks from out the sea
> Of God's eternal word, the voice of Time
> Deadens, – the shocks of faction, shrieks of crime,
> The shouts of folly, and the groans of sin.
>
> (7–14)

2
The Elided Father

I have got [Paine's Rights of Man] – If it do not cure my cough it is
a damned perverse mule of a cough – The pamphlet – From the row
– But mum – We don't sell it – Oh, no – Ears and eggs.
                    Thomas Holcroft to William Godwin, March 1791

Who said 'Ay, mum's the word'?
Sexton to willow.
                    Walter De la Mare

The Language of Nature

'The mighty debt which nothing can repay' in 'Ode, 1814' is finally
not (though it may cross the mind) the national debt swollen by finan-
cing the war with France, but rather a later manifestation of that
'mighty debt of grief'(431) that in 'The Vale of Esthwaite' the adolescent Wordsworth had avowed was owed primarily to his father for a
special kind of protective parentalism. Debts, however they may be
converted into investments, are always irksome at some level, and
Wordsworth found it unusually difficult to settle this particular one
because for obscure reasons it was of its singular nature hardly to have
been incurred. His recalcitrance in paying what he in that sense felt he
did not owe is suggested by the half-echo of Milton's Satan's resentment when faced with 'The debt immense of endless gratitude'[1] to God
in *Paradise Lost*.

'The Vale', Wordsworth's fragmentary and disjointed juvenile poem
(569 lines have been published of what may once have been many
more), written at the age of sixteen to seventeen in the loco-descriptive
genre interspersed with episodic narratives, swings from nightmare

hallucinations to factual autobiographical reminiscence and culminates in the recollection of his father's death, through which he first confronted a highly complex paternal identification overdetermined by the maternal relation. In order to explain to himself where he had arrived in his conflicted feelings about the event, he calls up the language of repentance belatedly to lament his father's death (so paying his debt) even as it demonstrates the paradigm of conversion that had itself qualified the role of the father and so, guiltily, distracted his mourning:

> For much it gives my heart relief
> To pay the mighty debt of grief,
> With sighs repeated o'er and o'er,
> I mourn because I mourned no more.
>
> (430–3)

The poem works its way round to confronting the trauma that had occurred when Wordsworth was thirteen:

> Long, long, upon yon naked rock
> Alone, I bore the bitter shock:
> Long, long, my swimming eyes did roam
> For little Horse to bear me home.
> To bear me – what avails my tear?
> To sorrow o'er a Father's bier.
>
> (422–7)

He was angry that the horse he expected his father to send to take him home for Christmas had not arrived, but his father was lying mortally ill from exposure at the time. It seems likely from this and the three later *Prelude* versions of the same incident that what in the original poem he referred to as 'a heavy load' (429) of guilt had resulted when impetuous expressions of vengeance had become unexpectedly self-fulfilling, and obscurely self-enhancing. It is more than the weather that is impacting on him and making his eyes swim with tears, and the retroactive 'shock' locates the Oedipal trauma not so much in the news of his father's death (Wordsworth obviously could not have known of it at the time, since it took place ten days later) as in his alarm at the intensity of his own past bitterness that had turned out so potently self-affirmative: 'Alone, I bore the bitter shock.' There is power gained as well as the premonition of abandonment in this defining moment of isolation, and the real shock turns out to be the related scandal that his father's death was such a secondary experience to the outcome of his mother's which it in effect served to reinforce.

All Wordsworth's accounts of this episode in the *Prelude* versions rely on several echoes from *Hamlet* particularly associated with the father's ghost that have been cumulatively noted, though never, I think, coherently, in terms of Marjorie Garber's observation that 'The appearance of ghosts within [Shakespeare's] plays is almost always juxtaposed to a scene of writing' (Garber, 18). In a later version of Wordsworth's father's death, in Part I of the two-part *Prelude* of 1799, the list of 'spectacles and sounds' (368) attached to the experience culminates in the image of 'the mist / Which on the line of each of those two roads / Advanced in such indisputable shapes' (365–7) – revising the exchange of language that Hamlet saw his father's ghost as inviting: 'Thou com'st in such a questionable shape' (*S*, I iv 1006).[2] Lacan's revision of Freud reveals the true object of Oedipal desire to be the phallus of language, and following that alternative narrative which for Wordsworth makes the ghost of the father the return of language trauma, the dialogue in the Wordsworthian encounter that initially seemed withheld by a paternal veto ('indisputable'), as the father refuses to share his power over the word (here represented by the withheld horse), turns out anyway to have been largely irrelevant to the fulfilment of some stronger desire. Wordsworth finds himself in the longer view to have been yearning not so much for the symbolic power his father's death would deliver as for some more familiar legitimization promised by the stronger impulse to accede to 'correct[ion]' of that desire and his own 'chastisement' (360, 355):

> The event,
> With all the sorrow which it brought, appeared
> A chastisement; and when I called to mind
> That day so lately passed ...
>   ...
>   ... I bowed low
> To God who thus corrected my desires.
>   (353–60)

Organizing these variations within the Oedipal triangle was Wordsworth's personal history of having enjoyed an earlier and exceptionally empowering complication of it. At this point, his stronger desire was not so much to acquire the word as to have done so in the distinctively repentant mode previously established. While he acknowledges the 'chastisement' of guilt over the loss of his father, the 'trite reflections of morality' (358) that he expresses in response do not match the depth of 'passion' (359) he subsequently experiences. 'God' may have 'thus corrected [his] desires' (to compete aggressively for the power of the word), but in such a way as in the end to provide him with the self-realizing exercise of penitence. Longer ago, his mother had taught him how to deal with the law of the father by internalizing it in this way, and everything seemed to have conspired to bring it to culminating effect. Within the natural order, which since his mother's death had served to reflect and embed through all disturbances the binding relation he had renewed with her, the castrating menace he might otherwise have felt to have been immanent in the 'Stormy, and rough, and wild' (342) day turns out to have been redirected to the removal of his father from the scene (the severe weather conditions he was experiencing were actually killing his father from exposure at the time). Waiting for his horse, his motives had been unclear, but later the defusing of his Oedipal urge within his presymbolic bonding, which was already waiting *for him*, became quite frankly invigorating: 'All these were spectacles and sounds to which / I often would repair, and thence would drink / As at a fountain' (368–70). Yet the internalized father has, of course, also been retained. The elemental violence represents an alternative self-empowerment that still achieves a special identification with his father's spirit (compare old Hamlet's 'I am thy father's spirit', I v 1006) by fusing any lingering sense of retribution with an enriching presentation of the natural environment:

> And I do not doubt
> That in this later time, when storm and rain
> Beat on my roof at midnight, or by day
> When I am in the woods, unknown to me
> The workings of my spirit thence are brought.
> (370–4)

A deeply intimate sustenance derives from the fading of that other, rivalrous mode of subjectification that more usually needs to pass through a wounding contest for the word of the father. At later times the absence of that passage of arms comes in aid of the unopposed access of an already entrenched inner power by enabling a deflection from the channel of conflict, guilty victory and appropriation. The result was the idealization of the (maternalized) father relation in the form of domesticated father-figures. In the notes Wordsworth dictated to Isabella Fenwick in 1843, he tells how his envy of another student's proficiency in Italian at Cambridge reminded him that the spirit of 'emulation' seemed personally dangerous to him, and how it became regulated by a moral register (the Sermon on the Mount) associated with a heavenly/dead father: 'it made me very thankful that as a boy I never experienced it. I felt very early the force of the words "Be ye perfect as your Father in heaven is perfect"' (Grosart, III 456).

By the time his father died, then, the maternal relation had been regulating Wordsworth's perception of all those natural scenes he was always to continue to find most memorable. What he saw that most mattered to him (and, fortuitously, what he most saw in the Vale of Esthwaite during his school-days from 1779 to 1787) was an exceptionally sheltered ecology and gentle topography which mirrored his settled trust in an all-embracing maternalism in the outer world. But this maternalism was also tough. If he had been 'Fostered alike by beauty and by fear' (*Prel* I 306) in the scenery of his childhood at Cockermouth and Hawkshead, the maternal relation had provided him with the over-riding framework of enclosure, not simply to withstand traumas of loss and guilt but in an abstruse way to thrive on them. The portrait he draws of himself in the 'Autobiographical Memoranda' as a boy with 'a stiff, moody, and violent temper' (*Memoirs* I 9) is wholly convincing when he explains how he used it to *court* 'chastisment' – as a demonstration, for example, of his immunity from a regime of patriarchal pieties founded upon brute intimidation and punishment:

> Upon another occasion, while I was at my grandfather's house at Penrith, along with my eldest brother, Richard, we were whipping tops together in the large drawing-room, on which the carpet was only laid down on special occasions. The walls were hung round with family pictures, and I said to my brother, "Dare you strike your whip through that old lady's petticoat?" He replied, "No, I won't." "Then," said I, "here goes;" and I struck my lash through her hooped petticoat, for which no doubt, though I have forgotten it, I was properly punished. But possibly, from some want of judgment in punishments inflicted, I had become perverse and obstinate in defying chastisement, and rather proud of it than otherwise. (ibid.)

Wordsworth's revision of Hamlet's Oedipalism is symptomatic. Hamlet had complained that his mother had inadequately mourned *his* father:

> within a month, –
> . . .
> *A little month*, or ere those shoes were old,

> With which she follow'd my poor father's body,
>
> . . .
>
> . . . marry'd with my uncle.
>
> (I ii 1003; emphasis added)

The inadequacy of the period given to mourning is disproportionate to what for Hamlet is an event of great magnitude, but in 'The Vale' Wordsworth aligns the insufficiency of his own response to his father's death with that of the mother, Gertrude. He plays down the (Oedipal) plot by minimizing the object of contention ('*little* Horse to bear me home', emphasis added), and attenuates the scale of his consequent development ('Nor did my *little* heart foresee / She lost a home in losing thee', 434–5; emphasis added) The sequence concludes with a puzzling ambiguity: 'Nor did it know, of thee bereft, / That *little* more than Heaven was left' (436–7; emphasis added). Of course, Wordsworth intends to say (hyperbolically) that hardly anything remained than his own death and reunion with his father in the next world. What his words also say, however, is that it was *almost* heaven ('little more than Heaven was left') *without* his father – which is hardly a small gain. What results indirectly from this appealing belittlement is, I am suggesting, the licensing of the subject's extraordinarily overdetermined entry into the symbolic order.

In this way, rather than fearing to have been secretly glad that his father is dead, Wordsworth is reminded that he in particular seems not to have needed to harbour any such motive. His father, John, had in fact been an absent father for most of the poet's life. He was a distant figure who, as land-steward and law-agent to the unpopular local magnate, the Earl of Lonsdale, had constantly to travel away on business. In early childhood, Wordsworth was brought up by his mother and her family, at whose home in another town (Penrith) he spent half the year from the age of three to six. He lived with his mother's family after her death, whenever he was not away at school, until he left for university in the year he completed drafting 'The Vale'. The reaction to his father's death, therefore, may be straightforwardly viewed as endorsing his father's marginal relevance to the actual circumstances of Wordsworth's social passage. But there were to be further intricacies attached to other sources of guilt and self-blame that arose between Wordsworth's writing the first account in his juvenile poem and his rewriting it for the *Prelude* versions. The complications came first from his own absence as a father, after he had for whatever justifiable reasons effectively deserted his first, illegitimate child and her mother in 1792.

Between the first account of his father's death in 'The Vale' and the subsequent *Prelude* version of 1799 Wordsworth had come to need to discover new strength from his special relation with the father to answer the consequences of his actual sexual transgression and his own first, anguishing experience of paternity. It was in the two-part *Prelude* of 1799 that Wordsworth began to develop the confession of a failure to mourn, as narrated in 'The Vale', into his revision of Hamlet's Oedipalism so as to arrive at a scheme of productive chastisement resulting in 'the workings of [his] spirit' (Pt. 1, 374). During the interim, the penitential paradigm was offering to form the basis of his entire cultural project, centred on authoring *The Recluse*, and his recognition of that entailed his creation of a distinctively authoritative poetic voice from the incremental effects of his additional, more recent traumas. By having to explain himself, what was to become ever more obviously the 'long and laborious Work'[3] of *The Recluse* seemed at first to be getting written already.

Wordsworth's encounter with his father's spirit, his rewriting of Hamlet's as *his* father's ghost, emerges as one shaped by an earlier formative relation that had become imprinted on the natural environment. Given his personal history, it meant that he had to define his special relation to language by discovering, from within the symbolic order, forms of representation for the particular terms on which he had entered it, and which had tended previously to be rather silently mirrored in his perceptions of the physical world. Intimations of transgression had been regulated by the kind of agency he summons to bring about the conversion of the anti-hero in 'Peter Bell', when, at the start of Part Third, he writes of the 'Dread Spirits' who have 'wandered from [their] course / Disordering colour, form, and stature!' (761–3), as in 'The Vale' and the Penrith Beacon episode of Book XI of *The Prelude*. There again, the admonitory realization takes the shape of the sudden presentation of language on the blank page: 'A *word* – which to his dying day / Perplexed the good man's gentle soul':

> The ghostly word, thus plainly seen,
> Did never from his lips depart;
> But he hath said, poor gentle wight!
> It brought full many a sin to light
> Out of the bottom of his heart.
> (754–60)

Wordsworth stresses that the agency has different modes of operation:

> Your presence often have I felt
> In darkness and the stormy night;
> And with like force, if need there be,
> Ye can put forth your agency
> When earth is calm, and heaven is bright
>
> (776–80)

– and the formulation he was developing for its representation in his poetry, involving a deviation from undisciplined inscription in the word of the father in search of the primary dyadic relation that had then to be brought back into expression, was that of the *language of nature*. Some fragmentary lines written in 1798, and included in Part II of the two-part *Prelude*, suggest how Wordsworth's expectation for the natural environment to speak for him took the form of the paternal inspiriting of scenes by sound rather than sight. When his habituation to visual reflexivity was challenged by a sense of other power, a still nurturing language could rudimentarily be discerned as apparently emanating from natural metabolism itself:

> For I would walk alone
> In storm and tempest, or in starless nights
> Beneath the quiet heavens, and at that time
> Would feel whate'er there is of power in sound
> To breathe an elevated mood, by form
> Or image unprofaned; and I would stand
> Beneath some rock, listening to sounds that are
> The ghostly language of the ancient earth,
> Or make their dim abode in distant winds.
> Thence did I drink the visionary power.
>
> (351–60)

For Wordsworth, such a controlled re-entry into (natural) language is so filled with the retained presence of what at first preceded symbolic otherness that it continuingly defers knowledge of the lack which all language entails. In an interplay between an illusion of fulfilment and frustration, it substitutes the recollection of a still possible kind of imaginary jubilation for the recognition of language's inevitably failing quest to replace the original and totally satisfying union with the mother:

> the soul –
> Remembering how she felt, but what she felt

Remembering not – retains an obscure sense
Of possible sublimity, to which
With growing faculties she doth aspire,
With faculties still growing, feeling still
That whatsoever point they gain they still
Have something to pursue.   (364–71)

Indeed, Wordsworth's poetry is so dependent on the recuperation of activities within the presymbolic that it invites comparison with Julia Kristeva's theorizing of a 'maternal function' that commences forming the 'subject-in-process' *before* Lacan's mirror stage. Kristeva uncovers the archaic and complex prefiguration of paternal law in this function which is already negotiating the logic of signification through the body-of-the-mother before the encounter with the symbolic takes place. The disposition to control, she believes, is imbibed with the mother's milk as the mother's prohibition regulates the nurture and evacuation of the infant's body and through weaning initiates the workings of negation. At this stage, the 'phallic mother' circumscribes the field of demand and stands in for what will become otherness, but in order to enter into the symbolic order of power and desire – to become a human subject – the infant has to separate from the 'maternal container' which it must 'abject' with the loving support of the 'imaginary father', her version of Freud's father in individual prehistory.[4]

Nevertheless, for Kristeva, the space in which the presymbolic maternal law obtains, which she calls the 'semiotic chora' after the unorganized signifying process of gesture, sound and rhythm (the 'semiotic' itself) which takes place there, will continue to be present as the irrepressible materiality, or signifying substance within the symbolic order. Semiotic drive, then, continues in dialectic with symbolic elements of stasis in the symbolic to produce signification, and it is this survival of maternal materiality inside the word of the father, on the border between what is constructed as nature and culture proper, that illuminates Wordsworth's formulation of the language of nature. Listening again to the 1798 fragment printed above, it is possible to hear in the 'growing faculties' and 'faculties still growing' that 'still / have something to pursue' one of those characteristic Wordsworthian overflowings of powerful feelings that Kristeva describes as *'the power of semiotic rhythms, which convey an intense presence of meaning in a presubject still incapable of signification'* (Kristeva, 1988, 62).

Dedicated Spirits

The beneficent horrors of spectral androgyny pervade the 'brooding Superstition' (27) of 'The Vale', that culminates in the autobiographical recollection of Wordsworth's father's death. When the potential of Gothic fantasy to heighten and distort becomes woven with the self-characterizing Oedipal theme from *Hamlet*, Wordsworth finds himself exploring the weird effects that his protracted relation with the mother had exerted on his own identification with the father-figure.

The poem's Gothicism is partly antiquarian, and picks up on local legend. In his *Guide to the Lakes* (1778), Thomas West records of the ruined Calgarth Hall, a castellated manor house which stood on the east bank of Windermere and which probably features centrally as the 'Gothic mansion' (l47) in this poem, 'spectres still are seen' (63–4). The building had long boasted two skulls, which in one version had come from two skeletons that had belonged to 'a famous doctress' (Armistead, 41) who once lived there. A more popular tale 'of immemorial standing' was that they were those of 'two poor old people, who were unjustly executed for a robbery' and that 'to perpetuate their innocence, some ghost brought them there' (ibid.). It was also claimed that the skeletal remains had been 'buried, burned, powdered, and dispersed to the winds, and upon the lake, several times, to no purpose as to their removal and destruction' (ibid.).[5] The ineradicable traces throughout the vicinity of the presence of a couple who had been held responsible for a capital crime of which they had themselves become the innocent victims might be expected to have exerted a particular appeal for Wordsworth.

Other childhood bogeys came to figure the latent guilt and fear of Oedipal conflict in Wordsworth's juvenile poetry, such as the fifteen-foot giant buried in St Andrew's churchyard next to his dame school at Penrith, and the skeletal woodcuts from Foxe's *The Book of Martyrs* in the library of Hawkshead Grammar School, which he describes as having impressed the Pedlar's early years: 'Strange and uncouth, dire faces, figures dire, / Sharp-kneed, sharp-elbowed, and lean-ancled too, / With long and ghostly shanks, forms which once seen / Could never be forgotten' (Figure 3).[6] Taken together, the anxiety fantasies that for Wordsworth people the areas around Penrith and Hawkshead merge into the narrative of gigantic buried presences who return in the form of animated skeletons, and who turn out to have been as much the objects as the perpetrators of violence. Instead of threatening vengeance, they bring with them words of fortitude and composure, like their later

Figure 3 Exhumation of Wickliffe, woodcut from *The Acts and Monuments of John Foxe* (1563)

avatar the Leech Gatherer. But what personalizes Wordsworth's Gothic in 'The Vale' is the coalescence of the threatening father-figure (as in the childhood spots of Books I and II of *The Prelude* discussed in Chapter 1) with the other, stronger presence of the maternal disciplinarian, who by circumscribing the terror of violence within the law of the father comes in the poem to shape the register of Gothic horror itself.

Local lore, deeply internalized, must have served to domesticate the literary vogue of the Gothic when it came to articulate Wordsworth's pre-established fantasies. Though the only 'Gothic' novel to have preceded 'The Vale' is Horace Walpole's *The Castle of Otranto* (1764), the poem is saturated with echoes of Gothic poetry, most extensively of Helen Maria Williams's 'Part of an Irregular Fragment, Found in the Dark Passage of a Tower', from her *Poems* (1786), which evokes the historical murders associated with the Tower of London. Crucially, in the Gothic Wordsworth discovered not only a reflective surface for imaging his own adolescent psychodrama, but also a register that helped him professionalize his inscription in a disciplinary literary discourse: it led him in the direction of an exemplary poetic voice. Though it seems opposed to the other minor Miltonic register of sentimental poetry that is interwoven with it here (mostly by juxtaposition) and that runs throughout the juvenilia – assimilated particularly from Charlotte Smith, to whose works a Hawkshead teacher, James Bowman, had introduced him – the poem ends up with a complex feminized figuration for the subject of both registers.

One work in particular guided Wordsworth's self-recognition in poetic language. His adolescent reading specialized in pseudo-medieval poems, of which his favourite was James Beattie's unfinished *The Minstrel*, published in two separately published books, 1770 and 1774. It offered him an important identification in its hero, Edwin, as Dorothy Wordsworth's remarks to a friend, describing him in the summer of 1787 (when 'The Vale' was being drafted) and later indicate. She quotes part of a stanza beginning 'In truth he was a strange and wayward wight, / Fond of each gentle, and each dreadful scene: / In darkness and in storm he found delight' and comments: 'That verse . . . always reminds me of him, and indeed the whole character of Edwin resembles much what William was when I first knew him – after my leaving Halifax' (*WL* I 100–1). Beattie's poem must have spoken extraordinarily for Wordsworth's own state of mind, as Legouis commented: 'it was left for Beattie to proclaim frankly the identity of poetry and melancholy' (1921, 155). Besides, as Kenneth Johnston has noted, the figure of the minstrel had been accorded a specifically northern lineage by Thomas Percy in his essay, 'The Ancient English Minstrel', published in his *Reliques of Ancient English Poetry* (1765) (83–4).

The Minstrel is about vocation. It was subtitled 'The Progress of Genius', and the design announced in its Preface is a simple formulation of a common project which became the story of *The Prelude*: 'to trace the progress of a Poetical Genius, born in a rude age, from the dawning of fancy and reason, til that period at which [Edwin] may be supposed capable of appearing in the world as a MINSTREL, that is, as an itinerant Poet and Musician' (see 1819, 6) (Figure 4). The lines that Wordsworth adopted from Beattie as his epigraph – 'Adieu, ye lays that fancy's flowers adorn, / The soft amusement of the vacant mind' – referred in the original to the death of Beattie's own inspiring father-figure, the medical professor John Gregory ('friend, teacher, pattern, darling of mankind!'), just before the second book was concluded, and that book aspires to greater maturity through suffering confronted in a specific idiom, by, that is, '[smiting] the Gothic lyre with harsher hand' (42). Intellectual ambition, announced in the recommendation that philosophy should be espoused rather than imagination, was to lead Beattie himself into other kinds of activity that in effect prevented him from completing the poem.[7] But within Beattie's poem Wordsworth encountered a deeply familiar and, for him, peculiarly adequate father-figure, the bardic hermit through whom Edwin's calling is confirmed. He is an

R.Westall R.A.del.   Cha.Heath fc.

The wild harp rang to his adventurous hand....
Book 1 Stanza 57.

Figure 4   Richard Westall, *The Minstrel* (1816)

old man (merged in a natural setting by a stone, with his own instrument lying beside him), whose description prefigures such Wordsworthian solitaries as the Old Cumberland Beggar and the Leech Gatherer (Figure 5):

> At early dawn the Youth his journey took,
> And many a mountain pass'd and valley wide,
> Then reach'd the wild; where, in a flowery nook,
> And seated on a mossy stone, he spied
> An ancient man: his harp lay him beside,
> A stag sprang from the pasture at his call,
> And, kneeling, lick'd the wither'd hand that tied
> A wreath of woodbine round his antlers tall,
> And hung his lofty neck with many a flowret small.
>
> (53)

The way in which phallic power and blood sports are disarmed by the managed artifice of nature seems already Wordsworthian, as does the myth of Edwin's evolution from shepherd-boy to troubadour. What must have appeared so wonderfully satisfactory for Wordsworth was the

Figure 5   Richard Westall, *The Hermit* (1816)

portrait of the youthful artist, the 'sketch of intellectual biography',[8] whereby Wordsworth could recognize the self-reflexivity of both a critical paternal identification *and* the presentation of congenial poetic registers that would enable him to assume a professional discourse. It was poetry about poetry.

'The Vale' rehearses that initiation. Its scenery is steeped in Wordsworth's family romance: the paternal marching mists (of the horse-waiting episode) and the hampered maternal progress (of the Penrith Beacon episode) provide the setting from which the autobiographical confessions emerge at the end:

> The solemn mists, dark brown or pale,
> March slow and solemn down the vale;
> The moon with sick and watery face
> Wades through the sky with heavy pace.
>
> (236–9)

More specifically, Wordsworth is fascinated by a female form that is exaggerated in height, that looks 'pale and ghastly', and that 'slowly wav'd her hand'. Later on, he encounters in a complementary white-shrouded male spectre a terrifying poet-figure, who bears on his arm a lyre:

> On tiptoe, as I lean'd aghast
> Listening the hollow-howling blast
> I started back – when at my hand
> A tall thin spectre seemed to stand
> . . .
> His bones look'd sable through his skin
> . . .
> And on one branded arm he bore
> What seem'd the poet's harp of yore;
> One hand he wav'd, and would have spoke,
> But from his trembling shadow broke
> Faint murmuring – sad and hollow moans
> As if the wind sigh'd through his bones.
> He wav'd again, we entered slow
> A passage narrow damp and low;
> I heard the mountain heave a sigh
> Nodding its rocky helm on high,
> And on we journey'd many a mile

> While all was black as night the while,
> Save his tall form before my sight
> Seen by the wan pale dismal light
> Around his bones so [   ] shed
> Like a white shroud that wraps the dead.
> Now as we wander'd through the gloom
> In black Helvellyn's inmost womb
> The spectre made a solemn stand,
> Slow round my head thrice wav'd his hand,
> And [?] mine ear – then swept his [? lyre]
> That shriek'd terrific shrill and [? dire]
> Shudder'd the fiend: the vault among
> Echoed the loud and dismal song.
>
> (325–8, 334–57)

The mountain's nodding crest of Helm Crag, Grasmere, is a Gothic allusion to Walpole's vast enchanted helmet of Otranto, but it is also more intimately associated with one of Wordsworth's privately over-determined Oedipal spots. Carol Landon has shown that the rough drafts at this stage present the location, Helm Crag, as the original of the mountain that uprears its head in the subsequent stolen boat episode of Book I of *The Prelude*:

> As when by solemn moonlight
> The shepherd rows his skiff
> From the dark rock that overhangs
> the dock, he [?kens] the top of a tall
> rock – at every measur[ed] stroke . . .
> Taller & taller [till *del.*] he drops his oars
> appalled.
>
> (Landon, 359–62)

Radically, it is the figure's poetic voice, his 'loud and dismal song', that so horrifies and compels the young initiate. But though the register of the Gothic awakens for Wordsworth some fearful intimation of the violent and cryptic origin of language itself, its appropiation is effectively being regulated by a deeply familiar white-robed figure holding a phallus in its hand, now a synecdoche for the discourse of poetry. As Wordsworth is actively finding his own poetic voice, it is the convention-ality of the Gothic register that facilitates his presumption – a literary conventionality that is being personally endorsed for him by the accustomed figuration (of an androgynous figure in white).[9] Literary discourse assumes the form of an approved relation to the word of the father that in turn serves to render it disciplinary.

Working inside the Gothic register, framing Wordsworth's revisionary Oedipalism, is an intertextuality with *Hamlet* which habitually recrudesces when he revisits the scene of language acquisition. In Wordsworth's poem, the commencing allusion to *Hamlet* invites an intensifying textual presence which it only seems to exorcize, as with the ghost in the play itself: 'Hark! o'er the hills with dewy feet / She comes, and warbles softly sweet' (83–4) recalls the first dismissal of Hamlet's father's ghost, 'But, look, the morn, in russet mantle clad, / Walks o'er the dew of yon high eastern hill' (S, I i 1001). Behind both of the subsequent encounters with the phantom mother (see Chapter 1) and minstrel father lies the text of Hamlet's meeting with his father's motioning and groaning ghost, as Wordsworth himself relives Hamlet's embarrassment – poised between two guilts: that of retaining the primary relation with the mother against the father when it has become unlawful, and that of disrupting the renewed primary relation by identifying with the (violently separated) word of the father.

This dilemma is reworked repeatedly in Wordsworth's later approaches to solitaries and is particularly evident in the description of the Discharged Soldier which became part of Book IV of *The Prelude*. There the apparitions from 'The Vale' reappear, exciting fluctuations of horror and sympathy:

> It chanced a sudden turning of the road
> Presented to my view an uncouth shape,
>
> . . .
>
> He was of stature tall,
> A foot above man's common measure tall,
> Stiff in his form, and upright, lank and lean –
>
> . . .
>
> His arms were long, and bare his hands; his mouth
> Shewed ghastly in the moonlight. . .
>
> . . .
>
> in his very dress appeared
> A desolation, a simplicity
> That seemed akin to solitude. Long time
> Did I peruse him with a mingled sense
> Of fear and sorrow. From his lips meanwhile
> There issued murmuring sounds, as if of pain

Or of uneasy thought...

       ...

I wished to see him move, but he remained
Fixed to his place, and still from time to time
Sent forth a murmuring voice of dead complaint,
Groans scarcely audible. Without self-blame
I had not thus prolonged my watch.

(401–34)

There are several resemblances between old Hamlet's ghost and the 'ghastly mildness' (493) of the soldier. Both are 'clad in military garb' (414), are suffering pitiably, carry themselves in a 'slow and stately' (I ii 1003) manner ('with / A stately air', 443–4), and gesture with hallucinatory politeness ('with what courteous action / It waves you to a more removed ground', I iv 1006):

Slowly from his resting-place
He rose, and with a lean and wasted arm
In measured gesture lifted to his head
Returned my salutation.

(437–40)

The encounter parallels the one described by Coleridge in 'The Ancient Mariner', the ballad both poets had originally sketched together and that was gestating during the winter of 1797–8 when Wordsworth wrote the fragmentary poem which later became part of Book IV. Linking the soldier and the mariner is the way the wedding-guest receives his lesson about transmuting unconsidered violence into a moral register of benevolence from a presence that initially appears to be a reanimated cadaver, described in the skeletal terms supplied to Coleridge by Wordsworth:

'I fear thee, Ancient Mariner!
I fear thy skinny hand!
And thou art long, and lank, and brown,
As is the ribbed sea-sand.

       ...

Fear not, fear not, thou wedding-guest!
This body dropt not down.'

(224–7, 30–1; the emphasis is Wordsworth's)

The experiences of both narrators are maturing, and even corrective. The wedding-guest, for example, is distracted from a scene of revelry ('"The guests are met, the feast is set; / May'st hear the merry din"', 7–8; '"Nodding their heads before her goes / The merry minstrelsy"', 35–6) to undergo sobering instruction. The preceding episode in Book IV is that of Wordsworth's solemn conviction that he was to become a poet of nature ('that I should be – else sinning greatly – / A dedicated spirit', 343–4), which also replaced an occasion of noisy and frivolous celebration ('I had passed / The night in dancing, gaiety and mirth – / With din of instruments', 319–21), and Wordsworth introduces his state of mind during the whole summer of these events in a phrase which aptly, and even in the case of the soldier literally, describes them as a 'Strange rendezvous . . . of grave and gay' (346–7). Moreover, Wordsworth's recognition of what was to be his adult role is presented as a transformation from a potentially intimidating manifestation into a state of 'blessedness' (346), when Wordsworth's self-recrimination over his 'heartless chace / Of trivial pleasures' (304–5) is admonished by the compensatory discipline of memory: 'And yet, in chastisement of these regrets, / The memory of one particular hour / Doth here rise up against me' (314–16).

The *rising* of the soldier also, though one from the half-dead, is after all unthreatening, as when the drowned schoolmaster resurfaced in Esthwaite Water in Wordsworth's early schooldays:

> At length, the dead man, 'mid that beauteous scene
> Of trees and hills and water, bolt upright
> Rose with ghastly face, a spectre shape –
> Of terror even
>
> (V 470–3)

– but an apparition that is '[hallowed] . . . / With decoration and ideal grace' (478–9). It is rather himself that Wordsworth has to fear. Hamlet says after the appearance of his father's ghost, 'Foul deeds will rise, / (Though all the earth o'erwhelm them) to men's eyes' (I ii 1004), and what both he and Wordsworth perhaps distrust is not so much a punitive visitation as the image of their own rivalrous fantasy. Wordsworth seems equally disturbed and, more curiously, attracted by seeing himself implicated in the disempowering of the figure before him. Typically for Wordsworth's solitaries, the soldier disowns the phallus except inasmuch as it has become a sign of weakness and necessary support:

> At this he stooped,
> And from the ground took up an oaken staff
> By me yet unobserved, a traveller's staff
> Which I suppose from his slack hand had dropped,
> And lain till now neglected in the grass.
>
> (459–63)

What fascinates Wordsworth in their conversation is something wanting in the emasculated war hero's touching meekness – a discontinuity between what Foucault calls 'the stigmata of past experience' (Foucault, 1984, 83), the material genealogy of this wasted apparition's revelation of the violences done to him, exploited and disowned by the state ('...in the tropic islands he had served, / Whence he had landed scarcely ten days past – / ...on his landing he had been dismissed', 446–8), and his refusal of Hamlet's father's call for revenge ('a quiet uncomplaining voice, / A stately air of mild indifference'):

> He all the while was in demeanor calm,
> Concise in answer. Solemn and sublime
> He might have seemed, but that in all he said
> There was a strange half-absence, and a tone
> Of weakness and indifference, as of one
> Remembering the importance of his theme
> But feeling it no longer.
>
> (472–8)

The original fragmentary version underlines the apparent defectiveness of the soldier's social inscription:

> He appeared
> Forlorn and desolate, a man cut off
> From all his kind, and more than half detached
> From his own nature.
>
> (Jonathan Wordsworth and Darlington (eds), 1970,
> 434: 57–60)

Yet Wordsworth is uncomfortable about patronising a father-figure to whom he does not feel securely superior, and lets us hear him uneasily trying on a hollow idiom of social condescension: '...I entreated that henceforth / He would not linger in the public ways, / But ask for timely furtherance, and help / Such as his state required' (489–92). If the soldier cannot fully command the situation, there is nonetheless authority in his silence, and the tables are turned with his reply:

> At this reproof,
> With the same ghastly mildness in his look,
> He said, 'My trust is in the God of Heaven,
> And in the eye of him that passes me.'
>
> (492–5)

Wordsworth himself is drawn to whatever might lie behind the soldier's unwillingness to communicate, since his own desires are filiated to such a figure who offers no resistance and relinquishes the initiative in verbal exchange; but he is also worried by the violence of his own gentlemanly self-assertion which is socially and psychologically implicated in the figure's oppression. A difficult identification is again facilitated by the recollection of Hamlet's father, and now as a victim. Wordsworth's 'Long time / Did I peruse him with a mingled sense / Of fear and sorrow' (419–21) half-echoes Horatio's description of the ghost's offering him 'A countenance more / In sorrow than in anger' (I ii 1003). In the upshot, Wordsworth requires words from the figure that will at once empower himself and yet neutralize the traces of his antagonism. He needs to find a language that can make a virtue of this father's defeat.

The turn to the other's impressiveness comes with the lesson of his passivity that is based on an appeal to scriptural expression, particularly Christ's teaching on resignation and trust in Luke XII ('And seek not ye what ye shall eat, or what ye shall drink, neither be ye of doubtful mind', 29), and maybe more distantly the parable of the Good Samaritan, who did not 'pass by' the 'half dead' victim (Luke 10: 30–2). Wordsworth describes his own practical charity and writes that, after leading the soldier to a 'lodging for the night' (459), 'At the door I knocked, / Calling aloud, "My friend, here is a man / By sickness overcome. Beneath your roof / This night let him find rest, and give him food"' (483–6), and that 'The cottage door was speedily unlocked' (496). At the back of Wordsworth's mind is the extended text, in Luke 12, which is the *locus classicus* for extolling the virtues of inactivity, and which does not exactly match his own protective zeal. Pre-echoing Wordsworth's 'He was of stature tall, / A foot above man's common measure tall' (405–6), Christ asks his disciples 'And which of you with taking thought can add to his stature one cubit?' (25). Christ enjoins them to be 'like unto men that wait for their lord when he will return from the wedding; that when he cometh and knocketh, they may open unto him immediately' (36). Both half-echoes serve to aggrandize the soldier as himself an imposing and lordly figure ('Solemn and sublime'), and play into the ultimate paternal promise of the text's central statement of assurance: 'Fear not, little flock; for it is your Father's good pleasure to give you the kingdom' (32).

To constitute the figure's fecklessness as surprisingly munificent and finally as the imparter of a self-reflective Christian register of redemption, further Shakespearean and biblical intertextualities are at work. The culminating narrative behind the episode is that of atonement – of the son's acceptance of his sacrifice to the law of the father. But here the father-figure himself is revealed not just at one with but also *as* the risen son. Aided by the knowledge of their hypostatic union and by the complication of Christ's self-sacrifice, as both sacrificer and sacrifice, Wordsworth's father-figure is himself showing him the way by having already internalized the practice of self-disempowerment that Wordsworth desires to emulate. The potentiality for a reversal of the father–son relation, the child as father of the man, is set to be carried over to the soldier from the association of Christ's resurrection ('Slowly from his resting-place / He rose') that was already immanent in Hamlet's father's ghost: the rising from the dead followed by the ascension that represents the ultimate reconciliation with the father. Hamlet adjures the ghost:

> but tell,
> Why thy canoniz'd bones, hearsed in death,
> Have burst their cerements? why the sepulchre,
> Wherein we saw thee quietly in-urn'd,
> Hath op'd his ponderous and marble jaws,
> To cast thee up again?
>
> (I iv 1006)

and the ghost, echoing Christ, resisting but obeying his mother's behest at the marriage in Cana ('mine hour is not yet come', John 2: 4), tells him '*My hour is almost come*, / When I to sulphurous and tormenting flames / Must render up myself' (I v 1006; my emphasis).

Even Wordsworth's uncertainty (' and I beheld / With ill-suppressed astonishment his tall / And ghastly figure moving at my side', 466–8) helps to find the links he is after. Their walk together resembles that of Christ with his disciples on the way to Emmaus whom his disappearance had 'astonished' (Luke 24: 22) though 'their eyes were holden that they should not know him' (16). Wordsworth's attempt at self-recognition in the soldier further recalls the gospels' description of the disciples' dubious examination of Christ's reanimated body-parts, particularly his hands and side. The ambivalence of fear and expectation that carries over from the scriptural accounts of the risen Christ into Wordsworth's meeting with the soldier contributes to a recurrent pattern of reprieved self-reproach in *The Prelude* that becomes climactically reactivated by his rendering of his involvement in revolutionary violence. In Book X, a similar deliverance is achieved through the wounds of Christ that he sees reflected in the butchery of the September massacres on his way back to England via Paris in October 1792. The later passage is also shaped by another noted *Hamlet* allusion (see Chapter 4), juxtaposed to a half-echo of the biblical account of the risen Christ, to offer in sum an acknowledgement of his inculpation in the bloody revolution, whose excesses he had not sufficiently reckoned with at the time, together with the almost incredible revelation of its having served to produce a saving discourse of restoration:

> The fear gone by
> Pressed on me almost like a fear to come.
> I thought of those September massacres,
> Divided from me by a little month,
> And felt and touched them, a substantial dread.
> (X 62–6)

The doubt of Thomas Didymus is directed by Wordsworth not only to a questioning as to whether the revolution as he had conceived of it could indeed have survived its implication in such atrocity, but also to the idea that, if it had, its blood-letting might be seen as somehow redemptive.

Though redemption is the narrative of the son's sacrifice to the law of the father, the comprehensive Christian scheme extends the simple expiatory notion that is stressed by St Paul in the Epistle to the Romans ('For what the law could not do, in that it was weak through the flesh, God sending his own Son in the likeness of sinful flesh, and for sin, condemned sin in the flesh: That the righteousness of the law might be fulfilled in us . . . ', 8: 3–4), and that was revived as the appeasing of an angry God in Calvin's *Institutes*, to the larger view in the Epistle to the Hebrews of Christ as the renewer and 'mediator of a better covenant' (8: 6). The Athanasian tradition of reading Christ's self-sacrifice 'in terms of a supremely liberating and victorious act of God in Christ, well prepared for by that supremely liberating and victorious act of Yahweh – the rescue of Israel from Egypt and the making of the Sinai covenant (Ashby, 57) is a continuation of the Hebrew tradition of sacrifice as 'the language through which relationship is established and communication carried on in material things' (ibid., 47). It is this further prospect of self-sacrifice that Wordsworth owns as providing the appropriate template for his literary discourse, in that it brings to expression the root initiation when the relation to the body had been surrendered to language, but under strict imaginary control. His particular mission, as he describes his sense of vocation in Book IV, is oblivious of the threat of castration: the language is as naturalized as the assumption of Milton's 'melody of birds' from *Paradise Lost*, VIII 527. Rather, he is dedicated to the remission of sin by representing his community almost incidentally – and certainly inexplicitly – in words at all:

> And in the meadows and the lower grounds
> Was all the sweetness of a common dawn –
> Dews, vapours, and the melody of birds,
> And labourers going forth into the fields.
> . . .
> I made no vows, but vows
> Were then made for me: bond unknown to me
> Was given, that I should be – else sinning greatly –
> A dedicated spirit.
>
> (336–9, 341–4)

Again, the figurative turn had been established in 'The Vale', where other tall white-robed figures – the Druids – minister to the realization of this necessary control:

> And hark! the ringing harp I hear
> And lo! her druid sons appear.
> Why roll on me your glaring eyes?
> Why fix on me for sacrifice?
> But he, the stream's loud genius, seen
> The black-arch'd boughs and rocks between
> That brood o'er one eternal night,
> Shoots from the cliff in robes of white.
> So oft in castle moated round
> In black damp dungeon underground,
> Strange forms are seen that, white and tall,

Stand straight against the coal-black wall.

(31–42)

The ephebe poet fears that he is to be sacrificed. He flees the 'mingled moan' (57) of tortured spirits and is terrified to find his harp being struck by '[a] grisly Phantom' (64). Yet, the threatening appearances are metamorphosed into natural forms (of waterfalls), and the grating noises after all turn into the dove's 'rustling' (68) and the pebble's 'gingling' (72) so as to dispel the nightmare of the Gothic register. The presiding Druidic forms, according to their customary ambiguity as both ceremonial killers and Celtic bards, have twin aspects as punitive agents (in dungeons) who turn out really to have been picturesque natural objects (underground streams and possibly stalagmites) and sounds, and are consequently happily positioned to resolve the desired Oedipal passage from Gothic to nature poetry.

In Book XII of *The Prelude*, a similarly moderating evocation of the Druids was to rise from the nightmare vision of gigantic primitivism and barbarous rites that had invested Stonehenge on Salisbury Plain in the 1793–4 poem located there:

> For oft at dead of night, when dreadful fire
> Reveals that powerful circle's reddening stones,
> 'Mid priests and spectres grim and idols dire,
> Far heard the great flame utters human moans,
> Then all is hushed: again the desert groans,
> A dismal light its farthest bounds illumes,
> While warrior spectres of gigantic bones,
> Forth-issuing from a thousand rifted tombs,
> Wheel on their fiery steeds amid the infernal glooms.[10]

The summoning up of Druidic sacrifice, when 'from huge wickers paled with circling fire / . . . horrid shrieks and dying cries / To ears of Daemon-Gods in peals aspire, / To Daemon-Gods a human sacrifice' (424–7), sustains at that moment the poem's unrelieved Gothic register, as a displacement of revolutionary and English state violence for the younger radical poet. *The Prelude* account covers the same ground but arouses a less rebarbative ancient past:

> I had a reverie and saw the past,
> Saw multitudes of men, and here and there
> A single Briton in his wolf-skin vest,

> With shield and stone-ax, stride across the wold;
> The voice of spears was heard, the rattling spear
> Shaken by arms of mighty bone, in strength
> Long-mouldered, of barabaric majesty.
>
> (XII 320–6)

The horrors of revolutionary purges and unjust war still merge with those of a vast wickerwork man filled with living men:

> and lo, again
> The desart visible by dismal flames!
> It is the sacrificial altar, fed
> With living men – how deep the groans – the voice
> Of those in the gigantic wicker thrills
> Throughout the region far and near, pervades
> The monumental hillocks, and the pomp
> Is for both worlds, the living and the dead.
>
> (329–36)

But mediated by his earlier reconstitution of the literary discourse of sacrifice in his account of the summer of when his poetic calling was being 'made for [him]', Wordsworth's displacement of the Reign of Terror and irresponsible English nationalism which had directed his use of the Gothic in the mid 1790s becomes transformed into the recognition of a more enlightened civilization by unfolding a larger significance of Druidic cultic practices. While he is partly repelled, Wordsworth is nevertheless also drawn to the institutionalization of sacrifice: 'monumental' and 'pomp' are transitional to controlled meaning and ceremony. More tellingly, the echo of Burke's vision of the organic society as 'a partnership' which 'cannot be obtained in many generations, it becomes a partnership not only between those who are living, but between those who are living, those who are dead, and those who are to be born' (*Reflections*, 120) frames his perception of the scene of violence as a phase in the vaster canvas of transgenerational exchange. Most characteristically, that shift has itself been conditioned by an even more foundational one – of coming to terms with representation as such:

> At other moments...
>   ... when 'twas my chance
> To have before me on the downy plain
> Lines, circles, mounts, a mystery of shapes

Such as in many quarters still survive,
With intricate profusion figuring o'er
The untilled ground (the work, as some divine,
Of infant science, imitative forms
By which the Druids covertly expressed
Their knowledge of the heavens, and imaged forth
The constellations), I was gently charmed,
Albeit with an antiquarian's dream,
And saw the bearded teachers, with white wands
Uplifted, pointing to the starry sky,
Alternately, and plain below, while breath
Of music seemed to guide them, and the waste
Was cheared with stillness and a pleasant sound.

(337–53)

Here, the figures on the turf, indicated by a metonymic 'white wand', demonstrate the conversion of 'deep groans' into 'a pleasant sound'.

When elsewhere in *The Prelude* Wordsworth conveys the subject's origin in similar images, he thereby indicates that the ritual tensions between (threatening) power and ceremony did indeed derive from its psychological archaeology, though he could only approach that site through figuration: 'But who shall parcel out / His intellect by geometric rules, / Split like a province into round and square? . . . Who that shall point as with a wand, and say / "This portion of the river of my mind / Came from yon fountain"?' (II 208–15). Kristeva's theory of sacrifice is particularly illuminating in making this social connection which is so crucial for Wordsworth. She sees it as an 'event' which is the social parallel of the break into the symbolic order that she calls the 'thetic phase'. For her, sacrifice replaces what, postsymbolically, is to be viewed as presymbolic violence with a located act of destruction that is directed against a specific victim. By positioning violence in this way, it becomes thetic and thus serves to establish the social order:

Far from unleashing violence, sacrifice shows how representing that violence is enough to stop it and to concatenate an order. Conversely, it indicates that all order is based on representation; what is violent is the irruption of the symbol, killing substance to make it signify. . . . sacrifice reminds that the Symbolic emerges out of material continuity through a violent unmotivated leap.

(Kristeva, 1984, 75 and 78)

For Wordsworth in particular, the apparently fortuitous homology between his radical preoccupation and the sacrificial scheme has to be rewritten into those registers that may be admitted into his poetic language. In the light of the Kristevan view, it is not the son as such who is seen to be sacrificed so much as the mother's body, or, more precisely, the maternal body as it survives in the son, the semiotic, which is regulated by becoming focused in the symbol.[11] By extension, Elisabeth Bronfen has argued that the female body especially is the site of violence for male creativity,[12] but in Wordsworth's case there is an unusually marked unwillingness to offer up his particularly fast hold on the mother's body, which he needs to be assured will return within the domain of the father to ensure the operation of redemptive discourses. There is, however, much potential guilt in 'killing [feminine] substance to make it signify', yet, as so often, De Quincey's elaboration of a Wordsworthian theme produces critical side-lights on its grounding texts. In his autobiography, De Quincey, who saw himself as a life-long sharer in the love of children, nonetheless finds himself retreating from the bedroom of his dead sister, Elizabeth, 'like a guilty thing, with stealthy steps from the room' (*DQ*, XIV 17). The *Hamlet* allusion ('it started like a guilty thing / Upon a fearful summons', I i 1001) places the writer beyond a foreclosing identification with the dead child to achieve an identification rather with the father's ghost. He knows, or feels that he has later learned, that the out-of-body experience that he undergoes at the site of his dead sister's body is the beginning of a conversion of loss into literature – the originating memory from which his writing career proceeds. For Wordsworth, too, in the Lucy poems the fantasized body of his dead sister (Dorothy) is the founding site of his autobiography, of his 'difference' as her elegist: 'But she is in her Grave, and Oh! / The difference to me' ('She dwelt among th'untrodden ways', 11–12). To him, Lucy is primary, she represents what he has had to lose though she has lastingly shed what in the Intimations Ode he describes as 'the fountain light of all our day, / . . . the master light of all our seeing' (152–3). Yet, as he realizes in the course of composing that poem – and this is the defining difference of *his* writing – for him, that illumination has had to be retained in a 'more habitual sway' (192): the 'visionary gleam' that has 'fled' (56) must be matched by a literary discourse that bespeaks the ghost of the father in a complementary way, forever pointing back towards the earlier formation. Having avowed that equivalence, Wordsworth can confront his guilt over leaving his 'past years' (136) behind, and contentedly identify with the ghost of the father that is itself in awe of their continuing influence, and see that deference gratefully as the foundation of his poetic art: 'I raise / The song of thanks and praise' for those 'High instincts before which our mortal Nature / Did tremble like a guilty Thing surprised' (140–8).

Whenever Wordsworth did distinguish a consolatory register, he was able to identify with the ghost of the father and offer his passage as cautionary for those – and they included finally all his readers – whom he felt sure would wish to make their cultural insertion on similar terms. 'Tintern Abbey' is paradigmatic in presenting his sister with the regime for her own emotional survival in the form of specific registers – such as the pantheistic 'one life' and moral philosophy – into which Wordsworth had reassuringly translated his own revision of revolutionary idealism. The offer is made in an admonitory voice that fuses those of both mother and father in enforcing his own language of self-sacrifice. Very similar to that of his own mother ('expressing a hope that I should remember the circumstance for the rest of my life'), the voice also resonates with that of Hamlet's father's ghost enjoining his son to 'remember me' (I v 1007) as a victim, but also with the Christ-like self-offering, 'this do in remembrance of me' (Luke, 22:19):

> Oh! then,
> If solitude, or fear, or pain, or grief,
> Should be thy portion, with what healing thoughts
> Of tender joy wilt thou remember me,
> And these my exhortations!
>
> (143–7)

Inbetweens

Wordsworth possessed a singularly abiding interest in his genesis, with the result that what Kristeva calls the maternal function preoccupies his positioning in the domain of the father where it consistently qualifies his relation to paternal authority and language itself. Mum's the word, and all the more so since the incidental shifts of allegiance which that positioning at different times informs have to be camouflaged in order to maintain its dominance. Because Wordsworth's inscription in the symbolic is so powerfully invested with maternalism, the expected resolution of sexual difference is reproblematized so as to call upon the indeterminacy of a process that dates back to presymbolic space: 'what can "identity", even "sexual identity" mean', as Kristeva writes, 'in a new theoretical . . . space where the very notion of identity is challenged?'

(1989, 214–15). As the tendency of Kristeva's work runs counter to those feminisms conceived in terms of identity politics and essentialist notions of gender, the affinities between it and Wordsworth's poetry make it especially helpful in relieving his poetry of some influential feminist misconstruals in order to recognize the intricately androgynous composition of his symbolic.

Many critics have argued along with Margaret Homans that the Romantic construction of subjectivity generally excludes femininity, and it is necessary to go determinedly against the grain of what have become entrenched Anglo-American feminist positions in Wordsworth criticism in order to follow the conflicted gendering of his recouped maternal function.[13] Anne Mellor's 'theoretical perspective' on 'Teaching Wordsworth and Women' is a case in point. She provides a straightforward statement of her critical and teaching practices based on the poet's representation of women, his gendering of nature and the imagination, and his social relations to women in his entourage. It is an approach that has strong social and pedagogic attractions, but one that has little time for the insights of its own founding mother, Virginia Woolf, in textualizing gender in the manner of Kristeva and other French women theorists. Mellor makes what she calls the 'polemical feminist argument' strongly: 'Wordsworth has not only embraced the patriarchal construction of the female as nature – and its attendant association of femininity with passivity, emotionality, irrationality, and corporeality – but also carried it one step further; he has denied to the female both her own language and the opportunity to speak. In short, he has constituted the female as not human' (1986, 145).[14] She answers her 'male students'' protest that Wordsworth's masculine figures are also nonindividuated projections of his own ego, anxieties, mental states, or philosophical concerns' by pointing out that 'Wordsworth's male characters are literally permitted to speak: Matthew, the Leech Gatherer, the old soldier, Michael – all speak their own words in Wordsworth's texts. But his women – Lucy, Margaret, Martha Ray, Dorothy – do not speak in propria persona; the words assigned to them are literally spoken by male narrators' (ibid.). There are, of course, many notable exceptions to Wordsworth's choice of male narrators. Females *are* given voice effectively – Goody Blake, for example, has one of deadly power, not to mention the admirably incorrigible little girl in 'We Are Seven' who is also definitely given the last word. But most of those for whom Mellor does not account are, significantly, mothers, such as the Forsaken Indian Woman, Margaret (in the story of her 'affliction'), the speakers of 'Maternal Grief' and

'The Cottager to her Infant', the Sailor's, the Mad, and the Emigrant Mothers, and so on.

That numerous mothers speak in the poetry is hardly surprising since in a way they are constantly speaking there – in the sense that Wordsworth's poetic language makes a point of always remembering at least part of the maternal function. The persistence of his special relation to language, however, came under urgent and prolonged pressure from Coleridge's plan for the great philosophical poem. In *The Contours of Masculine Desire*, Marlon Ross has probed the psychological dynamics behind Coleridge's dictate for an unproblematized kind of masculinity in Wordsworth's poetry. Ross's chapter on 'Fathers and Sons, Brothers and Lovers: Engendering Desire from the Margins of Masculine Rivalry' maintains that 'Gender difference becomes a model for distinguishing the strong poet from other male poets' (88), and that accordingly 'when Coleridge wants to praise his rival [Wordsworth], he does so by exploiting categories of gender: "Wordsworth has the least femineity in his mind. He is all *man*"' (ibid.). Romantic 'influence' is accordingly constituted by Coleridge in terms of the absolute subject theorized for him in the German idealist tradition: 'The ideal state is one of absolute influence, the power to sway without ever having been swayed, the final cause that has no cause outside itself – the state of God' (ibid.). Such a fantasy of absolute identity (of in effect becoming Lacan's 'transcendental signifier') posits the achievement of ultimate symbolic stasis unchallenged by semiotic flux in which the paternal function reigns supreme, but, inasmuch as Coleridge ever tried to define it, it is the language of idealist philosophy not poetry.

Ross's analysis of Coleridge's 'To William Wordsworth: Composed on the Night after His Recitation of a Poem on the Growth of an Individual Mind' pursues his account of Coleridge's strategy of '[turning] the rivalry of male equals into the pseudorivalry of female other [Coleridge himself] with male subject' (94). But in the work to which Coleridge's poem refers, as Ross writes, Coleridge admonishes Wordsworth that he 'has mistaken externally derived power for self-generated power' (101):

> Of tides obedient to external force,
> And currents self-determined, as might seem,
> Or by some inner Power; of moments awful,
> Now in thy inner life, and now abroad,
> When power streamed from thee, *and thy soul received*
> *The light reflected, as a light bestowed.*
>   (14–19; emphasis added)

In effect, despite his gendered self-deprecation, Coleridge thereby obliquely insists on the insufficiency of imaginary power and keeps the upper hand by retaining the master philosophical register for *The Recluse* that Coleridge describes in his *Table Talk*, but that Wordsworth was to be incapable of realizing in his poem:

> Wordsworth... should assume the station of a man in repose, whose mind was made up, and so prepared to deliver upon authority a system of philosophy. He was to treat man as man – a subject of eye, ear, touch, taste, in contact with external nature – informing the senses from the mind, and not compounding a mind out of the senses... Something of this sort I suggested – and it was agreed on. It is what in substance I have been all my life doing in my system of philosophy. (*TT* I 307–8)

By focusing on the doctrine, Coleridge's account avoids the specific problems of poetic language which he left, impossibly, to Wordsworth, whom he advertised, like some splendid poetical quack, as 'the first & greatest philosophical Poet – the only man who has effected a compleat and constant synthesis of Thought & Feeling and combined them with Poetic Forms' (*LSTC* II 1034). Instead, Coleridge offers only a theoretical register that would effectively repress the materiality of the maternal function.[15]

The Coleridgean misconstruction of Wordsworth's self-originating masculinity was reinforced by many others in the Wordsworth circle. Henry Crabb Robinson, for example, loyally dismissed John Wilson's derivative *Isle of Palms* as the work of 'A *female* Wordsworth', displaying 'A plentiful lack of thought, with great delicacy and even elegance of taste, but without riches or strength of imagination' (*HCRBW* I 140). Encouraged by friends and what Ross calls the masculinizing 'feminine appreciation' of Dorothy and his wife, Mary, Wordsworth produced work that increasingly polarized into the self-consciously minor scope of domestic affections and the repeatedly frustrated attempt to actualize the voice of the vicariously masculinist *Recluse*. In 'Character of the Happy Warrior', composed 1805, for example, he describes what he was trying to settle as the model for his own self-conception of heroic dutifulness: 'He who, though thus endued as with a sense / And faculty for storm and turbulence, / Is yet a Soul whose master-bias leans / To homefelt pleasures and to gentle scenes' (57–60). He speculates that Napoleon's upbringing had been responsible for his distorted sense of power, in that 'the sternness of the brain' had never had the opportunity

Figure 6 B. R. Haydon, *Wordsworth on Helvellyn*

to 'temper ... Thoughts motherly, and meek as womanhood' ('I grieved for Buonaparte', 7–8). The female Wordsworths were eager to act the part of his epic precursor, Milton's daughters, and wanted to see Wordsworth as ultimate and isolated, as, for example, the 'lonely Summit' ('There is an Eminence, – of these our hills', 17), Stone-Arthur, after

Haydon's portrait of 'Wordsworth on Helvellyn' (Figure 6) ('it is perfection' Dora Wordsworth said on her death-bed: see Blanshard, 167).[16] Yet Wordsworth, infuriatingly for them, consistently refused to conform to his counterpart role and seemed incapable of fulfilling his side of the bargain. He turned out repeatedly to be lesser than they expected, inferior to their construction, as one of De Quincey's anecdotes (not without its own self-interest) describes during a summer evening's walk with 'Wordsworth, his sister, and Mr. J –, a native Westmorland clergyman': 'Mr. J –, a fine towering figure, six feet high, massy and columnar in its proportions, happened to be walking, a little in advance, with Wordsworth; Miss Wordsworth and myself being in the rear . . . during which time, at intervals, Miss Wordsworth would exclaim, in a tone of vexation, '"Is it possible, – can that be William? How very mean he looks!"' (*DQ*, II 140).

The neglect of Wordsworth's counter-position is worth pondering. Ross, for example, does not consider what is effectively Coleridge's roundabout *feminization* of Wordsworth when measured by his own masculinist theory, nor wonder why Wordsworth's poetry is itself so consistently received as unmanly by its contemporaneous criticism: the word 'puerile' and its synonyms are among the adjectives most commonly applied to the poetry in Wordsworth's lifetime.[17] How has it remained possible for the masculinist construct to weather the most damaging exposure of its univocalist pretensions in the elaborate textual history of *The Prelude* as it has been uncovered from Ernest de Selincourt's 1926 parallel edition to Jonathan Wordsworth's 1995 Penguin edition of the *four* versions (supplemented by Duncan Wu's recent *The Five-Book Prelude*, 1997) that have cumulatively worked to expose the poem as notoriously unstable and contradictory? Yet Mellor's later book, *Romanticism and Gender*, continues to censure Wordsworth effectively for having been (mis)read as a patriarchal producer *par excellence*, though the considerable critical corpus that deconstructs this pretension in his poetry is openly acknowledged.

In her chapter on 'Writing the Self / Self Writing: William Wordsworth's *Prelude* / Dorothy Wordsworth's *Journals*' in *Romanticism and Gender*, Mellor again writes boldly that the poem, 'one of the most influential literary autobiographies ever written', is a prime example of the 'Masculine Romanticism [that] has traditionally been identified with the assertion of a self that is unified, unique, enduring, capable of initiating activity, and above all aware of itself as a self' (145), and in order to substantiate her case about *The Prelude* being the production of 'a specifically *masculine* self' (147) she concentrates on readers in the Coleridgean tradition, such as Meyer Abrams and 'many others' like him, who have seen the poem as 'depend[ing] upon . . . the historical emergence of the individual (male) self of social contract theory and economic capitalism' (152). Interestingly, it is only when she comes to the section on Dorothy that deconstructionists and French women theorists are suddenly taken seriously for the analysis of 'other ways of constructing the self than that attempted by William Wordsworth'. It is, however, only by recourse to the same forms of analysis that the recalcitrances in Wordsworth's own gendering (which Mellor herself describes) can be properly weighed:

> Wordsworth initially genders the mind as feminine . . . As the mind moves ever further away from, or above, nature, it finally becomes simultaneously masculine and feminine: 'the mind / Is *lord* and *master*, and that outward sense / Is but the obedient servant of *her* will' . . . But Wordsworth recognizes that his hold on male supremacy is as insecure as his hold on his autonomous self. At the very end of this poem dedicated to a revelation of the male poet's possession of a godlike imagination 'in all the might of its endowments' . . . Wordsworth acknowledges that this very imagination, 'the main essential power' which throughout *The Prelude* he has tracked 'up her way sublime' . . . is resistantly female. Wordsworth thus reveals the stubborn Otherness of all that he has labored so long and hard to absorb into his own identity: the originary power of the female, of the mother, of Nature. (150–1)

That is obviously not 'a specifically *masculine* self'.

Still, arriving at the recognition of Wordsworth's androgynous imagination does not in itself extricate him from the masquerade of a disguised masculinism. Gayatri Chakravorty Spivak has written persuasively of Wordsworth's incorporation of femininity: '[He] claims for the full-grown poet an androgynous plenitude which would include within the self an indeterminate role of mother as well as lover', and she illustrates Wordsworth's ploy from one of the culminating passages of the final book of *The Prelude*, on 'intellectual love':

> And he whose soul hath risen
> Up to the height of feeling intellect
> Shall want no humbler tenderness, his heart
> Be tender as a nursing mother's heart;

> Of female softness shall his life be full,
> Of little loves and delicate desires,
> Mild interests and gentlest sympathies.
>
> (XII I 204–10; see Spivak, 334)

For her this kind of androgyny merely amounts to a patriarchal variant in that it excludes the fully developed woman: 'woman shut out. I cannot but see in it the sexual-political program of the Great Tradition' (336). Again, her perspective on ideology and gender necessarily focuses more on the history of reception than the specifics of Wordsworth's case, including his own exclusion, in some ways, from full development. In another study that includes a consideration of Wordsworth and gender, Antony Easthope has echoed Spivak's argument and that of Diane Long Hoeveler in her exploration of 'an androgynous ideology' produced by 'the appropriation of feminine qualities by male heroes' (xiv) by pointing out that 'If you exclude woman, you deny heterosexual desire, you deny paternity and leave the way open for a man to imagine himself as son *and* lover, father *and* mother of poems, male *and* female at once' (Easthope, 93). Easthope goes further in seeing Wordsworth's androgyny not only as counter-feminist but also as a masculinist ruse: 'when Mick Jagger wore a frock at the Hyde Park concert on 5 June 1969 it affirmed a masculinity so strong it could even contain femininity' (92). But these are very different androgynies,[18] and a failure to appreciate the priority given to the resilient maternal function in Wordsworth's misses the much more radical indeterminacies going on beneath his symbolic transvestism.

That the invocation of Kristeva's ideas is no prophylactic against sexual politics is demonstrated in two of the series of three essays by Mary Jacobus that constitute the most sustained feminist critique of *The Prelude* so far (see 1989). In '"Splitting the Race of Man in Twain": Prostitution, Personification, and *The Prelude*', as part of an orchestrated argument Jacobus employs Kristeva's account of the splitting mother from *Powers of Horror* to distinguish between two mother-figures in Book VII. One is what she calls the 'Romantic' woman figure of Mary of Buttermere, whose babe has to be given up to render the mother, as Wordsworth writes, 'Without contamination' (351). 'The infant's burial tranquillizes her unquiet life', writes Jacobus, 'allowing her to stand in for the purified, pre-sexual, Lake District poet' (208). The other kind of 'outcast' mother-figure, who characteristically takes the form of a prostitute, with another kind of child, who survives and is explicitly male, is seen in the mother and beautiful child in the theatre:

> foremost I am crossed
> Here by remembrance of two figures: one
> A rosy babe, who for a twelvemonth's space
> Perhaps had been of age to deal about
> Articulate prattle, child as beautiful
> As ever sate upon a mother's knee;
> The other was the parent of that babe –
> But on the mother's cheek the tints were false,
> A painted bloom.
>
> (366–74)

In the fantasy that follows (of the child's being 'embalmed / By nature', 400–1; see Chapter 1), Jacobus argues that the boy's 'fall has been displaced on to the forgotten mother' (218) and that the mother has been, in Kristevan terminology, 'abjected': 'In order to save the boy, Wordsworth has to get rid of the mother' (221).

In the application she is making, Jacobus risks confusing the abjection of all women with the *necessary* abjection of the mother. The phase of abjection described by Kristeva inaugurates the pre-Oedipal narrative, when the infant expels itself from the mother's body which is seen as viscerally disgusting, and is in fact indispensable in giving effect to the 'desire for separation, for becoming autonomous' (see Oliver, 55) in both sexes. Without its prefiguring of symbolic division, the maternal function would become foreclosed and there could be no entry into language and culture. But in Jacobus's analysis of the two commonsense mother-figures, it looks as if neither could ever win in Wordsworth's poetry. If one survives intact, she is really the son in disguise; but if she is rejected as repulsive, a less common story in Wordsworth's poems, that is in order for the son to thrive. In effect, two kinds of inquiry are unhelpfully overlapping here: one has to do with the sociopolitical history of constructions of motherhood and the other relates to the story of Wordsworth's subject-in-process which, for him, is exceptionally interested in the retention of the maternal function. As an individual example of male psychology, Wordsworth's poem does and does not substantiate the linkage implied, because besides their individual fates these mothers have additional roles in Wordsworth's overall scheme of maternal empowerment.

Jacobus appears to be on secure ground when she deals with the passage describing Wordsworth's encounter with the prostitute later in Book VII:

> Full surely from the bottom of my heart
> I shuddered; but the pain was almost lost,
> Absorbed and buried in the immensity
> Of the effect: a barrier seemed at once
> Thrown in, that from humanity divorced
> The human form, splitting the race of man
> In twain, yet leaving the same outward shape.
>
> (421–7)

I would argue that the trauma of the experience is so critical because what Wordsworth here represents as his first experience of 'blasphemy' (385) and 'open shame' (386) interrupts the regulatory negotiation of Wordsworth's pre-established split woman figure by detaching her transgressive aspect from the full penitential design. The twin mother-figures in Buttermere and at the theatre, on the other hand, do together reconstitute that composite structure, enabling their joint offspring to remain undefiled despite passing through 'the fiery furnace' (399) and in some sense withholding them from all that might lie beyond the fall into sexual difference:

> through some special privilege
> Stopped at the growth [they] had – destined to live,
> To be, to have been, come, and go, a child
> And nothing more, no partner in the years
> That bear us forward to distress and guilt,
> Pain and abasement.
>
> (401–6; my alteration)

Just as, for this composite, the London boy is desired to merge with Mary's dead child, so the London demirep may be blended in the remarkably circumspect and cautionary demeanour of her northern counterpart. As an unmarried mother who had been the object of a bigamist's seduction, Mary's story had become a popular scandal. One of James Gillray's more restrained plates, 'Mary of Buttermere. Sketch'd from Life, July, 1800' (see Figure 7), gains its point simply from this notoriety. It was perhaps impossible for Gillray to produce any plausible picture of candidly 'unsoiled modesty', but the body curves, apparent

Figure 7 James Gillray, *Mary of Buttermere: Sketch'd from Life, July, 1800*

through her low-cut muslin dress, and her flowing, loosely bound, and flower-entwined tresses, as she hands over glasses of foaming ale, unmistakably bring out for the general voyeur the hospitable charms that have been betrayed. The 'Maid of Buttermere' herself, then, had a history of shared transgression that her full career had successfully absolved.

This last perception is important, because of course Wordsworth himself never can become simply 'the purified, pre-sexual, Lake District poet' again – the writer always would be post-sexual – and by *standing in* for him Mary represents a more varied, if resolved, history. But both mothers in question are unpartnered, and their relation to their children may be seen either to subsume paternal presence, in the name of the mother, or exclude it. The danger for both mothers comes not from underplaying the power of the mother so much as potentially overplaying it. For both mother and child the danger is exclusion, resulting in social foreclosure. Abandoned to her own resources and in an urge towards protective infanticide, a lone mother might exert her own phallic status in making a virtue of arresting a position that defends the infant from the stern and violent face of the father. This course is that fulfilled by Mary of Buttermere and other husbandless women, such as Martha Ray in 'The Thorn', who, we are sinisterly led to believe, may not have permitted her baby to risk the kind of betrayal she had had to undergo, and Betty Foy in 'The Idiot Boy' who really did not want little Johnny any other way than 'burring' his semiotic echolalia as a token of (her) maternal phallicism: 'And with a hurly-burly now / He shakes the green bough in his hand' (60–1). Indeed, the loving father can himself reinforce the adequacy of phallic maternity for purposes of protection or restitution. The village schoolmaster, Matthew, who ostensibly shuns the potential anguish of another loss, following that of his daughter, in the 'blooming Girl' ('Two April Mornings', 43) in the churchyard is a case in point. He also 'did not wish' (56) the later girl to be his, because, more obliquely, he already retains a completely fulfilling relation to his dead daughter, a relation which has for him come to be adequately represented in his oneness with nature, the phallus for which the father continues to uphold:

> Matthew is in his grave, yet now,
> Methinks I see him stand,
> As at that moment, with a bough
> Of wilding in his hand.
>
> (57–60)

As Wordsworth's own ambition was to encourage the mother's continuing hold, he was deeply attracted to the condition of unageing children, like that described in 'The Danish Boy' and the Winander boy passage in Book IV of *The Prelude*, which might be viewed as having achieved representation in the language of nature. But the fantasy on offer in his account of Mary of Buttermere, of never having to move outside the bond with the loving mother – 'Happy are they both, / Mother and child' (359–60) – while it reacts to the pains and mayhem of modern urban culture encountered in London, does not in itself seem to address the poem's besetting problem, of having to create a language that does and does not exit from that relation. Yet Wordsworth's appeal to that fantasy is after all one with active discursive implications for cultural and political practices, not least for poetry itself.

Along the path of Wordsworth's greater desire – for cultural representation, which lies beyond semiotic oneness and circles around imaginary union, the subsumed paternal presence necessarily attends. The imaginary relation with the mother, following the abjection of her material body, in fact requires the co-presence of an imaginary father to ensure her continuing desirability, and this incipient paternal function is both masculine and feminine: Kristeva calls it the 'father–mother conglomerate' (see Oliver, 77). As Kelly Oliver writes, it can even be seen as 'the mother's love itself' proceeding from 'an identification with her desire for the Phallus'.[19] In short, the imaginary father is an undeniable part of the ideal, loving mother's history, and in strongly identifying with that function the child can indeed become the father of the man.

Jacobus excludes the presence of this rudimentary paternal function entirely from Wordsworth's maternalism, though it is highly distinctive of his poetry. The loving and lovable imaginary father who cherishes the developing being is most manifest, for example, in Michael's fatherhood:

> For often-times
> Old Michael, while [Luke] was a babe in arms,
> Had done him female service, not alone
> For pastime and delight, as is the use
> Of fathers, but with patient mind enforced
> To acts of tenderness; and he has rocked
> His cradle, as with a woman's gentle hand.
> (152–8)

It occurs memorably in the 'matron's tale' from Book VIII of *The Prelude*, which relates at unusual length the episode of a shepherd-father rescuing his son who has become cut off from social passage, 'Right in the middle of the roaring stream' (305). The father successfully brings the boy back to the community:

> The shepherd heard
> The outcry of his son, he stretched his staff
> Towards him, bade him leap – which word scarce said,
> The boy was safe within his father's arms.
>
> (308–11)

Wordsworth's own gentle instructiveness in the poetry addressed to his daughters, Caroline and Dora, is clearly guided by the same function (see Chapter 1), as in 'Address to My Infant Daughter', written for Dora in 1804, where he explicitly refers to 'Mother's love, / Nor less than mother's love in other breasts' (28–9). But it is far more diffuse throughout his works and turns out to be the underburden of all his writing, for example, of less obvious and more light-hearted reprises, such as the end-piece to *Benjamin the Waggoner*, overtly about alterations in local transport.

The description of Benjamin's dependable progress through the various seasons in the Vale of Grasmere expresses Wordsworth's sense of an always anticipated presence that he has long enjoyed seeing held in imaginary suspension on the surface of the lake:

> – Yes, I, and all about me here,
> Through all the changes of the year,
> Had seen him through the mountains go,
> In pomp of mist or pomp of snow:
> Or with a milder grace adorning
> The landscape of a summer's morning;
> While Grasmere smoothed her liquid plain
> The moving image to detain.
>
> (225–33)

But Benjamin's forced absence has deprived Wordsworth of what is radically a maternal presence, and the later fleet of vehicles that have replaced Benjamin's waggon expose their cargo to the elements, as the waggon had never done:

> And oft, as they pass slowly on,
> Beneath my windows, one by one,
> See, perched upon the naked height
> The summit of a cumbrous freight,
> A single traveller – and there
> Another; then perhaps a pair –

The lame, the sickly, and the old;
Men, women, heartless with the cold;
And babes in wet and starveling plight;
Which once, be weather as it might,
Had still a nest within a nest,
Thy shelter – and their mother's breast!

(252–63)

Wordsworth's invariable theme touches on tragic resonances of parental deprivation and longing for reinstatement:

Then most of all, then far the most,
Do I regret what we have lost;
Am grieved for that unhappy sin
Which robbed us of good Benjamin; –
And of his stately Charge, which none
Could keep alive when He was gone!

(264–9)

The 'familiar face' of the imaginary father (which keeps returning, as Wordsworth's revision of Hamlet's father's ghost) is clearly glimpsed here at the grass roots, and in the end Wordsworth cannot but repay the 'mighty debt of grief' he owes to his dead parent with the kind of poetry his beneficence has helped to create:

Nor is it I who play the part,
But a shy spirit in my heart,
That comes and goes – will sometimes leap
From hiding-places ten years deep;
And haunts me with familiar face,
Returning like a ghost unlaid,
Until the debt I owe be paid.

(209–15)

This haunting face in *The Prelude* – the 'common face of Nature [that] spake to [him] / Rememberable things' (I 615–16), 'the features / Of the same face' that climactically present him with the language of nature in the Simplon Pass (VI 568–9) – finds its sure way into the analysis of Wordsworthian motherhood in Book VII. By the 1850 text, another presence has joined the maternal gaze in the London theatre: 'child as beautiful / As ever sate upon a mother's knee' (370–1, 1805) has become

'Child as beautiful / As ever clung around a mother's neck, / Or father fondly gazed upon with pride' (339–41). Most strikingly, an image of cross-gendered 'tenderness' (601) is added in the subsequent description of the 'brawny Artificer' (which is one of the most significant of all the later *Prelude* additions):

> A Father – for he bore that sacred name –
> Him saw I, sitting in an open square,
> Upon a corner-stone of that low wall,
> Wherein were fixed the iron pales that fenced
> A spacious grass-plot; there, in silence, sate
> This One Man, with sickly babe outstretched
> Upon his knee, whom he had thither brought
> For sunshine, and to breathe the fresher air.
> Of those who passed, and me who looked at him,
> He took no heed; but in his brawny arms
> (The Artificer was to the elbow bare,
> And from his work this moment had been stolen)
> He held the child, and, bending over it,
> As if he were afraid both of the sun
> And of the air, which he had come to seek,
> Eyed the poor babe with love unutterable.
>
> (603–18)

Here the imaginary father has been materialized. Economically insecure within his own domain, excluded from fenced-in property, and almost outlawed in having to 'steal' to sustain life, he mirrors the mother's love in a masculinized modality ('in his brawny arms'), and re'-enters the presymbolic to co-operate in the infant's nurturing ('with love unutterable').

What Wordsworth ultimately wanted out of the maternal function was a very particularly controlled poetic discourse, and he sought to generate it intuitively from intertextualities with feminine literary registers, often in the work of women writers like Dorothy Wordsworth. In so doing, he stands accused of appropriating female voices. Germaine Greer, for example, has argued that Wordsworth, in a representative move, completely took over the work of Anne Finch, Countess of Winchelsea, in his selection from it for the anthology of poetry he compiled for Lady Mary Lowther in 1819. She writes that 'Wordsworth was anxious to claim [Finch], even at the cost of misrepresenting her' (3), and she sees him as 'cavalierly [dealing] with those parts which he did not understand' (4). Short selections from 'The Spleen', 'Petition for an Absolute Retreat', and a slightly mutilated 'A Nocturnal Reverie' are seen as being made to mirror Wordsworth's own preoccupations rather than doing justice to the woman writer's full accomplishments, which dramatize rather her own frustrations, coterie allusiveness, and female friendships. Greer refers to Wordsworth's 'proprietary feeling' (7) in his comments for the poems printed in Alexander Dyce's *Specimens of British Poetesses*, 1827, and other selections, and adds that he regarded 'A Nocturnal Reverie' 'as if it had been written by himself' (9).[20] To a greater or lesser extent, anthologists are always and inevitably open to this kind of charge, as are all writers whose influences have been traced, and a similar selective affinity applies equally to Wordsworth's adaptation of male precursors. Wordsworth in fact freely extracts from the male poets he includes in the presentation album, though thirty-two of the ninety-two manuscript pages contain Finch's work, and Greer is claiming an unusually coercive and self-interested male relation to Finch's texts which specifically interferes with a woman's writing by emphasizing a partial quietism and asociality, as seen in the culmination of his extract from 'A Nocturnal Reverie':

> Their short-liv'd jubilee the creatures keep,
> Which but endures while tyrant-man does sleep:
> When a sedate content the spirit feels,
> And no fierce light disturbs whilst it reveals;
> *But silent musings urge the mind to seek*
> *Something too high for syllables to speak;*
> 'Till the free soul to a compos'edness charm'd,
> Finding the elements of rage disarm'd,
> O'er all below a solemn quiet grown,
> Joys in the inferior world, and thinks it like her own.[21]

Wordsworth's editorializing is instructive, because it demonstrates the principle within the intertextualities of his poetic discourse. Greer's presentation of Anne Finch is clearly directed by Virginia Woolf's treatment of that more obviously conflicted seventeenth-century woman writer, the Duchess of Newcastle, a noted eccentric. Finch's writing is not so self-contradictory, and her taste for detailed natural observation has often appealed, as Greer notes, to later generations of poets besides Wordsworth. Nevertheless, it had an exceptional attraction for Wordsworth, and the issue remains whether Wordsworth's attentions are effectively serving to construct a limited kind of femininity or whether he is rather recognizing a woman writer's ability to speak for something he shares within himself which he had found difficult to bring to expression, along the lines of that 'fellowship / Of modest sympathy' (75–6) which he describes as 'admitting' (71) him into the world 'Of printed books and authorship' (75) in Book VI of *The Prelude*. He is doubtless doing both, directly or indirectly, but his deepest interest lies not in enforcing a diminished scale of social experience and speechlessness as woman's lot, but in an achieved structure of correspondences within silence that Finch has exemplarily succeeded in articulating and which he wishes to see culturally represented at large. In that way, Anne Finch is one of his poetic mothers: she had taught him how to write.

3
Describing the Revolution

Wordsworth's politics were always those of a poet, circling in the larger orbit of causes and principles, careless of the transitory oscillations of events.

J. R. Lowell in 'Wordsworth', 1876

To believe that the world is in harmony, to feel oneself in harmony with it, that is peace; that is the inner festival.

Jules Michelet

Squaring the Circle

For Wordsworth, the French Revolution was and was not, in the manner of Ronald Paulson's general account, 'the particular "bricolage" – whatever was at hand at the moment – for the author or writer who wanted to talk about *something else*' (5). What for him was primarily a personal trauma found uncannily apt historical representation in the series of quandaries that the revolution presented him with, including the deposition of Louis XVI and subsequent September massacres, the declaration of war between England and France, and the Reign of Terror (officially inaugurated in October 1793 when the revolutionary government legitimized popular violence) leading to the execution of the 'Girondin' leaders with whom he had been closely associated. The shocks they generated could be resolved only by resubjugating himself to an overriding discipline in order to pursue a seamless path through French and English politics in the 1790s. After that, as he became gradually freed from the complications of adversarial positionality in England, the intensifying formation increasingly absorbed the reactionary discourses of church and state. But, though his poetry became inscribed with conservative discourses of authority and tradition, its political specificity was always secondary to the urgent private needs it addressed, in a way suggested by a luminous remark of James Chandler (referring to Wordsworth's account of the revolution given in Books X and XI of *The Prelude*): 'Burke's comments seem to anticipate Wordsworth's crisis so completely simply because Wordsworth used Burke's terms to reconstruct it' (1984, 57). Crucially, Wordsworth was also impelled retroactively to deny the historical in order to heal the private cleavage that the revolution had represented to him – a fit which made Wordsworth *the* representative spokesman for political shiftiness in Britain during the period. Before consciously reconstructing his crisis in post-revolutionary discourses, however, Wordsworth had been obliged to face the awareness that he was in effect reading his own traumatic history in his exposure to revolutionary knowledge.

The historical trauma so powerfully engaged that occasioned by Wordsworth's entry into the symbolic order because it was itself bound up in the moment when, as Foucault writes, language itself changed to become self-reflexive: 'From the nineteenth century, language began to fold upon itself, to acquire its own particular density, to deploy a history, an objectivity, and laws of its own. It became one object of knowledge among others, on the same level as living beings, wealth and value, and the history of events and men' (1971, 296). A. J. P. Taylor observed that 'only from the time of the great French Revolution have there been revolutions that sought not merely to change the rulers, but to transform the entire social and political system. The French Revolution originated revolutions in the modern sense and it was not until after it that people knew what revolutions were like' (17). Thereafter, Thomas Paine had argued in *The Rights of Man* (1791–2), society became inalterably post-revolutionary and, because no counter-revolution could abolish the new knowledge, it could never be unthought: 'There does not exist in the compass of language, an arrangement of words to express so much as the means of effecting a counter-revolution. The means must be an obliteration of knowledge; and it has never yet been discovered, how to make a man *unthink* his thoughts' (141). The French Revolution had opened up an irrepressible gap which, as Henri Grégoire (the prelate who was Bishop of Blois during Wordsworth's stay there in 1791–2 and who was responsible for introducing massive educational reforms) expressed it in January 1794, was a blank which could only be filled with some other version of human nature: 'there is still an enormous gap between what we are and what we could be. Let us hurry to fill this gap; let us reconstitute human nature by giving it a new stamp' (Hunt, 2).

A space for ideology had appeared in which 'the past' had come to stand for an optional conservative ideology of traditionalism: the *ancien régime* had been invented, while the new post-Enlightenment society (now, as Kant wrote, come of age)[1] began its task of self-definition. Paine maintained the necessity of marking the difference: 'Every age and generation must be as free to act for itself, *in all cases*, as the ages and generations which preceded it' (63–4), and the entry into the new domain of knowledge and 'freedom' was, as William Godwin argued, one into political maturity:

> Nothing can be more necessary for the general benefit, than that we should divest ourselves, as soon as the proper period arrives, of the shackles of infancy; that human life should not be one of eternal childhood; but that men should judge for themselves, unfettered by the prejudices of education, or the institutions of their country. (246)

But something yet undefined, and called 'the nation', was being given supreme power in France, as the Abbé Sièyes declared: 'The nation is prior to everything. It is the source of everything. Its will is always legal' (124). In the vacuum of authority, because the various constitutions and national assemblies could not represent any fixed centre of meaning, the ensuing competition between various groupings to arrogate the right to speak for the new nation took the form of the supervision and revision of popular and traditionalist discourses, such as the carnivalesque, Roman republicanism, and royalist symbols. But though the revolution attempted to define itself as an enduring republic by re-closure in consensus discourses it had in reality set signifiers free.

The great national Fête de la Federation was a case in point. It was to be an enduring but much varying symbol of the revolutionary society for Wordsworth. Held a year after the fall of the Bastille on 14 July 1790, it joyfully commemorated the king's acceptance of a new, more democratic constitution and the reunion of the people with the royal family, and was still in touch with pre-revolutionary folk and religious festivals, before the subsequent staging of official spectacles had fully set in to promote factional agendas other than simply reconstituting the sovereign people: 'Outside Paris, there was an unselfconscious mélange of elements, all counting towards the new, loyal, non-aristocratic France. Tricolours, the traditional may trees, lighted torches, processions of the young and old, saints' and corporation days, and heterodox oaths were mixed together' (Parker, 53). When Wordsworth and his travelling companion, Robert Jones, arrived in Calais, the party had started: 'Europe was rejoiced, / France standing on the top of golden hours, / And human nature seeming born again' (VI 352–4). Street manifestations, such as those into which they were swept – dancing in a ring, the farandole, the crowd elated with wine, song and the agape or love-banquet – tapped into the popular celebration of carnival, with its rites of seasonal rejuvenation and its presentation of the world upside down. In *The Prelude* he describes how in 1790

> We took our way, direct through hamlets, towns,
> Gaudy with reliques of that festival,
> Flowers left to wither on triumphal arcs
> And window-garlands
>
> > (VI 361–4)

and he

> above all remembered
> That day when through an arch that spanned the street,
> A rainbow made of garish ornaments
> (Triumphal pomp of Liberty confirmed)
> We walked, a pair of weary travellers,
> Along the town of Arras
>
> > (X 450–5)

But by his return in summer 1802, when the Peace of Amiens made it possible to revisit France during the temporary truce, even the memory of those festive flowers had withered. In between had come the savage revelling of the Terror, when 'Domestic carnage . . . filled all the year / With feast-days' (X 329–30).

In the lyrics of March, the month when the treaty was signed, he attempts to recreate the exultation of the revolutionary fête in less degradable but still derivative signs of hope: 'My heart leaps up when I behold / A rainbow in the sky' (1–2); but in the first part of the Intimations Ode (whose composition dates from that time) he is obliged to acknowledge an undeniable sense of loss and betrayal:

> Ye blessèd Creatures, I have heard the call
> Ye to each other make; I see
> The heavens laugh with you in your jubilee;
> My heart is at your festival,

. . .
Whither is fled the visionary gleam?
Where is it now, the glory and the dream?
(36–57)

Revisiting Calais on 15 August 1802, he was moved to contempt when greeted with the bitterly contrasting celebrations for Napoleon's birthday, after his proclamation as Consul for life, and in 'Festivals I have seen that were not names' he objected to the dangerous cult of individual personality.

Passing once more through Arras, he finds the place-name has become overlaid with blighting associations as the 'place from which / Issued that Robespierre, who afterwards / Wielded the sceptre of the atheist crew' (X 455–7), parodically reigning over the Terror. Ironically, English traditions had come to offer truer expressions of the virtues of social harmony and peace which the French festivities of 1790 had seemed to be promising, whereas his recollection of the historical fête had become that of a fixed signifier divorced from the signifieds of the revolution's different regimes over the years:

I could almost
Have quarrelled with that blameless spectacle
For being yet an image in my mind
To mock me under such a strange reverse.
(X 462–5)

The awkward slippage between signifiers and signifieds had been inherent in the earlier years of the revolution before any new language of power had held effectively. As Carlyle was to point out in his scornful rejection of Roux's simplistic Christianizing of the revolution, it was most specifically the attempt to include the knowledge of the Terror, bordering on both institutionalization and anarchy, that had questioned the adequacy of previous forms of expression for what had materialized:

heaven knows, there were terrors and horrors enough: yet that was not all the Phenomenon; nay, more properly, that was not the Phenomenon at all, but rather was the *shadow* of it, the negative part of it. And now, in a new stage of the business, when History, ceasing to shriek, would try rather to include under her old Forms of speech or speculation this amazing new Thing; that so some accredited scientific Law of Nature might suffice for the unexpected Product of Nature, and History might get to speak of it articulately, and draw inferences and profit from it; in this new stage, History, we may say, babbles and flounders perhaps in a still painfuller manner. (*The French Revolution*, II 293)

All that could yet be done was '[to renounce] the pretension to *name* it at present' (294). Up to the steadying of Cambacérè's *Projet de Code Civil*, 1796, which led eventually to the promulgation of the *Code Napoléone* between 1804 and 1810, there was an erratic wavering between the new definitions and actual developments that Burke had foreshadowed at the start: 'The wretched scheme of your present masters is not to fit the Constitution to the people, but . . . to fit their country to their theory of the Constitution' ('Letter to a Member of the National Assembly', in Blakemore, 14). A rigorous programme of onomastic reform took measures to close down anarchic polysemism and to get rid of old names. As Jacques-Pierre Brissot, (who had introduced Wordsworth into the Legislative Assembly), argued on the eve of the revolution's inner violent splitting in August 1792, 'if all we did was to convince all men to speak the same language, the press would soon spread the French Revolution everywhere' (quoted by Johnston, 320). Steven Blakemore recounts (recalling that 'On 3 December, 1792, Robespierre argued against granting Louis XVI a trial because his "name alone brings the scourge of war upon the agitated nation"'), all 'the names, titles, and words evoking the old order had to be destroyed', including the French Calendar (85). But, though neologisms and coinages (such as 'sansculotte', 'terrorist', 'Jacobin', or 'le peuple')[2] were installing a new political terminology, revolutionary discursivity was proving to be unstable *by definition*. In response to the kind of imprisonment in the past that Paine expressed in his fear of being 'immured in the Bastille of a word' (see Olivia Smith, 46), Article 11 of *The Rights of Man* stated that 'Every citizen may speak, write and print freely' (see Paxton, 171) – a proposition that was only slowly to reveal the potential of its own undoing.

As reforming discourses became factionalized and appropriated by competing and successive regimes, it was manifest that rather than the invention of ultimate, universal languages, what had developed was a new awareness – a fall into self-knowledge – of the power of language itself: in François Furet's formulation, 'speech substitute[d] itself for power' and 'The semiotic circuit (became) the absolute master of politics' (see Hunt, 23). Power talks: it could commandeer language that no longer signified consensus. When Lyons, a city that had declared for the constitution of 1791, was brought to heel by the republican armies, Georges Couthon, who was among those commissioned, in Simon

Schama's phrase, 'to re-Jacobinise' it, wrote to Saint-Just in October 1793 that 'People needed to be taught their "alphabet" all over again' (see Schama, 779–80).

The particular dilemma for Wordsworth was that the revolution became exceptionally packed with precisely the self-knowledge he wished to repress: his own reconstitution in the liberated power of the word. As he wrote in Book XI of *The Prelude*, 'Enough, no doubt, the advocates themselves / Of ancient institutions had performed / To bring disgrace upon their very names' (849–51), and 'a shock had then been given / To old opinions' so that his own mind had been 'Let loose and goaded' (860–1, 863). Through a series of radical re-readings of the revolution, challenged by key events – especially the king's deposition and the September massacres (leading eventually to the authorized Terror of the Revolutionary Government), and England's declaration of war on France – Wordsworth arrived at the irrespressible knowledge of self-division. An other self was discovered in the revolution, that he had originally taken to be enacting the unproblematic spreading of his ideal ego, and the traumatic realization reawakened all the feared otherness of language itself. From 1791 to 1794 he negotiated a more or less precarious inscription in revolutionary knowledge, which he recounts in Books IX and X of *The Prelude*; but from 1795 to the time when those books were actually composed, in 1804–5, he employed a series of philosophical and political registers to redefine that inscription as after all one of imaginary stability. Compelled by history to acknowledge discursive contradictions by which his subjectivity had been constituted, he remained psychologically compelled to construct a poetic language that could subsume them in imaginary closure.

In *The Prelude* Wordsworth describes himself on his arrival in Paris in November 1791, and later at Orleans, as curiously disengaged. He duly visited the most notable scenes, pocketing a relic of the demolished Bastille, but with a feeling of disappointment, of something lacking. After he had moved to Orleans in December, despite having read 'the master pamphlets of the day' (*Prel* IX 97),[3] he was still 'indifferent' to the great events: 'I scarcely felt / The shock of these concussions, unconcerned, / Tranquil almost, and careless' (IX 86–8).[4] 'Tranquility' was something Wordsworth would come to value differently when he came to interrogate such clichés in the light of subsequent seismic experiences. But until his enthusiasm was kindled by his aristocratic-republican mentor, Michel Beaupuy, in Blois some time between January to mid-April and July 1792, he had 'looked for something which [he] could not find' (IX 70) – an excitement that he assuredly did come to feel when, censorship and prosecution removed, revolutionary knowledge found vent in such Girondist journalism as Antoine-Joseph Gorsas's *Courrier des LXXXIII Départements* and Jean Louis Carra's immensely popular *Annales Patriotiques*:

> The land all swarmed with passion, like a plain
> Devoured by locusts – Carra, Gorsas – add
> A hundred other names, forgotten now
> Nor to be heard of more; yet were they powers,
> Like earthquakes, shocks repeated day by day.
> And felt through every nook of town and field.
>
> (IX 178–83)

At this stage, Rousseauist utopianism and Girondist rhetoric produced shocks that were animating. He had joined in that heady mood in which, as Schama has written, 'visions opened up of possible societies that might be capable of integrating the imperious "I" within the comradely "We"' (162). The pervasive revolutionary idiom of sensibility and virtue was automatically assimilated into the accustomed effect of literary registers, which from childhood through youth had provided a self-styling that prevailed within whatever cultural practices were inserting him into history. For the displaced and introspectively bookish ex-student, the merging of the private and public realms represented a regulated enlargement through an invitingly disencumbered passage: he later saw himself at the time as still 'a child of Nature, as at first, / Diffusing only those affections wider / That from the cradle had grown up with me' (X 752–4). The extract from Book X that Wordsworth published in 1809 entitled 'The French Revolution as it Appeared to Enthusiasts at its Commencement' was an attempt to recapture the unopposable fairy-tale ambience that in 1791 had imbued revolutionary watchwords and declarations:

> Oh! times,
> In which the meagre, stale, forbidding ways
> Of custom, law, and statute, took at once
> The attraction of a country in romance!
> When Reason seemed the most to assert her rights,
> When most intent on making of herself
> A prime Enchantress to assist the work
> Which then was going forward in her name!
>
> (5–12)[5]

Wordsworth's recollection of those few months was one of enchantment. Though the Loire valley was particularly well-cultivated and comparatively prosperous, offering 'scenes / Of vineyard, orchard, meadow-ground and tilth' (X 5),[6] in *The Prelude* Beaupuy does give one telling instance of economic break-down in the Loiret countryside in his picture of 'a hunger-bitten girl' (IX 512): '"Tis against that / That we are fighting"' (IX 519–20). But, though movingly articulated by 'the voice / Of one devoted' (406–7), the chivalric crusade against an economic predicament conceals an unformed conception as to *who* exactly the actual, though undeclared, enemy was to be.

For Wordsworth, the revolutionary nation was still radically undivided. He claims that his zeal was defined 'in opposition' that had 'burst / Forth like a Polar Summer' (260–1) against the royalist officers, with whom he boarded at Orleans and who had ostracized Beaupuy at Blois. His conviction grew that 'their discourse' was 'Maimed, spiritless' (265–6), appealing to a nationalist rhetoric that had come to have a different force from that to which he was himself attached: 'Every word / They uttered was a dart by counter-winds / Blown back upon themselves . . . and, in their weakness strong, / I triumphed' (261–7). Yet Wordsworth's rejection was arguably not radically of their social order – the ambiguities of liberal nobles like Beaupuy were as yet unresolved – but rather of their betrayal of a still viable knightly code. 'Chivalry', due to the 1781 *loi Ségur*, which restricted army commissions 'to noble families that could trace their lineage back at least four generations' (Schama, 162), was necessarily the prerogative of the nobility. One motivation for the measure – the desire 'to protect at least some portion of the public realm from the invasiveness of money' (ibid.) – was to find willing re-expression in Wordsworth's subsequent allegiance to the English republican nobility, claiming a proud descent that represents his anti-capitalist critique in the 1800s: 'In our halls is hung / Armoury of the invincible Knights of old' ('It is not to be thought of that the Flood', 9–10). That part of Wordsworth was still confusedly not unresponsive to those royalists who since the king's enforced return from Varennes had been deserting to join the army of invasion, 'bent upon undoing what was done' (IX 137), is suggested by the Burkean echo in his Shakespearean phrase for them – 'The Chivalry of France' (343)[7] – even while 'tears dimmed [his] sight' (275) for the 'patriot-love / And self-devotion' (278–9) of the volunteers who marched off to join Lafayette's revolutionary army to the strains of 'Ça Ira'.[8]

The medium by which his politics became invested with 'chivalrous delight' (503) was Renaissance poetry – Milton, Ariosto, Tasso and Spenser.

Wordsworth is claiming – encouraged by his rewriting of the revolution now – to be recuperating the primacy of this register throughout: that his reception of the revolution was always fundamentally literary. It dehistoricized the actual moment, when 'From earnest dialogues [he] slipped in thought, / And let remembrance steal to other times' (446–7), 'even the historian's tale / Prizing but little otherwise than [he] prized / Tales of the poets' (207–10). The admiring identification with Beaupuy, later heroized as a model of the ultimate self-sacrifice (he 'perished fighting . . . For liberty', 431–3, during the civil war in the Vendée, as Wordsworth thought),[9] was primarily with an embodiment of the ideal ego:

> He through the events
> Of that great change wandered in perfect faith,
> As through a book, an old romance, or tale
> Of Fairy, or some dream of actions wrought
> Behind the summer clouds.
>
> (305–9)

Wordsworth's poem of the time, *Descriptive Sketches* (1793), looking back to his pre-revolutionary Alpine expedition of 1790 and his idealization of Swiss republicanism, similarly expects to extend a juvenile idiom of the sentimental picturesque to embrace the mood of revolutionary exaltation in 1792. But the poem continually loses confidence in the adequacy of the register to shape the later experience, and, in the words of the Cornell editor, the poem is structured by 'cycle[s] of rising hopes followed by disappointment' (Birdsall (ed.), x). In particular, the apostrophe to France fails to inscribe the shock of the new in the trite Phoenix pageantry of an Elizabethan masque that is certainly *not* regenerated:

> Yet, yet rejoice, tho' Pride's perverted ire
> Rouze Hell's own aid, and wrap thy hills in fire.
> Lo! from th'innocuous flames, a lovely birth!
> With it's own Virtues springs another earth:
> Nature, as in her prime, her virgin reign
> Begins, and Love and Truth compose her train.
>
> (*Descriptive Sketches*, 1793 version, 780–5)

One recognition of the painful discontinuities being effected is recorded in what he describes in *The Prelude* as the 'violence abrupt' (IX 472) by which old convents were being programmatically dismantled. He alludes in the earlier poem to the expulsion of the monks from the Grande Chartreuse in 1792:

> The cloister startles at the gleam of arms,
> And Blasphemy the shuddering fane alarms;
> ...
> Vallombre, 'mid her falling fanes, deplores,
> For ever broke, the sabbath of her bow'rs.
>
> (60–1, 78–9)

But it merges into the prevalent tone of defeatist melancholy. The active British revolutionary, Thomas Holcroft, in his review for the *Monthly Review*, tellingly deconstructed Wordsworth's personal vision of a Rousseauist natural paradise. He quotes the passage beginning 'But doubly pitying Nature loves to show'r / Soft on his wounded heart her healing pow'r' (13–14) to point out the self-contradiction of the discontented figure in the Edenic landscape: 'Here we find that *doubly* pitying Nature is very kind to the traveller, but that his traveller has a *wounded heart* and *plods* his road *forlorn'* (see Birdsall (ed.), 301). The ending, with its woeful echo of *Paradise Lost* undercutting that of 'Lycidas', promises a very different world from that of the Fête de la Federation:

> To-night, my friend, within this humble cot
> Be the dead load of mortal ills forgot,
> Renewing, when the rosy summits glow
> At morn, our various journey, sad and slow.
>
> (810–13)

The depression is undoubtedly related to the private troubles of his affair with Annette. She had been teaching him French, helping him with 'a half-learned speech' (IX, 195), but a far more disturbing re-initiation into the domain of the father came with her pregnancy while he was writing this work. Wordsworth's avowal of his political commitment in *The Prelude* climaxes in a rapturous political idealism that is suggestively conveyed as a love-affair with the people: 'my heart was all / Given to the people, and my love was theirs' (124–5), and it may well be that the first recoil from an unqualified trusting 'To Nature for a happy end of all' (604) came with the conception of his natural daughter, born in December 1792, and the belated awareness that an unplanned step had been taken in passionate surrender.

Certainly, a distinctly new stage of unmistakable self-alienation came in October 1792 when he lingered in Paris on his way back to England for almost six weeks after the revolution had taken on a more brutal shape. *The Prelude* records Wordsworth's sense of horror, despite his claiming to be still 'enflamed with hope' (X 38), after the declaration of the Republic on 22 September. He tried unsuccessfully to read the scenes of the ominous and horrific recent events – the Temple, where the newly deposed king and royal family were imprisoned, and the Place de Carrousel, in front of the Tuileries palace, where, following its storming in August, some 800 of the king's staff and defenders had been burned after surrendering the Palace:

> upon these
> And other sights looking as doth a man
> Upon a volume whose contents he knows
> Are memorable but from him locked up,
> Being written in a tongue he cannot read,
> So that he questions the mute leaves with pain,
> And half upbraids their silence.
>
> (48–54)

The alien 'tongue' was that of Marat's *L'Ami du Peuple* and more recently of his *placards*, shrilly voicing the popular hysteria that found expression in those scenes, 'Heaped up with dead and dying' (48), and in the subsequent slaughtering of over 1000 prisoners in September, quite other from the chivalric register Wordsworth had seemed till then to find so deeply familiar. He began to understand that the 'revolution' was a signifier that did not enjoy imaginary coherence, and he could no longer edit out the 'substantial dread' (66) of violent opposites, finally exposing his own subjectification. For the force of this moment, we have Wordsworth's testimony as late as 1835: 'the scenes that I witnessed during the earlier years of the French Revolution when I was resident in France, come back on me with appalling violence' (*WL* III 39).

Extraordinarily, the sudden insight is framed in quotation marks. A split occurs in the language of the text declaring the separation of an other voice, that, distinctly heard in the past, now oracularly breaks into meta-recital:

> 'The horse is taught his manage, and the wind
> Of heaven wheels round and treads in his own steps;
> Year follows year, the tide returns again,

Day follows day, all things have second birth;
The earthquake is not satisfied at once'.

(70–4)

In 1792 the Assembly had moved to the manège, the former riding school next to the Tuileries. It became the theatre of the Girondins' crusading rhetoric that was for a time the revolution's controlling power,[10] but the unbridled indocility of Jacobin militancy now threatened that discipline. There is an important shift of emphasis here, as the pattern of regularity gives way to constant, but random, menace. The development of thought moves from the literal English meaning of 'revolution' as rotation, on the Copernican model of heavenly cycles – which described the benign circularity of Wordsworth's own sense of recurrently revolving from past to present to past – to the more modern, French reading, stressing an unpredictable break with the past.[11]

The distinction is crucial to Wordsworth's misperception of what would happen in France. George Woodcock defines the English view as 'a swinging back towards a better and more innocent past' which 'has never been entirely eliminated from radical thinking' (3). The Restoration of Charles II following the Commonwealth interregnum in 1688 was accepted by Whigs, Tories and radicals of the time as the Glorious Revolution which reinstated the true English constitution, and such a vision, though contrary in its sense of direction to that of the English millenarians of the 1790s, was certainly in line with Wordsworth's primary interest in the re-establishing of a lost past. It was to become entrenched as the distinctively British version, which for Burke reconciled the American Rebellion with the evolved principles of 1688: 'When this child of ours wishes to assimilate to the parent, and to reflect with a true filial resemblance the beauteous countenance of British liberty, are we to turn to them the shameful parts of the constitution?' ('Speech on American Taxation', 1961, 59). It was, in fact, redefined in response to the aberration of the French Revolution, and, most influentially, Macaulay's Whig view of British history was to be based on the incorporation of the experience of temporary rebellion leading to the Commonwealth which only served to re-authorize the full course of the English Revolutionary scheme: 'because we had a destroying revolution in the seventeenth century ... we have not had a preserving revolution in the nineteenth' (1882, III 413).

This was the discrimination that Wordsworth was waking up to in Paris, which suddenly felt like a jungle 'where tigers roam' (82). In Shakespearean tragedy he later found a voice that he had not wished to hear for what was to turn into violent usurpation, hailed within himself: 'I seemed to hear a voice that cried / To the whole city, "Sleep no more!"' (76–7). In 1794, writing to his Cambridge friend, William Matthews, Wordsworth convicted the 'present ministry' of being 'already so deeply advanced in iniquity that like Macbeth they cannot retreat' (*WL* I 135). Ten years later, when he composed his account of his revolutionary history, his own earlier implication in the words of the regicide Macbeth through which Wordsworth writes 'I wrought upon myself' (75) announces also a premonition of the killing of Louis XVI the following January. Wordsworth's full revolutionary knowledge is prematurely hinted at this stage, as immanent in the account is the future career of atrocities, culminating in the Terror: 'The fear gone by / Pressed on me almost like a fear to come' (62–3). But in 1792 Wordsworth was still resisting the message of the Place de Carrousel, the square where he had indeed met the gaze of an alienated self, and where he had begun to realize that he would somehow have to come to terms with the interrupted cyclicity of the revolutionary settlement of 1688, and, in short, square the circle.

Arguing in a Circle

The dethronement and massacres of 1792 caused the first tremor to threaten the security of Wordsworth's commitment to the French Revolution. From then until he ultimately rejected it, his ongoing engagement was marked by a series of further vacillations between alienation and fervour for either French or English political and social practices, national and regional. Along a chain of chiastic transferrals, he was to move from French republicanism to English republicanism to English constitutionalism. In retrospect, he could see rightly that the gradualism of his transit to what emerged as an opposite party positioning had been inscribed throughout with a special relation to discursification itself that had always (apart from some tumultuous years in the early 1790s when he did not write what has consistently been received as his most characteristic or lasting poetry) tended to conservatism. The leaning of his thought at every stage had been towards return, repetition and continuity. In short, apart from a confusing and painful detour, he had consistently been an adherent of what was at the same time becoming defined as the Burkean nation, whereas the antagonism of the liberal critique of his political changes has been mostly addressed not so much to his intrinsic conservatism as to his break with the democratizing principles of the French Revolution. Yet the interlude of his engagement in French politics and its aftermath was after all an historical acting out of the primary paradigm that shaped all his life and works. The period which operated as the hinge of political redirection lasted, with several epicycles of investment in and withdrawal from the revolution, from October 1792 in Paris to the completion of *The Borderers* and the composition of the first version of 'The Ruined Cottage' in 1797.

In order to bring out the peculiar continuities in his 'apostasy',[12] they may be placed against the grain of the political criticism of the French Revolution's most unswerving English defender and Burke's chief Romantic adversary, Hazlitt. Hazlitt's 1823 essay for *The Liberal*, 'Arguing in a Circle', plays on the figure of circularity throughout, setting up the proper context for democratic dispute as anti-hierarchical:

> [The public] is the most tremendous ring that ever was formed to see fair play between man and man; it puts people on their good behaviour immediately; and wherever it exists, there is an end of the airs and graces which individuals, high in rank, and low in understanding and morals, may chuse to give themselves. (*H* XIX 267)

Hazlitt's own expanding argument comes round to denouncing the forces of reaction in Europe – most topically the interference of the Holy Alliance in Spain, whereby the royalist French army had enabled Ferdinand VII once more to reject the constitution of 1812 – and then to link them, by virtue of Canning's policy of non-interference, with the present Tory administration and a Britain which 'must remain neuter while a grievous wrong is acting . . . because the name of liberty alone (without the cant of loyalty) has lost its magic charm on the ears of Englishmen' (271). He deprecates in particular the influence of Burke, whom he arraigns, anachronistically – and this is the crucial move – as an apologist for the recent developments of European 'Legitimacy', even after the isolation of Britain following the Congress of Verona the previous year ('We want a Burke to give the thing a legitimate turn at present', ibid.), and so builds up the picture of a truculent conservativism that had effected a violent intervention in the otherwise certain advances initiated by the French Revolution: 'The "Reflections on the French Revolution" was a spiteful and dastard but too successful attempt to *put a spoke in the wheels* of knowledge and progressive civilization, and throw them back for a century and a half at least' (273). Hazlitt's chain of reasoning sees wheels within wheels, and the issue becomes: which version of revolution – 1688 or 1789 – carries more authority? For Hazlitt, it is a non-issue: it is clear which trajectory leads to brutality and social divisiveness, and in place of the slowly assuaging rotation of the 1688 Revolution, loyalism to the British constitution is stigmatized with the crimes of continental absolutism, with which the deserters of the *'Lake School'* (276) become climactically associated. Hazlitt turns conservative traditionalism on its head by inventively presenting the Lake Poets as tear-aways. The 'tergiversation' (278) of that 'apostate' group are presented as those of 'turn-coats' who have switched between 'violent extremes' (277). They have veered away from the assured path of the French Revolution, and, from Hazlitt's viewpoint, come to occupy a conceptual gap, led on simply by self-interest. Hazlitt's progressivist revolution has itself accommodated that of 1688, leaving no room for the traditionalist outlook to represent the French version as epiphenomenal (in the way of the Commonwealth period) to its own vaster national scheme. Instead, Hazlitt's reading forces the new monarchists back into a vicious Burkean circle, and effectively cancels out what from the perspective of the conservative imagination was an outer all-embracing and pacifying world-view – one which for Wordsworth in particular, whom Hazlitt does not here name, had hidden depths.

Of all the Wordsworth circle, the complexities of Wordsworth's own revolutionary knowledge is most inadequately represented in Hazlitt's historiography. Wordsworth's 'mummifying' of his personal past, though it paralleled the historical preoccupation of nostalgists for the old order, is hugely in excess of the mere opportunism that Hazlitt explicitly attributes to Southey. Hazlitt's punning understanding of political corruption depended on its concealing the death of a bygone system of government: 'Burke strewed the flowers of his style over the rotten carcase of corruption, and embalmed it in immortal prose' (271). But for Wordsworth the past *was* held in suspension in the poetic language of *The Prelude*.

What Wordsworth saw as the climactic 'Change and subversion' (X 233) of his revolutionary knowledge – a 'stride at once / Into another region' (240–1) – occurred in February 1793 after his return to England, when, following the French declaration of war against England and Holland, England finally took up arms against the French:

> No shock
> Given to my moral nature had I known
> Down to that very moment . . .
> . . . that might be named
> A revolution, save at this one time.
> (233–7)

What he had previously thought of as alternative representations of the coming universal society, (an English village community and revolutionary France), suddenly became irreconcilable: 'not, as hitherto, / A swallowing up of lesser things in great, / But change of them into their opposites' (762–4). Referring to Madame Roland's last words, 'Oh Liberty, what crimes are committed in thy name!', he reiterates the impact of his own discovery that the same words could signify contradictory things, and that, at 'a time / In which apostasy from ancient faith / Seemed but conversion to a higher creed' (283–5), those discrepancies were within in his own mind. He had to resolve 'a conflict of sensations without name' (265) by choosing which version of patriotism he should re-authorize in the name of his ideal republic. The dilemma had come unexpectedly, since the solidarity of 'the English people' (211) in supporting the bill abolishing the slave trade had appeared to demonstrate a univocal consensus – 'a whole nation crying with one voice' (212) – analogous to that which had appeared to redefine the French state at the commencement of the revolution. Now, kneeling in an English church, he could not subscribe to a service of thanksgiving 'To [the] great Father' (269) for the Duke of York's successful siege of Dunkirk, and remained silent. Instead, he continued to espouse the French declaration of war as an expression of universal revolution, still echoing Brissot's 'crusade for universal liberty' (Schama, 597), and secretly 'Exulted in the triumph of [his] soul / When Englishmen by thousands were o'erthrown' (260–1) in the Battle of Hondshoote.

Nothing need have checked Wordsworth's moral support of the official enemy during its ensuing reverses – as Belgium was liberated, the Holy Roman Empire declared war on France, the royalist revolt broke out in the Vendée, and Dumouriez and Louis Philippe deserted. Just as he had felt compelled to endorse the sacrifice of his fellow-countrymen to the purity of the revolution, there is no evidence that he did not approve the establishment of the Committee of Public Safety in April with its dictatorial power as a necessary step.[13] His anti-Pittite and anti-war animus, represented in 'Salisbury Plain' (composed between summer 1793 and May 1794), must have suffered greater provocation by the Scottish treason trials of Muir, Palmer and others, resulting in their transportation in 1793. Yet, despite the gagging acts, introduced to suppress the Corresponding and other societies, and the freezing of the popular constitution in the suspension of the Habeas Corpus for eight years from 1794, the British Constitution was in some degree vindicated by the acquittal of Horne Tooke, Hardy, Thelwall and the other leading members of the London Corresponding Society, charged with treason in an English court in 1794. Trial by jury could well have stood favourable comparison for Wordsworth with the methods of the Committee of Public Safety, when, with the arrest of Brissot and the purge of the Girondins in June – their leadership was to be guillotined from 24 to 31 October – the inner contradictions of the revolution were again manifest.

In *The French Revolution*, Carlyle evokes 'Poor Deputy Gorsas', who stole

> in August, to Paris; lurked several weeks about the Palais *ci-devant* Royal; was seen there one day; was clutched, identified, and without ceremony, being already 'out of the law', was sent to the Place de la Revolution. He died, recommending his wife and children to the pity of the Republic. It is the ninth day of October 1793. Gorsas is the first Deputy that dies on the scaffold; he will not be the last.   (II 322)

Carlyle got the date wrong (actually 7 October), but he believed he had gained first-hand information about this particular execution, when around 1840 Wordsworth told him that he had personally witnessed it. Wordsworth seemed to produce fresh evidence of 'the public emotion his death excited', and 'testified strongly to the ominous feeling which that event produced in everybody, and of which he himself seemed to retain something: "Where will it end, when you have set an example in this kind?"' (1881, II 335). Apart from this single mention there is no other allusion in any of Wordsworth's writings to the requisite visit to France, though it would fill in an important lacuna in his known biography, from early August to mid October 1793.[14] But the execution, witnessed or not, was so disturbing a memory to Wordsworth because it did bring him face to face with what he had become intimately involved with, and in so doing it demonstrated the definitive severing of his revolutionary knowledge from what, despite previous disturbances, had remained his resilient Rousseauist–Girondist interpretation. Beyond that, since in earlier, headier days Gorsas's journalism had provided Wordsworth with the revolutionary language required to sustain his self-representation (though Gorsas had condoned the September massacres, he had moved towards the Girondins against the Commune and the Montagnards), his fate now re-enacted the castration of Wordsworth's subject in language by exposing the arbitrariness of their shared discourse. Henceforth, he now saw, revolutionary discourse would chase after the plenitude it was itself always destroying ('Where will it end?')

The worst horror, therefore, was that the revolutionary Wordsworth, in a parody of what would be resolved as the discourse of self-sacrifice (see Chapter 2), was not only the victim but also, as Nick Roe has argued, the executioner.[15] In fact, the role of *bourreau*, or headsman, had previously been revealed to be unstable by none other than Gorsas himself. At the end of 1789, the National Constituent Assembly had decided in its deliberations on electoral law that the executioner, Charles-Henri Sanson, was to be treated on the same basis as every other honourable citizen, just as it was simultaneously discovered that aristocrats were using a house in his possession for issuing subversive pamphlets.[16] Gorsas led the press hunt with the allegation that all the caste of executioners with their almost dynastic successions and intermarriages were crypto-feudalists who were conspiring to restore the *ancien régime*. In the event, Sanson was triumphantly acquitted, to be chosen in due course to decapitate Louis XVI. After himself assenting to Louis's death in *A Letter to the Bishop of Llandaff*, composed in February or March 1793 – a step which even Paine had opposed – Wordsworth had inevitably become implicated in a manifestly conflicted judicial system that was on the verge of serving, as its new masters, the terrorist usurpers of the king. In the unpublished *Letter*, Wordsworth made his most self-compromising statements on the acceptability of political killing by dismissing 'the personal sufferings of the late royal martyr' as those of one who was himself a kind of murderer, and argued the case for progressive violence: ' . . . a time of revolution is not the season of true Liberty . . . in order to reign in peace [Liberty] must establish herself by violence . . . Political virtues are developed at the expence of moral ones . . . ' (*Prose* I 33–4). Yet, addressing a noted liberal churchman and 'Christian teacher', Bishop Richard Watson, Wordsworth made it clear that this outlook depended on its being part of an indispensable programme of regulated control, a 'stern necessity', producing 'a convulsion from which is to spring a fairer order of things', and that it was the work of professional cultural mediators to expound such an enlightened discourse of Oedipal replacement:

It is the province of education to rectify the erroneous notions which a habit of oppression, and even of resistance, may have created, and to soften this ferocity of character proceeding from a necessary suspension of the mild and social virtues; it belongs to her to create a race of men who, truly free, will look upon their fathers as only enfranchised. (*Prose* I 34)

But the *Letter*, like his other most overtly political and Godwinian work, 'Salisbury Plain' (1793–4), which came out only in a much revised version in 1842, remained unpublished at that time, and in its case never was brought out for the rest of his life. Domestic British repression may have been only one reason for Wordsworth's inability wholly to authorize them for entry into the public arena. In a rapidly changing context, it was in the execution of Gorsas that Wordsworth first woke up to the ongoing nature of revolutionary violence, and began to intuit what lay ahead: that rather than representing the imaginary regulation of a violently grasped subjectivity, it had come to signify the unquenchable thirst for factional and even individual power that, for him, would find ultimate embodiment in Napoleon. He saw that the revolution sustained by maniacal violence was annihilating rather than defending the concept of a unified nation, separating 'the old man from the chimney-nook, / The maiden from the bosom of her love, / The mother from the cradle of her babe, / The warrior from the field' (X 330–3). Those in control of what was happening were out of control of themselves. The mechanical efficiency of the guillotine, an instrument designed with a humanitarian intention, had come not merely to do its job almost automatically, but also to mimic the exhilarating demonstration of power that was unopposed by considerations of suffering or compunction. Wordsworth's illustration for this exhibition of devastatingly facile power, fixated on its ever greater exercise, is a toy windmill held by a child who

> is not content,
> But with the plaything at arm's length he sets
> His front against the blast, and runs amain
> To make it whirl the faster.
>
> (342–5)

In short, in the scene of Gorsas's execution Wordsworth's reawakened alienation *within* revolutionary discourse began also to shift into alienation *from* his representation by the dominant power of sansculottism. An effort legitimately to empower victimhood, political but also more radical than politics alone could bring about, became his leading preoccupation in the poetry of the rest of the decade.

Robespierre, arrogating the supreme dictatorial power to which Louvet had accused him of aspiring, was *the* spokesman for Jacobin terrorism, in which Wordsworth saw the image of subjectivity out of imaginary control – a diagnosis that was also the blueprint for his rejection of Godwinian rationalism in *The Borderers*, as later, consummately, of

Napoleonism. Blakemore has written of the 'arbitrary, linguistic powers' of which Robespierre was 'the arch-representative', and quotes Taine, who saw him as a vulgar pedant:

> a man corrupted by his own language, a man whose mind became the *cuistre*, 'that is to say, the hollow, inflated mind which filled with words and imagining that these are ideas, revels in its own declamation and dupes itself that it may dictate to others' ... 'The empty term he selects is used in a contrary sense; the sonorous words *justice*, *humanity*, mean to him piles of human heads, the same as a text from the gospels means to a grand inquisitor the burning of heretics.' (87)

Similarly for Wordsworth Robespierre dictated a regime in which words were separated from things, whereby pious slogans became abstractions representing a will-to-power in the semblance of moral and political idealisms. On the very day, 8 June 1794, that Robespierre celebrated his vacuous power-cult in the Festival of the Supreme Being (prior to mass executions), Wordsworth wrote to his radical friend William Matthews that he condemned 'the infatuation profligacy and extravagance of men in power' and, though he remained a convinced republican, he '[recoiled] from the bare idea of a revolution' (*WL* I 124) as he had come to know it.

Consequently, Wordsworth responded to the news of Robespierre's being guillotined on 28 July 1794 with a prophetic feeling of triumph, as the reassertion of what he had always felt must prove insuppressible. The announcement '*Robespierre was dead*' (X 535) was one of those major communications – as with his poetic vocation in Book IV when 'vows were then made for [him]' – that presented him with 'the voice / Of [his] own wish' ('Ode to Duty', 42–3). His 'passionate intuition' (587) that the Republic's 'triumphs' would still 'be in the end / Great, universal, irresistible' (584–5), leading to 'the ultimate repose of things' (584–5), was reconfirmed when his new 'sympathy with power' (416) had seemed to find expression in the subduing of rampantly undisciplined subjectivity. '[T]he day of vengeance yet to come' (274), on which his anger had fed in the English church the previous year, was legitimately visitable on all opponents of his imaginary revolution, from whatever side: originally Pitt's regime, then the Revolutionary Government declared in December 1793 with its atrocities in France, and later, unhesitatingly, Napoleon.

Wordsworth's 'hymn of triumph' (543) was his regulated version of the 'cruel joy of the people',[17] avenging the deaths of the Girondin leaders with whom Wordsworth identified, in a private transformation of the revolutionary 'Te Deum' performed all over France. His singularly overdetermined subjectivity celebrated its victorious control over potential anarchy: 'the madding factions' were to be 'tranquillized' (554). Characteristically, it is through literary discourse that the imaginary is re-established, authorized by given intertextualities derived from the Old Testament, and also bearing a revisionary discourse of Miltonic republicanism:

> few happier moments have been mine
> Through my whole life than that when first I heard
> That this foul tribe of Moloch was o'erthrown,
> And their chief regent levelled with the dust.
>
> (466–9)

This false and fallen god who, as Milton writes, led 'the wisest heart / Of Solomon . . . by fraud to build / His Temple right against the Temple of God' (*Paradise Lost*, I 400–2) and who was the first of those who 'with cursed things / His holy Rites, and solemn Feasts profan'd' (389–90), figures Robespierre's perversion of the early revolutionary festivals and of the vindication of revolutionary violence. His sacrificial cult specialized in the destruction of children: 'First Moloch, horrid King besmear'd with blood / Of human sacrifice, and parents tears' (392–3). In effect, he represented the muddying of Wordsworth's allegiances by grotesquely parodying the regal power he had tried – in Robespierre's case for a time successfully – to usurp.

What binds *The Prelude* together in memory – the contemporaneous perception of actual events with their retellings – is the continuing insistence of Wordsworth's imaginary order. Though the discourses and their registers necessarily change, as each trauma in Wordsworth's experience recalled the original trauma of language-acquisition, and produced a new language to encompass it, nevertheless, in that sense, 'The form remains, the Function never dies' (*The River Duddon*, 'Conclusion', 6). Different versions of a poem engage new languages that serve to address more recent crises in order to resolve (even as they describe) the principal traumas of childhood and the revolution in a fundamentally continuous psychological pattern.

In this way, the Miltonic register with which Wordsworth restores imaginary sway in Book X of autumn 1804 had accrued to his more recent advocacy of British 'Liberty' – the term he used in 1807 to categorize his political sonnets of the early 1800s – rather than belonging to the time of the events it is invoked to recall from ten years before. But, though it had by then come to answer the urgent problem of legitimizing violent retribution that had challenged him in 1794, its application conceals the lack of *any* confident new idiom in which to assimilate the trauma of Robespierreanism back at that time. Over time, he was to arrive at the realization that the revolution had in fact presented him with increasingly empty rhetoric. His considered opinion in 1802 was that as far as he was concerned throughout the revolutionary years France had produced a blank:

> Perpetual emptiness! unceasing change!
> No single Volume paramount, no code,
> No master spirit, no determined road;
> But equally a want of Books and Men!
> ('Great Men have been among us;
> hands that penned', 11–14)[18]

This was the stultification that is enacted in the career of the Solitary in *The Excursion* (1814), which shadows that of Wordsworth up to the point at which he is faced with the need for the compensatory discourses which the whole poem is constructed to provide, according to Coleridge's suggestion of 1799 for

> a poem . . . addressed to those, who, in consequence of the complete failure of the French Revolution, have thrown up all hopes of the amelioration of mankind, and are sinking into an almost epicurean selfishness, disguising the same under the soft titles of domestic attachment and contempt for visionary *philosophes*. (*LSTC* I 527)

If the Solitary's reading of the opening events in France in Book III is more reminiscent of Coleridge's own millenarianism, his rude awakening is that of Wordsworth himself, with its nightmare return of detached individualism, hollow (Godwinian) rationalism and despair. At first, the revolution had seemed to offer the Solitary a social vision that, by extending his undifferentiated family symbiosis, might replace it when that became shattered. The deaths of his wife and children involve those of Wordsworth's own children, Thomas and Catherine, in 1811–12, the most recent in the series of such traumas to befall Wordsworth. For the Solitary the derangement resulted in the dangerous 'abstraction' (III 706) of 'intellectual power' (700) that, explicitly echoing Rivers's in *The Borderers*, 'through words and things, / Went sounding on, a dim and perilous way!' (700–1) But the Solitary 'was reconverted to the world' (734) as the traditional language of spiritual hope seemed fulfilled in history, with the fall of the Bastille. When rapturous universalism turned to caballing, however, 'confusion reigned' (774), and he himself for a time became the vehement mouthpiece of rhetorical 'Abstraction' (796). Eventually, he came to realize that he was engaged in nothing other than a fight for power 'in a struggling and distempered world', in which he acknowledged 'a seductive image' of 'a troubled mind' (804–5).

The protraction of the Solitary's malady derives from his inability to discover any alternative discourse in which to sustain 'The splendour, which had given a festal air / To self-importance' (II 194–5). His mountain-vision of the New Jerusalem in Book II is conceived in the language of Revelations: 'That which I *saw* was the revealed abode / Of spirits in beatitude' (873–4). But to try to represent the panorama of nature in those glorifying terms exposes him to a kind of trite artificiality:

> Fabric it seemed of diamond and of gold,
> With alabaster domes, and silver spires,
> And blazing terrace upon terrace, high
> Uplifted; here, serene pavilions bright,
> In avenues disposed; there, towers begirt
> With battlements that on their restless fronts
> Bore stars – illumination of all gems!
>
>   . . .
>
> Right in the midst, where interspace appeared
> Of open court, an object like a throne
> Under a shining canopy of state
> Stood fixed
>
>   (839–45, 861–4)

His most revitalizing moment of experience is subdued to a biblical register that may fleetingly distract him from his historical experience, but that in no way comes to terms with it. The illusoriness of the scene does not match up to the revelation of the revolution, and provides no substantial representation for his post-revolutionary subjectivity: '"I have been dead," I cried, / "And now I live! Oh! wherefore *do* I live?" / And with that pang I prayed to be no more!' (875–7).

Wordsworth's case, however, was to be different, as he was gradually to become the Wanderer of his own poem, creating a literary discourse through which to redefine the key national institutions of Tory state and Anglican church. But in 1794, no persuasive discourse was immediately available to him, either in France or England. His bitterest expressions in *The Prelude* concerning his political feelings during these years are reserved for his bad political fathers, Pitt and his government, whom he describes as 'Giants in their impiety alone' (X 652). He believed that their declaration of war on France had served to bolster Jacobinism, and he retained contempt for their domestic repressions and the network of paid informers from which he and Coleridge were to suffer at Alfoxden in 1797: 'in their weapons and their warfare base / As vermin working out of reach, they leagued / Their strength perfidiously to undermine / Justice, and make an end of liberty' (653–6).[19] Nevertheless, at the actual time of hearing of Robespierre's fall Wordsworth's dilemma was being opportunely relieved by re-apprehending 'The ultimate repose of things' in an effective re-insistence of the imaginary relation to natural objects that in childhood had soothed the original shock of subjectification and now returned to pacify its reawakening by the Terror.

In the spring of 1794, Wordsworth had been reunited with Dorothy for several weeks in the Lake District. The family reunion offered the promise of a re-enfoldment within the symbiosis of infancy – a state that later incorporated their brother John, whose drowning in 1805 is mourned in 'Elegiac Stanzas Suggested by a Picture of Peele Castle'. That poem, written in 1806, (in search of an enduring aesthetic of the sublime to support his latest domestic tragedy), looks back to the convalescent holiday at Rampside in summer 1794, during which Wordsworth learned of Robespierre's death, as a time when his perception of the scene of the castle reflected in Morecambe Bay had been overdetermined by imaginary harmonies recaptured from boyhood:

> Thy form was sleeping on a glassy sea.

> Beside a sea that could not cease to smile;
> On tranquil land, beneath a sky of bliss.
> (4, 19–20)

'Peele Castle' laments the later shattering of the regained equanimity of 1794, and has effortfully to reconstruct continuity with an embattled literary discourse of resilient nationalism. Nevertheless the cumulative experience of that summer had previously fortified Wordsworth by re-establishing the remembered serenity that was about to find expression for the subjugation of Jacobinism in his extraordinarily personally freighted register of nature poetry.

It was in this mood that Wordsworth felt ready to develop a more active interest in a prominent strain in contemporary British radicalism – Godwinian philanthropism – that he had begun to consider earlier that year as another mirroring language for his political idealism. Its apparent voicing of Wordsworth's own moderated position offered a significant translation from the scene of French affairs, as the attentions of the reorganized committees in Paris and later the newly constituted Directory (from 1 November 1795) turned towards internal economic issues and foreign diplomacy. But in the course of 1795 he began after all to detect the unsuitability of Godwinian philanthropism as an imaginary langauge, fearing, as he relates in *The Prelude*, in its underlying rationalism ('The human reason's naked self', X 817) the reiterated menace of undisciplined subjectivity.

The failure of his attempt to sustain a radical discourse is demonstrated in the impasse of *The Borderers* (1796–7). Unable by then to identify with either Mortimer's naive idealism or Rivers's cynical individualism, Wordsworth could not locate any political discourse in which to acknowledge and contain his revolutionary knowledge. Rivers more particularly portrays the process of 'the perversion of the understanding' that Wordsworth had witnessed 'while the Revolution was rapidly advancing to its extreme of wickedness' (*Prose*, [The 1842 Note], *The Borderers*, 813). His imagining of individual freedom, pre-echoing the Solitary's, involves not only the overthrow of a Bastille of historical abuses of power, but also the pre-emption of the new social disciplining of the carceral society, represented for him by submission to customary compunction:

> Three sleepless nights I passed in sounding on
> Through words and deeds, a dim and perilous way;
> And wheresoe'er I turned me, I beheld
> A slavery, compared to which the dungeon
> And clanking chain are perfect liberty.
>
>   (IV ii 102–6)

He has learned that 'wondrous revolutions' (III v 144) can be made by ethical experimentation, and revels in the empowering arbitrariness revealed by the Terror: 'I saw that every shape of action / Might lead to good – I saw it and burst forth / Thirsting for some exploit of power and terror' (IV ii 108–10). His new sense of power is based on the realization that, when rights had become equivocal and values contradictory, new regimes, political and moral, were to be invented at will. Wordsworth's essay on his character describes how his 'low hankering after the *double entendre* of vice' is 'awakened' by 'the revolutions through which his character has passed' ([On the Character of Rivers], *The Borderers*, 65) – a trait that issues in Rivers's own proposition that 'The faintest breath that breathes can move a world' (III v 85), reducing revolutionary knowledge to semantic caprice: 'Murder! what's in the word?' (III v 92)

As the abhorrent other self that had been revealed to Wordsworth, Rivers is often seen as demonstrating a critique of Godwinism, but while Rivers's detachment from conventional moralities recalls one effect of Godwinism, when it comes to revolutionary violence Godwin's own analysis added to the muddle that he brought upon Wordsworth at the time, leading him to '[yield] up moral questions in despair' (X 900). A crux is Godwin's strictures on the mentality of assassins in 'Of Tyrannicide', Chapter IV, Book Four, of *Enquiry Concerning Political Justice*, 1793, where he argues that the same violent act may be the language of both the murderous will-to-power and the freedom-fighter: 'The pistol and the dagger may easily be made the auxiliaries of vice, as of virtue' (*Enquiry*, 294). The terrain of such ethical indeterminacy, when 'The boundaries ... are gone' (295) and when what is instinctively repugnant represents itself as admirable in 'a tranquil gaiety' that 'changes the use of speech, and composes every feature the better to deceive' (ibid.), is recognizably that of *The Borderers*.[20] Godwin's example of such hypocrisy is 'the conspirators kneeling at the feet of Caesar, as they did the moment before they destroyed him!' (ibid.)

Through Godwin, Wordsworth invests Rivers's analysis of the assassin's power with allusions to Shakespeare's *Julius Caesar*, the cult revolutionary text shadowed by 'The abuse of greatness ... when it disjoins / Remorse from power' (*S*, II i 747). For Rivers, greatness *is* precisely this disjoining:

> Remorse,
> It cannot live with thought, think on, think on,
> And it will die. What? in this universe,
> Where the least things control the greatest.[21]

Intertextualities with Shakespearean tragedies help Godwin organize the Oedipalism of the tyrannicidal act. Rivers's conscience-stricken sleeplessness recalls Brutus's, as well as that of Wordsworth (and Macbeth) in the *Prelude* account of Paris 1792, when in his 'high and lonely' room 'With unextinguished taper [he] kept watch' (X 57 61) and 'seemed to hear a voice that cried / To the whole city, "Sleep no more!"' (77). More deeply resonant for Wordsworth is Godwin's description of behaviour that 'delights in obscurity' and 'avoids all question, and hesitates and trembles before the questioner' (294), conjuring Hamlet's father's ghost who 'started like a guilty thing, / Upon a fearful summons' (I i 1001). Like Wordsworth's 'indisputable shapes' in his account of experiencing his father's death, Godwin's assassin differs from the 'questionable shape' of old Hamlet in arrogating the phallus to himself, and thereby associates himself with the tyrannical cycle. Unlike Wordsworth, however, the political murderer has no confident excuse, and cannot put one into words, whereas for Wordsworth, both in the account of his waiting for the horses and in the Intimations Ode, where he echoes Godwin's *trembling* ('High instincts before which our mortal Nature / Did tremble like a guilty Thing surprised'), the encounter with the paternal presence will become cautiously reviewed as only the first stage of a re-empowering of the imaginary position ('But for those first affections, / Those shadowy recollections, / ... / Are yet the fountain light of all our day, / Are yet the master-light of all our seeing' (143–59; see Chapter 2).

Brutus's 'Between the acting of a dreadful thing, / And the first motion, all the interim', after he has been '[Whetted] ... against Caesar' (II i 747) by Cassius, helps to mark out the pivot of the Wordsworthian imagination and its conversion of transgression into a special kind of poetic language. Godwin quotes it in his critique, but whereas the original continues: 'Like a phantasma or a hideous dream', Godwin substitutes a suggestively truncated half-line: 'is mystery and reserve' (295). Half-echoes of Brutus's speech, mediated by Godwin, culminate in Rivers's attempt to convert Mortimer:

> Action is transitory, a step, a blow
> The motion of a muscle – this way or that
> 'Tis done – and in the after-vacancy
> We wonder at ourselves like men betray'd.
> Suffering is permanent, obscure and dark,
> And has the nature of infinity.
>
> (III v 60–5)

Wordsworth reads a different sense into 'motion' (effecting the action) from Shakespeare's (proposal) to alter Brutus's 'interim' between conception and deed into an open-ended 'after-vacancy', following the deed. For the Wordsworthian imagination, Brutus's 'state of a man, / Like to a little kingdom', which 'suffers then / The nature of an insurrection' (II i 747), continues to be suffered within, seeking resolution; but Rivers's revolutionary knowledge is irreversible, and his immediate answer to the unspoken question 'What have I done?' is that he has grasped the power of permanent revolution. Wordsworth found himself, as he wrote of this interim period in *The Prelude*, stuck between the discourses of revolutionary politics and literature. He was in a predicament reminiscent of his response to the execution of Gorsas – torn between the roles of Jacobin prosecutor and royalist prisoner, even metaphorically of Marie Antoinette or one of the large number of nobility who had been condemned by the Revolutionary Tribunal:

> Dragging all passions, notions, shapes of faith,
> Like culprits to the bar, suspiciously
> Calling the mind to establish in plain day
> Her titles and her honours.
>
> (X 889–92)

In the ambiguous figuring, the innocent workings of the mind that are outlawed by rationalist inquisition are represented as aristocrats. Wordsworth was indirectly owning that his deepest affective sympathies had perhaps more in common with the old order than with those who had abused power in the new. Some curiously disabling linkages were recuperable between Jacobinism and Godwinism on the one hand, and the *ancien régime* and some self-characterizing pieties on the other. Rather than reconciling transgression in a disciplinary regime, the new order had reverted to becoming compulsively punitive.

Cold Carnival

Following the stoning of the king's coach at the opening of parliament, the scenario for an ideological civil war in England was prepared by government repression effectively silencing political publications, and introducing the 'two Bills' outlawing treasonable practices and unlawful assemblies in December 1795. That Wordsworth's prophesy of the restitution of a controlled revolution had *not* come to pass in France was to become evident through the following years with the wars of conquest, especially the French invasion of Switzerland in January 1798, which was the beginning of the end for Wordsworth: 'after Buonaparte had violated the Independence of Switzerland, my heart turned against him, and the Nation that could submit to be the Instrument of such an outrage' (*WL* IV 97). Napoleon's *coup d'état* in November 1799 was to be the final straw.

His rejection of Godwinism was the result of his search for an alternative vehicle for the reconstruction of primary unity – what in *The Prelude* he referred to as the 'saving intercourse / with (his) true self' (X 914–15) that Dorothy had promised and that reawoke 'Those mysteries of passion which have made, / And shall continue ever more to make / In spite of all that reason hath performed, / And shall perform, to exalt and to refine / One brotherhood of all the human race' (IX 84–8). From 1794 Dorothy's intense absorption in the natural world, as Wordsworth writes in 'Tintern Abbey', helped calm, with its 'gleams / Of past existence' (149–50), the disorientation which the frustration of separation from Annette and Caroline and his hostility to the British government had brought about since his return to England. In that poem he alludes to his original visit to the Wye Valley, after his return in 1793, as that of a man on the run from his other newly alienated self: 'More like man / Flying from something that he dreads, than one / Who sought the thing he loved' (71–3). He depicts himself at that time as savagely courting regression to a purely sensuous mode of perception, trying, impossibly and so desperately, to regain his primitively steadied subjectivity, or 'I', held by the focus of the organic 'eye', in order to regain

> a feeling and a love.
> That had no need of a remoter charm,
> By thought supplied, or any interest
> Unborrowed from the eye.
>
> (81–4)

Now, after half that world-shattering decade, it is both gone and still present, in the tense combination of intensity and tranquillity in Dorothy Wordsworth's responsiveness to natural objects, so fixated that it isomorphously images an imaginary dyad both to the observer and to the observer's observer, as the brother's relation to the sister mirrors hers to the natural world. By now, Wordsworth was fully and confidently invested in his chosen discourse of poetry, a practice legitimized by his formulation of the language of nature. As he exchanged 'The language of [his] former heart' with Dorothy, and read '[His] former pleasures in the shooting lights / Of [her] wild eyes' (118–20), he offered her an initiation into the scheme of his achieved poetic language. The reiterated insistence of a controlled entry into the symbolic by an I/eye (that in *The Prelude* is 'the most despotic of our senses', XI 174, yet here 'made quiet by the power / Of harmony', 48–9) was to insure her from the griefs that beset disorganized intensity. Through this move, 'nature and the language of the sense' (109) speak, in that the dyadic relation in which mind merges with the natural world has itself become the dominant subject of whatever registers or discursive styles it comes to inhabit.

In the second half of the 1790s Wordsworth mostly abandoned political discourses to explore the capacity of literary discourse chiefly to represent human suffering as the ground for reforming social organization. In the course of composing 'The Ruined Cottage' (1797–8), Wordsworth pondered on the power of a painful inner adjustment to withstand 'all the grief / The passing shews of being leave behind'[22] and prove more radically satisfying than the restless quest of subjectifying desire. His meditation revolves around the border between the articulation of human meanings and silence. Rather than simply lamenting or welcoming human extinction, the poem examines the puzzling area of response created by the sustaining of *both* emotions. Proceeding from the effect of all human signs in inscribing natural objects with fatality –

> Beside yon spring I stood
> And eyed its waters till we seemed to feel
> One sadness, they and I. For a bond
> Of brotherhood is broken
>
> (82–5)

– the narrator is taught to construe the inevitable destruction of individual meanings as more painfully registered from a position of unregulated subjectification, inflected in what the Pedlar terms 'an untoward mind' and 'the weakness of humanity' (193–4). Yet the poet-narrator's hard-won resilience is finally expressed in terms of a restituted 'bond / Of brotherhood', which after all offers an insistence that may be inferred to derive from a relation to a common mother. In effect, he shares with Margaret his own residual intimation of dyadic union: 'it seemed / To comfort me while with a brother's love / I blessed her in the impotence of grief' (498–500). His response to the trauma of Margaret's death recalls the positioning that the loss of Wordsworth's mother had formerly reinforced and that, strengthened again by having to withstand another tragic story, he is able reciprocally to confer on Margaret herself. But the hidden promise in making her one with nature lies in that relation's emerging, however barely, as the principle behind all lasting social practices, and is here recoverable as

That secret spirit of humanity
Which, 'mid the calm oblivious tendencies
Of nature, 'mid her plants, her weeds, and flowers,
And silent overgrowings, still survived.

(503–6)

The acknowledgement to Margaret herself can only be *of* Margaret, or epitaphic, in this way, but for Wordsworth's particular agenda at that time the act of mourning serves also to refound a timely poetic discourse that can prevail over all the serial crises of differentiated subjectivity, whether they proceed from political disillusionment or private guilt.

As Wordsworth completed 'The Ruined Cottage' he poured out the lyrical ballads which probed and celebrated the poetic restoration of the 'primary laws of our nature . . . the essential passions of the heart . . . our elementary feelings . . . the passions of men . . . incorporated with the beautiful and permanent forms of nature' (Preface to *Lyrical Ballads*, Prose I 124). Politically, the as yet unspecified register of impersonal and communal affections in 'a spiritual community binding together the living and the dead: the good, the brave, and the wise, of all ages' (*Prose* I 339) was that of Burkean organicism, which took on a nationalist nuance after his second exile during the freezing winter of 1799 that Wordsworth and Dorothy spent holed up in Goslar. There, Dorothy's imaginary gaze is fixed on the distinctly English scene of 'the last green field / That Lucy's eyes surveyed!' ('I Travelled Among Unknown Men', 15–16), and Wordsworth's desire is firmly redirected towards the home fires: 'And she I cherished turned her wheel / Beside an English fire' (11–12). His literary discourse then became overtly politicized once more by taking on the Miltonic voice of British republicanism in the anti-Napoleonic 'Liberty' sonnets of 1801–2. Formerly, it had readily associated with French republicanism in the early 1790s as providing the ambiguous precedent for the exemplary execution of their king and abolilition of monarchy, though in *The Prelude* Wordsworth stresses that the French originally sought to emulate the English constitutional model of the Glorious Revolution, when he writes that they honoured himself and Jones as 'their forerunners in a glorious course' (VI 412). By the 1800s, his republicanism had reassumed its more distinctly English character, addressed equally against unrestrained French imperialism and the 'Rapine, avarice, expense' ('Written in London, September, 1802', 9) of what in the Fenwick note he refers to as 'the vanity and parade of [his] own country, especially in great towns and cities' (*PW* III

455). Such a puritanical attitude to luxury links Wordsworth's critique of the French Revolution to that of the internal industrial and agrarian revolution and its faith in progressivism that had now begun to engage him more urgently. Implicit in the empowerment of literary discourse itself had been the microcultural model of 'Plain living and high thinking' ('O Friend! I know not which way I must look', 11) in the 'prefect Republic of Shepherds and Agriculturalists' (*Prose* II 206) in the Lake District, which was representative of those rural societies that were now under sentence of social and economic break-up. Wordsworth responded to this newly focused crisis with the regionalist pastoralism of the second volume of the second edition of *Lyrical Ballads* (1802), in such poems as 'Michael' and 'The Brothers'.

Urban life now presented him with the other face of the national psyche in the spectacle of the popular mob, in which the sum of his revolutionary knowledge became impacted. For Book VII of *The Prelude*, he wrote in 1804 of his visit in September 1802 to St Bartholomew's Fair, held at Smithfield, where in the 1550s Protestant martyrs were burned in the reign of Queen Mary. He places it squarely as an example of the Bakhtinian carnivalesque:

> What say you then
> To times when half the city shall break out
> Full of one passion – vengeance, rage, or fear –
> To executions, to a street on fire,
> Mobs, riots, or rejoicings? From those sights
> Take one, an annual festival, the fair
> Holden where martyrs suffered in past time,
> And named of St Bartholomew.
>
> (645–52)

Some characteristic folk features suggestive of liberating, democratic reversals had enlivened *Lyrical Ballads*, in poems like 'The Idiot Boy' – Wordsworth told Isabella Fenwick that he 'never wrote anything with so much glee' (*PW* IV 478) – which is a burlesque exhibiting one of the commonest of all carnival shows, an idiot riding horseback (especially back-to-front): 'Perhaps he's turned himself about, / His face unto the horse's tail' (322–3). The boy's inversion of night and day belongs to the same custom: '"The cocks did crow to-whoo, to-whoo, / And the sun did shine so cold!"' (450–1) But though the upside-down world of the folk ballad typically revels in the subversion of authority symbols, creating for example its own 'boy-bishops', when 'The child is father of the man', Wordsworth's is a cold carnival: its resistances are pre-disciplined by psychological insistence put to moral and social purpose according to the festive decorum of the Fête de la Federation of 1790.

The carnival of St Bartholomew Fair, on the other hand, summarizing the disorganized and disenfranchized volatilities of the modern capital, epitomized for Wordsworth the anarchic energies of sansculottism. London was by then the largest city in Europe, with a population of almost three-quarters of a million, and, unlike any other British centre, was undefined by any dominating industrial activity.[23] Overall, like the Fair, it presented 'an unmanageable sight' (709) – it had not been 'taught its manage' – and was packed for Wordsworth with revolutionary overtones, and evocations of French massacres. At the time of the Terror of 1793 in particular, the massacre of St Bartholomew's Day, 1572, when the Huguenots were butchered in Paris, was frequently alluded to in the speeches of the Convention and in dramatic scenarios and political pamphlets. Marie-Joseph Chénier's play, *Charles XI*, which was written as the revolution was brewing and first performed amid public uproar in 1789, notoriously centred on the king's ordering of the massacres. The resonance may have been strengthened for Wordsworth by the particular outrages perpetrated at the Smithfield Fair of 1802: this was the occasion when Lady Holland's mob 'abused, knocked down, or robbed, almost every person they met' (Morley, 447). It may also be coloured by Burke's reference to the parallel: 'Your citizens of Paris formerly had lent themselves as the ready instruments to slaughter the followers of Calvin, at the infamous massacre of St. Bartholomew' (*Reflections*, 249). Burke continues in an interrogative phrase that pre-echoes Wordsworth's 'What say you then / To times when half the city shall break out / Full of one passion...?': 'What should we say to those who could think of retaliating on the Parisians of this day the abominations and horrors of that time?' (ibid.). Wordsworth's description certainly reveals a Burkean phobia for the nether world, especially when (as in James Gillray's propagandist prints, which are the prime contemporary example of the political carnivalesque) it is invested with political power and becomes a 'parliament of monsters' (692). The higgledy-piggledy carnival world of spewing orifices and unashamed promiscuity represents the threat to the orderly, organic, national tradition posed by both contemporary revolutions: it is like 'one vast mill...vomiting' (693–4). Even more primitively, it disturbs the structure of ordered meaning ('melted and reduced / To one identity by differences / That have no law, no meaning, and no end' (703–5), creating, as David Simpson writes, 'the absence of meaning through the very overlapping of possible meanings' (64). Instead, as Wordsworth's exemplum of rural education, the opening of the succeeding Book VIII presents his alternative 'summer festival' (10), Grasmere Fair, attended by 'a little family of men' (7). The customary exchange of livestock and fruit assumes enormous proportions when it is situated within the counter-discourse of Wordsworth's nature poetry:

> Immense
> Is the recess, the circumambient world
> Magnificent, by which they are embraced.
> They move about upon the soft green field;
> How little they, they and their doings, seem,
> ... and yet how great,
> For all things serve them.
>
> (46–55)

When his *bête noire*, Pitt, resigned in January 1801, the anti-Jacobin programme of the Tories was moderated as the party splintered into conflicting factions, and there followed what Fox himself called 'The euthanasia of politics' (see Trevelyan, 110), in which the existing regime could concentrate on the one-nation popular front against Napoleon, buoyed up by Nelson's victory in April of 1801, when he destroyed the Danish fleet off Copenhagen. Southey's comment on Napoleon's part in the preliminaries for the Peace of Amiens, signed in March 1802 – that it 'restored in me the English feeling which had long been dreaded; it placed me in sympathy with my country' (Simmons, 103) – expresses the experience of conversion that was shared by many of his formerly radical generation who now openly joined in support for the defensive coalition. Representatively, after the Declaration of War, in May 1803, Wordsworth began training as part of the body of Grasmere volunteer militia preparing for the anticipated French invasion, and in 'Lines on the Expected Invasion, 1803', he called on both royalist and republican traditions, of Falkland and Montrose, Pym and Milton, to unite in the nation's common cause:

> Come ye – whate'er your creed – O waken all,
> Whate'er your temper, at your country's call;
> Resolving (this a free-born Nation can)
> To have one Soul, and perish to a man.
>
> (15–18)

At the turn of the century Wordsworth took his closest political representative to be Fox, who had been the chief British opponent of the war against France. As the letter of appeal which he sent with a presentation copy of *Lyrical Ballads* (1800) demonstrates (see *WL* I 312–15), Wordsworth was then offering his regionalist pastoralism as an intervention in domestic politics, but, as partisan debate became blurred, its implicit registers of benevolent patriarchy and traditionalism were destined to overtake Miltonic republicanism in speaking for his nation. Inflected in the kind of social preparation that Wordsworth advocates as being needed to control the semiotic chaos of Bartholomew Fair, presenting 'differences / That have no law, no meaning', is a new respect for constitutional continuity and monarchism, 'with a feeling for the whole' (VII 713). Such imaginative control, 'Not violating any just restraint' (733), not only exorcized the excesses of popular disorder, but also indirectly revalidated the traditional forms of British government as expressions of the communal solidarity that Wordsworth felt had originally fired the revolution. In this way, the Wordsworthian construction of 'nature' takes on a more explicitly Burkean colouring of 'Composure and ennobling harmony' (741):

> The mountain's outline and its steady form
> Gives a pure grandeur, and its presence shapes
> The measure and the prospect of the soul
> To majesty.
>
> (723–6)

In particular, the constitutional idea of 'restoration' now more evidently took over, with its implied rejection of revolution in its modern sense – the title for Book XI became 'The Imagination, How Impaired and Restored'. It was informed by Burke's argument for the accommodation of social change according to the old Whig constitution of the Glorious Revolution of 1688 which was effected by a revolution, in his words, 'made to preserve our *antient* indisputable laws and liberties' (*Reflections*, 117). Burke's famous lament for the passing of 'the age of Chivalry' found a kind of reinstatement in Wordsworth's 'Ode to Duty', when he tired of 'unchartered freedom' (37) and 'chance desires' (38) and wished to 'feel past doubt / That [his] submissiveness was choice' (44): 'Never, never more, shall we behold that generous loyalty to rank and sex, that proud submission, that dignified obedience, that subordination of the heart, which kept alive, even in servitude itself, the spirit of an exalted freedom' (*Reflections*, 170). In a revision to Book VII made in 1832 (the year of the Great Reform Bill which Wordsworth fretfully opposed), an unhampered apostrophe swims to the surface, praising the 'Genius of Burke' (*1850*, 512), who

> the majesty proclaims
> Of Institutes and Laws, hallowed by time;
> Declares the vital power of social ties
> Endeared by Custom . . .
>
> (525–8)

Distinct traces of this new allegiance emerged in the poetry of 1804, the year he began to extend and complete the thirteen-book *Prelude*. In that year also he completed the Intimations Ode, revealing his eagerness to regain the 'glories' of 'that imperial palace whence he came' (83–4), and endeavouring the restoration of lost powers. In his essay for *The Liberal* in January 1823, 'On the Spirit of Monarchy', Hazlitt acutely makes out the harmonics in 'And by the vision splendid / Is on his way attended' (73–4) by quoting it to show how 'The imagination keeps pace with royal state' (*H* XIX 256). Wordsworth was to witness a disgusting parody of restoration in that year as Napoleon was declared Emperor, and, as Wordsworth writes, in order to 'rivet up the gains of France' (X 932), had the Pope crown him. The coronation was the culminating expression of power out of control, just as with the old order, and in it – in Wordsworth's devastating phrase – he saw 'the dog / Returning to his vomit' (934 5). The result was another parodic feast, a meretricious show, 'an opera phantom' (940). But, in contradistinction, Wordsworth was interested rather in re-establishing the legitimacy of an uncorrupted social framework still touched by the promise of *his* revolution. Just after completing the Ode, he wrote in *The Prelude*: 'Our simple childhood sits upon a throne' (V 532). Wordsworth had effectively crowned the primary position of the mirror stage as it extended its imaginary sway within the presiding discourses of what (since 1 January 1801) had become the United Kingdom.

4
Changing Spots

KING RICHARD: *Lions make leopards tame.*
MOWBRAY: *Yea, but not change their spots.*

Shakespeare, *Richard II*

Power Poetry

An overdetermined Oedipal plot is involved in the pledging of Wordsworth's allegiance to constitutional monarchism that relies on his special relation to the word of the father. The constitution of 1688 had already normalized the monarchy as *the* established and securely ordered institution of power. Yet contemporary events had reversed the ruling discourses of the court in France into those of a new revolutionary knowledge, which, in order to be subsumed into English politics, had to be represented as a formidable but finally ineffective challenge that after all served to confirm the supremacy of the English constitution. Wordsworth's subscription to that naturalized narrative of revolution was consolidated by his particular Oedipal settlement. Governmentally and dynastically, the king is a paternal figure whose authority is under constant threat, and who must either be unthroned, as in France, or legitimately succeeded, as in England, where the succession had been disputed and sometimes broken, yet recurrently strengthened by withstanding rivalrous opposition. As a history of governance, British monarchism evidently reflected the pattern of restoration in Wordsworth's psychological case history: both spoke for a poet who at different times had grasped the language of violent opposition, had then found himself lost for appropriate words, and had then discovered that the language of his true desire was already there, to become revalued as the settlement born of revolt.

Specifically, Shakespearean drama provided the literary register that ministered to Wordsworth's management of social and political involutions. Hazlitt's notable dictum on the workings of poetic pleasure in *Coriolanus* describes the expansive effect of coming into line with the 'timely utterance' of the 'aristocratical ... faculty' of the imagination: 'The cause of the people is indeed but little calculated as a subject for poetry: it admits of rhetoric, which goes into argument and explanation, but it presents no immediate or distinct images to the mind ... The language of poetry naturally falls in with the language of power' (*H* IV 214). Hazlitt proceeds, as Jonathan Bate has suggested, to implicate 'the political apostasy of Wordsworth, Coleridge, and Southey' (1989, 165) in the gravitation of poetry to the centres of power, actually quoting Wordsworth's solemnization of patriotic violence in his 'Ode 1815': '[Poetry] has its altars and its victims, sacrifices, human sacrifices. Kings, priests, nobles, are its train-bearers, tyrants and slaves its executioners, – "Carnage is its daughter." – Poetry is right-royal ... our vanity or some other feeling makes us disposed to place ourselves in the situation of the strongest party' (214–15).[1] The Lake Poets all eventually joined the line of Burke, of whom Hazlitt, intending no compliment, wrote that 'Politics became poetry in his hands' ('Arguing in a Circle', *H* XIX 272).

Wordsworth's fate was significantly different from that of his revolutionary alter egos, the Solitary and Vaudracour in the Romeo and Juliet story of Vaudracour and Julia that was insinuated into Book IX of *The Prelude* as a displacement of his own relationship with Annette. Vaudracour, a man who becomes competely isolated within an unjustly conflicted social system and who dies in his twenty-fourth year, represents the trap of revolutionary disillusionment when he failed any longer to be roused by 'the voice of freedom, which through France ... resounded' (931–2), and was led to the renunciation of all social inscription: 'he never uttered word / To any living' (912–13). Paradoxically, however, the frame of Shakespearean tragedy, while it registers the gist of Wordsworth's own doomed affair, nonetheless supplies Wordsworth with a medium in which to place it, while it couches his own misadventure, and so, above all, to create poetry out of it. The danger of the issue is not flouted: indeed, the worst scenario of castration in the characterization of an inexorably severe father who disinherits his son is confronted. But the generation of the poetry itself is telling a divergent tale of another, benevolent, poetic father – Shakespeare – who enables Wordsworth to dramatize a history that, as a result, has not wholly been his own.

The difference *is* the poetry, and its writing is the act that overcomes the historical and personal trespass. Wordsworth highlights the parallelism while seeming to play it down:

> such theme
> Hath by a hundred poets been set forth
> In more delightful verse than skill of mine
> Could fashion – chiefly by that darling bard
> Who told of Juliet and her Romeo,
> And of the lark's note heard before its time,
> And of the streaks that laced the severing clouds
> In the unrelenting east. 'Tis mine to tread
> The humbler province of plain history.
>
> (635–43)

The Shakespearean analogue is uninhibitedly sustained – in situation (a fatal family opposition), incident (the rash swordplay that leads to sudden death and outlawry), and diction and allusion:

> The house she dwelt in was a sainted shrine,
> Her chamber-window did surpass in glory
> The portals of the east, all paradise
> Could by the simple opening of a door
> Let itself in upon him.
>
> (589–3)

In his peculiar revision of Harold Bloom's theory of Oedipal transmission, Wordsworth's anxiety is addressed, according to the scheme of restoration, to acclaiming influence by a poetic forefather, here exemplarily Shakespeare, whose borrowed word is empowering without contestation. It follows the same seamless succession as the 'phrases and figures of speech which from father to son have long been regarded as the common inheritance of Poets' that Wordsworth refers to in the 1800 Preface to *Lyrical Ballads* (*Prose* I 132).

In search of his particular literary discourse, Wordsworth listens for 'phrases and figures' that reflect the structure of his own particular Oedipal passage to give representation to the restoration of his ideal ego. His discovery of appropriate substitutions is characterized by that mild ecstasy of self-recognition when 'the clouds are split / Asunder' ('A Night-Piece', 11–12), and the representation of a former, dumb subjectivity is simply presented to him in the symbolic order. In the juvenile 'The Dog – An Idyllium', Wordsworth describes just this rising up of a self-reflective (as well as erotically desirable) poetic image in the course of strenuous composition – 'Great pains and little progress' (IV 103) as he writes in the related *Prelude* account – which bestows pleasurable self-expression:

> while I gaz'd to Nature blind,
> In the calm Ocean of my mind
> Some new-created image rose
> In full-blown beauty at its birth
> Lovely as Venus from the sea.
>
> (18–22)

Rising from the ocean, as 'The perfect image of a mighty mind' (69) emerges from the 'still ocean' (46) of the sea-mist in the Ascent of Snowdon passage in Book XIII of *The Prelude*, via 'that breach / Through which the homeless voice of waters rose' (62–3), is a form of self-representation that overflows spontaneously. The image is a phallus that speaks for both his imaginary position *and* the Other, because while it marks sexual difference (as 'Venus') it nonetheless effaces all trace of parental generation, like the 'unfathered vapour' (527) of the imagination that suddenly rises from the text that Wordsworth wrote for what became Book VI of *The Prelude*. These impressive moments of jubilant self-reflection, when Wordsworth discovers himself being articulated, placate his singular demand to be the unalienated object of the Other's desire, announcing the resurfacing of the imaginary structure within the symbolic order.

In this way, Wordsworth's poetry is always at one level simply descriptive, repeating the negotiation of that particular border of symbolic passage. But the correspondences within the intertextualities are not always or obviously preformulated. The poet has in differing degrees actively to discern them in a process of selective reflexivity which organizes the commutability of the intertexts. *Hamlet*, however, was exceptional in that its Oedipal scenario first brought Wordsworth's own case to the point of self-expression in the juvenilia (see Chapter 2), and thereafter it reappeared, to supervise the operations of other and subsequent post-traumatic inscriptions. After the deaths of his parents, chief among all the ensuing traumatic reminders of his first Oedipal struggle was Wordsworth's misreading of his revolutionary knowledge.

Whenever Wordsworth wrote about the revolution, either directly or obliquely, he was engaged in an act of revision, through which he both confronted and came to terms with the stratifications of a personal and historical paternal presence. In his critique of Wordsworth's dramatized discussion of the French Revolution in Books III and IV of *The Excursion*, De Quincey, despite himself, helps understand how Wordsworth could not simply set aside the revolution, but had learned his lasting lesson from it. De Quincey faults Wordsworth, as well as his characters – 'the philosophical Wanderer' and 'the learned vicar' – for failing to understand that the revolution '*has* succeeded; it is far beyond the reach of ruinous reactions; it is propagating its life; it is travelling on to new births – conquering, and yet to conquer' (*DQ* V 255–6). Yet that declaration does not state the critic's own (reactionary) position, which is closer to Wordsworth's than the one he chooses to visit on him by naively confusing the author entirely with his personae, charging that 'If [the Solitary], at first, hoped too much', '[Wordsworth's] philosophers, and therefore his own philosophy...afterwards recant too rashly' (256). In a footnote, De Quincey more genuinely assures the reader that he does not himself 'unconditionally [approve] of' the revolution, but that, using a mechanical model, 'the case was one which illustrated the composition of forces': 'The Revolution, and the resistance to the Revolution, were the two powers that quickened – each the other – for ultimate good' (ibid.). The excessive pedanticism and repetitiveness of De Quincey's self-elaboration indicate his anxiety to carve out a position of his own distinct from Wordsworth's, but, as so often, his own position is wrestling with a Wordsworthian intertextuality, and here it becomes an Oedipal contest with Wordsworth's own kind of Oedipalism. Whereas Wordsworth desires to appropriate the word of the father without obvious difference, De Quincey desires his appropriation of Wordsworth to appear more divergent than it is. In fact, between the Solitary and the Wanderer had come Books X and XI of *The Prelude*, as De Quincey knew – and in fact echoed in order to construct his own position.

De Quincey's criticism of Wordsworth's later account of the revolution in *The Excursion* is in fact influenced by his reading (in manuscript) of the earlier account in *The Prelude*, and by his acute sensitivity to Wordsworth's poetic language.[2] His view that the revolution 'is travelling on to new births' echoes Wordsworth's own perception that '"All things have second birth"' (73), following Louis's bloody deposition and the September massacres in Book X. In the passage in which Wordsworth unfolds his reactions to these events, De Quincey would have picked up the return of the Shakespearean register, and particularly the presence of the ghost of *Hamlet*, which so characteristically visits the scene of Oedipal encounter in Wordsworth (and De Quincey), and which here attends the process of its historicization, as De Quincey in turn relays it: 'the French Revolution did not close on the 18th Brumaire, 1799, at which time it suffered eclipse; at which time it entered a cloud, but not the cloud of death; at which time its vital movement was arrested by a military traitor, but ... this Revolution is still mining under ground, like the ghost of Hamlet, through every quarter of the globe' (256).

Wordsworth's leading self-dramatization for his dilemma in 1792, caught within painfully conflicted revolutionary discourses, is that of a tragic hero who both figures it and contributes to the poetic language in which to give it expression. The echo from *Hamlet* in describing the short time lapse since the gruesome events – 'I thought of those September massacres, / Divided from me by a little month' (X 65–6) – once again (see Chapter 2) takes up Shakespeare's

> – Frailty, thy name is woman! –
> A little month; or ere those shoes were old,
> With which she follow'd my poor father's body,
> Like Niobe, all tears: – why she, even she, –
>   ...
> ...marry'd with my uncle.
> <div align="right">(<i>S</i>, I ii 1003)</div>

'Tintern Abbey' had drawn on the same soliloquy's rejection of an impious world ('How weary, stale, flat, and unprofitable / Seem to me all the uses of this world!', 1002) informs Wordsworth's 'fretful stir / Unprofitable, and the fever of this world' (52–3), while the end of 'The Ruined Cottage' had distantly called on the same soliloquy, with its wish that 'this too too solid flesh would melt, / Thaw and resolve itself into a dew!' (ibid.), and its contempt for 'an unweeded garden, / That grows to seed; things rank, and gross in nature, / Possess it merely' (1002–3), finally to come to terms with a later scene of loss and destruction:

> She sleeps in the calm earth, and peace is here.
> I well remember that those very plumes,
> Those weeds, and the high spear-grass on that wall,
> By mist and silent rain-drops silvered o'er,
> As once I passed, did to my mind convey
> So still an image of tranquility,
> So calm and still, and looked so beautiful

> Amid the uneasy thoughts which filled my mind,
> That what we feel of sorrow and despair
> From ruin and from change, and all the grief
> The passing shews of being leave behind,
> Appeared an idle dream.
>
> (941–52)

There, Wordsworth had deflected the erotic overtones of a ravaged and unprotected female with which his story started – 'and this poor hut, / Stripped of its outward garb of household flowers, / . . . offers to the wind / A cold bare wall whose earthy top is tricked / With weeds and the rank spear-grass' (104–8) – into the counter-wish for pure personal dissolution, which in his case was not extinction but also literary discursification.

Hamlet's language is extraordinary for its preoccupation with ambiguities and puns, and it prompts a high degree of linguistic self-consciousness in response. Coleridge, who 'thought it essential to the understanding of Hamlet's character that we should reflect on the constitution of our own minds' (*CLL* I 543), suggestively noted that 'Hamlet opens his mouth with a playing on words, the complete absence of which throughout characterizes *Macbeth*' (*Literary Remains*, ed. Bate, 315), and he attributed the former's verbal instabilities to a combination of 'exuberant activity of mind', fashion, resentment, and 'suppressed passion . . . of a hardly smothered personal dislike' (316), resulting in the hyperactive articulation of displaced aggressivity. Oedipalizing the confusions in Hamlet's hostilities, from Freud's 'Psychopathic Characters on the Stage' to Ernest Jones to Lacan, has focused on his unconscious desire for his father's death, but, as Marjorie Garber points out, there is a continuing self-investment in the ghostly word, which, as well as recalling loss, also insists on marking absence – ''Tis here! / 'Tis here! / 'Tis gone! [*Exit Ghost*]' (I i 1001): 'Hamlet always stops. The very source of what makes Hamlet's arm waver at every moment is the narcissistic connection that Freud talks about in his text on the decline of the Oedipus complex: one cannot strike the phallus, because the phallus, even the real phallus, is a *ghost*' (131).[3] But, if it is not possible to take up arms against the phallus, word power may be used to mitigate itself – returning to Coleridge's insight to address Wordsworth's reworking – to 'smother' as well as vent the antagonism that has brought the linguistic unconscious into being.

The construction of 'nature' being achieved recalls the mother-relation within a position that had preceded the knowledge of sexual division, but it represents a subject who has undeniably gained it. In circumventing the subjectification attendant on rivalry for the power of the father, the fatherly Wanderer withdraws into his imaginary function to offer a kind of language which, however faintly, was always already there, like 'nature' itself.

That construction, which proceeds to dominate the composition of *The Prelude*, is interested in disregarding the father's absence, or removal, and here, in revolutionary Paris, it accordingly becomes compromised with the mother's (Gertrude's) refusal to mourn his death. As in 'The Vale of Esthwaite' (see Chapter 2), though Hamlet censures the insufficiency of Gertrude's grieving (a month was too short to represent true sorrow), the position from which Wordsworth demands all the mother's attention would welcome her remissness. In Wordsworth's appropriation ('Divided from me by a little month'), though the brevity of the space of time between his present visit and the preceding atrocities should logically make those events more shockingly immediate, it also represents, in line with his Oedipal revision, a relieving *belittlement* of the trauma, since Gertrude's guilty neglect can also be taken to express a welcome diminution of the impact of domestic (and political) crime on Wordsworth himself. At play in the passage, therefore, is not a cancellation of the horrors that have taken place but rather an accompanying sense that the brunt of his knowledge of them marked the turn that was eventually going to deliver the more self-fulfilling cultural discourses and poetic registers he sought.

The promise of poetic language had become uppermost. Wordsworth's internal conflict between his endorsement of the revolution and his 'resistance' to it for 'ultimate good' (in De Quincey's terms) is precisely the scenario of Books X and XI of *The Prelude* abridged in the critical passages, written in early summer 1804, on his dawning alienation from revolutionary knowledge (X 38–82), when he was

> upon these
> And other sights looking as doth a man
> Upon a volume whose contents he knows
> Are memorable but from him locked up,
> Being written in a tongue he cannot read,
> So that he questions the mute leaves with pain,
> And half upbraids their silence.
>
> (48–54)

Besides re-arousing the original shock of language acquisition, the experience had brought about an historical subjectification that needed replotting in order to recuperate imaginary coherence. But beyond the political revision at stake, listening attentively to Wordsworth's retelling, it is possible to tune into a process of revisionary adaptation that depends on a network of Shakespearean intertextualities, of *Hamlet* and other plays, whereby Wordsworth's reconstitution of *his* revolution has in effect come to construct his desired poetic language.

The Shakespearean effect on Wordsworth was partly theatrical. Among the metropolitan spectacles evoked in Book VII of *The Prelude*, 'Residence in London', Wordsworth was especially struck by various kinds of theatrical display, whether in the law-court, the pulpit, parliament, or on the stage itself. The popular entertainments of 'Half-rural Sadler's Wells' (289) were a constant attraction, when, down from Cambridge in 1791, Wordsworth was drawn to the animating scenes of the capital, and 'Life was . . . new, / The senses easily pleased' (440–1). Theatrical presentation, holding him spellbound in a way that characterizes the intensity of his most memorable childhood experiences, gave him

> Pleasure that had been handed down from times
> When at a country playhouse, having caught
> In summer through the fractured wall a glimpse
> Of daylight, at the thought of where I was
> I gladdened more than if I had beheld
> Before me some bright cavern of romance,
> Or than we do when on our beds we lie
> At night, in warmth, when rains are beating hard.
>   (479–88)

The 'country playhouse' was possibly that alluded to in a simile in one of the unpublished Matthew elegies as 'a play-house in a barn / Where Punch and Hamlet play together' (*PW* IV 454: 71–2), and it may even have been the venue for an early unsophisticated theatrical experience of *Hamlet* (though Wordsworth wrote to Beaumont: 'I never saw Hamlet acted my self', *WL* I 587). The comparison recalls the 'magician's airy pageant . . . A spectacle to which there is no end' (734, 741) which the post-revolutionary imagination had to recreate within the Cave of Yordas, another 'cavern of romance', in Book VIII of *The Prelude*. These interior goings-on also reinforce the empowering sense of protected invulnerability that followed his father's death and the upshot of waiting for the horses, 'when storm and rain / Beat on [his] roof at midnight' (XI 385–6). What Wordsworth is here recounting is the way in which his experience of the London theatre during this year before his confrontation with the pre-Terror in Paris had played out the workings of his imaginary ego in such a way as to provide him with a recent recuperation when it became challenged by revolutionary knowledge. In retrospect, a whole range of impressions from the London period took on a deepening and more importunate influence as he came to see them more generally reflecting what in the 1850 *Prelude*, adapting a quotation from Hamlet's advice to the players to describe the content of topical melodrama, Wordsworth referred to as the 'forms and pressures of the time' (288).

By 1804, Wordsworth was prepared to escape from a locking identification with Hamlet in order to act – to seize the word, albeit on his own terms – and delay no longer, but rather achieve his own competence in the poetic language of *The Recluse*. Yet the continuing danger of Wordsworth's remaining entrapped in Hamlet's position is highlighted in Coleridge's lecture records and critical notes on *Hamlet*, which contain a roundabout critique of Wordsworth's failure to compose the philosophical poem Coleridge has envisaged, while showing Coleridge's failure to understand both the peculiar puzzlement of Wordsworth's relation to language and his attempted resolution of it.

Wordsworth may well have had *Hamlet* in mind in December 1804 because at that time he wrote to Sir George Beaumont about a celebrated boy actor, William Betty, (one of whose specialities was the leading role), and expressed the hope that the child would 'rescue the English theatre from the infamy that has fallen upon it and *restore the reign of good sense and Nature*' (*WL* I 519; emphasis added). Earlier that year, on 6 March, Dorothy wrote to Coleridge that Wordsworth 'is sitting beside me reading Hamlet' (*WL* I 451). Around that time too, Hamlet may have been linked with the completion of *The Prelude* by the great poem's symbolic father, Coleridge himself, who would have to have become irrelevant before it could indeed be finished by Wordsworth himself. Though in 1819 Coleridge recorded – it remained uncorroborated – that Hazlitt had vouched for the fact that the main lines of Coleridge's exposition of Hamlet's character had been developed in conversation at Nether Stowey in 1798, it was in February of 1804 that Coleridge referred, also in a letter to Beaumont, to a discussion with him on *Hamlet*. Coleridge's note of record that 'the Play, or rather ... the Character' was that 'in the intuition and exposition of which [he] first made [his] turn for Philosophical criticism, and especially for insight into the genius of Shakespeare, *noticed*' (*CLL* II 293) shows the exceptional investment he had in the characterization, as having defined the nature of his own intellectual powers after giving up poetry himself. The precise times when Coleridge developed his Schlegel-like version of 'The Character of Hamlet' and when it became known to his circle, including Wordsworth, are problematic, but his notes on its genesis reveal some resentment for Wordsworth himself, who, he writes, 'from motives which I do not know or impulses which *I cannot* know, . . . has thought proper to assert that Schlegel and the German Critics *first* taught Englishmen to admire their own great Countryman intelligently' (ibid.).[4] Coleridge repeats the complaint in a letter of 1818, in which he reviewed the course of his own life that had led to his becoming a public lecturer, and sees it as symptomatic of the wasted promise he had bemoaned in his poem 'To William Wordsworth. Composed on the Night after his Recitation of a Poem on the Growth of an Individual Mind': 'Sense of past youth and manhood come in vain, / And genius given and knowledge won in vain; / . . . / . . . and all, / Commune with Thee had open'd out' (II 407: 69–73). He goes on to claim that his interest in establishing the precedence of his own Shakespeare criticism over A. W. von Schlegel's derives from his sense of hurt that it should be Wordsworth, 'for whose fame I had felt and fought with an ardour that amounted to absolute Self-oblivion' (*LSTC* IV 839), who had failed to do him justice.[5] The more or less obscure rivalry between Coleridge's theoretical and Wordsworth's poetic registers, as a result of which Coleridge transposes his own claim for originality to the field of dramatic criticism, leaves traces in the notes for 'The Character of Hamlet', which adopts the terms of Coleridge's long-standing debate with the Wordsworthian imagination, and indirectly casts Wordsworth's quandary in the role of Hamlet.

Coleridge's celebrated conjecture about Shakespeare's purpose in writing *Hamlet* – 'I conceive him to have wished to exemplify the moral necessity of a due Balance between our attention to outward objectives, and our meditation on inward thoughts – a due Balance between the real and the imaginary World' (*CLL* I 539) – relies on his diagnosing an overbalance of the imaginative power in Hamlet in terms that not only represent what Lamb and many others have taken to be a self-delineation (following Coleridge's own comment in his *Table Talk*: 'I have a smack of Hamlet myself, if I may say so', 1835, I 69) but that also significantly lead back to Wordsworth: 'The effect . . . is beautifully illustrated in the inward brooding of Hamlet: the effect of a superfluous activity of thought. His mind unseated from its healthy balance, is for ever occupied with the world within him, abstracted from external things: his words give a substance to shadows: and he is dissatisfied with commonplace realities' (*CLL*, I 544). Less evident than the reworking of Hamlet's 'the native hue of resolution / Is sickly'd o'er with the pale cast of thought' (III i 1017) is an echo ('throwing a mist over all common-place actualities') of Coleridge's recent description of Wordsworth's gift in *Biographia Literaria* as the transformation of 'subjects . . . chosen from ordinary life' so as to dispel 'the film of familiarity' (*BL* II 6–7) by 'spreading the tone, the *atmosphere*, and with it the depth and height of the ideal world around forms, incidents, and situations, of which, for the common view, custom had bedimmed all the lustre, had dried up the sparkle and the dew drops' (I 80). The resonances between Coleridge's descriptions may imply that for him Wordsworth too has 'a smack of Hamlet' in that his idealizing strength could easily turn into the introspective abstraction of *The Prelude*, which is really Hamlet's (and therefore Coleridge's) terrain. As if to drive the lesson home, Coleridge uses Wordsworth's own warning, Rivers, whom he quotes, to define Hamlet's tendency as 'great, enormous, intellectual activity, and a consequent proportionate aversion to real action': 'Action is transitory – a step, a blow, / . . . / Suffering is permanent, obscure and dark, / And shares the nature of infinity' (1539, 1543–4). '[R]eal action' for Wordsworth would, of course, mean proceeding with the composition of *The Recluse*. But his willingness to waylay himself by making a virtue of inactivity had already been illustrated by his use of the same extract. The speech is the densest in Wordsworh's play, and, despite the circumstances of its delivery, its tragic complexity led to his adopting its insights as the epigraph for the violent history of *The White Doe of Rylstone*, the poem in which he had explicitly shunned the activity of external incident. Wordsworth considered that 'The mere physical action was all unsuccessful; but the true action of the poem was spiritual – the subduing of the will, and all inferior passions, to the perfect purifying and spiritualising of the intellectual nature' (*PW* III 548).

There is also a hint in Hamlet's diagnosed habit of 'giving substance to shadows' of an engagement with Wordsworth's own attempt to define the workings of his imagination in the passages related to his description of crossing the Alps in Books VI and VIII of *The Prelude*. In the Cave of Yordas simile, the putative traveller is initially absorbed by fascinating indeterminacy:

> He looks and sees the cavern spread and grow,
> Widening itself on all sides, sees, or thinks
> He sees, erelong, the roof above his head,

> Which instantly unsettles and recedes –
> Substance and shadow, light and darkness, all
> Commingled, making up a canopy
> Of shapes, and forms, and tendencies to shape,
> That shift and vanish, change and interchange
> Like spectres – ferment quiet and sublime.
>
> (VIII 715–23)

But this pleasurable activity, as the subject, like Coleridge's Hamlet, tries 'giving substance to shadows', culminates in a sense of loss that comes with the 'perfect view' (726) of the interior. The stultification is associated with the act of reading, whereby a formerly unopposed imaginary spreading has been reduced to language: 'Till, every effort, every motion gone, / The scene before him lies in perfect view / Exposed, and lifeless as a written book' (725–7). That, ironically, the simile refers precisely to what Wordsworth is pursuing in his own poem – that is, textual performance, 'a written book' – manifests the origin of his writing block on the Coleridgean project as a series of embarrassments deriving from that with language itself. Yet through the various textual stages of the passages involved we can witness the gradual emergence of what to Wordsworth will prove an acceptable idiom of the imagination in which to write his own book, the rest of the 1805 *Prelude*, without surrendering the self-reflexivity that had impeded composition. But not *The Recluse*.

Overall, Coleridge's association of Hamlet with Wordsworth is saying more than that a prince should not be a poet: it is also describing a kind of poetry that shies away from social and cultural effectivity in the way he believes *The Recluse* should not. Hazlitt's companion portrait of Hamlet makes a similar point, and it also echoes Wordworth's own figuring of self-justification for not being able to resolve his political quandary ('And long orations which in dreams I pleaded / Before unjust tribunals', X 412–13), extending to the whole process of composing *The Prelude*, *rather than* the great work: '[Hamlet] may be said to be amenable only to the tribunal of his own thoughts, and is too much taken up with the airy world of contemplation to lay as much stress as he ought on the practical consequences of things' (Bate, *Romantics on Shakespeare*, 326). Wordsworth does not leave the Cave of Yordas with the poem Coleridge is demanding, but in the second half of the simile (VIII 728–41) he defines his inchoate recognition of the non-alienating power of his own appropriate poetic language. When the traveller / Wordsworth re-examines the literal text of the cave's interior, he finds that the former, more self-accommodating way of reading starts to return:

> the senseless mass,
> In its projections, wrinkles, cavities,
> Through all its surface, with all colours streaming,
> Like a magician's airy pageant, parts,
> Unites, embodying everywhere some pressure
> Or image, recognised or new, some type
> Or picture of the world...
> ...
> A spectacle to which there is no end.
>
> (731–41)

The language-shock has been assuaged by the reassuring evocation of what look like the imaginary registers of fairy-tale and romance, but which also return as representations of selected social and cultural discourses of social hierarchy, established church and monarchism: 'the warrior clad in mail / The prancing steed, the pilgrim with his staff, / The mitred bishop and the throned king' (738–40).

The Coleridgean diagnosis of Hamlet's fatal interiority recalls the development of this attempt by Wordsworth to convey the internal manoeuvrings of the imagination:

> It is the nature of thought to be indefinite: while definiteness belongs to reality. The sense of sublimity arises, not from the sight of an outward object, but from the reflection upon it: not from the impression, but from the reflection upon it. Few have seen a celebrated waterfall without feeling something of disappointment: it is only subsequently, by reflection, that the image comes back full into the mind, and brings with it a train of grand or beautiful associations. Hamlet feels this...
>
> (*CLL* I 544)

But Coleridge's characterization of Hamlet settles on the workings of narcissistic reflexivity, which undercuts a more effective and outward-looking kind of subjectivity. The inward 'train' or 'pageant' of imagery along which the subject-formation seeks representation is seen as symptomatic of Hamlet's continuing failure to achieve discursive power: 'in him we see a mind that keeps itself in a state of abstraction, and beholds external objects as hieroglyphics' (ibid.), as Wordsworth deciphers the 'workings of [his] one mind' (VI 568) in the Simplon Pass as 'Characters of the great apocalypse, / The types and symbols of eternity' (570–1). For Wordsworth, however, his cultural work is not merely the reduplication of his own psychological malaise so much as the authentication of moral and nationalist discourses in terms of his own history. Nor does his narcissism obstruct the upshot of his self-diagnosis in the way Coleridge complains of Hamlet: 'He mistakes the seeing his chains for the breaking of them' (*CLL* I 544), but rather, as in the 'Ode to Duty', it is converted into the critical acceptance of a self-disciplinary blueprint for all discursification: 'I supplicate for thy control / . . . / And in the light of truth thy Bondman let me live!' (35, 64)

Accordingly, Wordsworth's self-echoings from his juvenilia in the end recover an inscription in Shakespearean textuality which, felicitously, has now also become an inscription into a political discourse. In the later eighteenth and early nineteenth centuries, some of the 'multivolume collections of British poetry' materially constructed 'Shakespeare' as an important register of nationalism in the constructions of 'Great Britain' and of what Wordsworth called 'the tongue / That Shakespeare spake' ('It is not to be thought of that the Flood', 11–12).[6] The more specifically anti-Gallic construction of his genius had been pitted against Napoleon by Schlegel, and in both England and Germany, as Jonathan Bate writes, he 'served as a weapon against the hegemonic tendencies of French neo-classical culture' (Bate (ed.), 9). The sort of public deference, for instance, that was implied in Pitt's suspending parliament in order that members might attend Betty's performance of *Hamlet* is illustrated again by Coleridge's lecture on *Hamlet*, delivered in Bristol in 1813, which is reported as having begun with a comparison between Macbeth and Napoleon, and ended with an allusion to 'the successes of the Allies' (*CLL* I 546): 'England, justly proud, as she had a right to be, of a Shakespear, a Milton, a Bacon and a Newton, could also boast of a Nelson and a Wellington' (226).

The intricate windings of Wordsworth's path towards poetic restoration, as it was marked out in crossing the Alps, are directed by both the need for a language for *The Recluse* and his alarm at acquiring it in any other than the form he demands. Following the same route, in Book X, revolutionary knowledge becomes the necessary transgression which he must control by reconciling different voices over time, and for that operation particular Shakespearean dramatic texts were exceptionally responsive to Wordsworth's inner discord with their dialogical range of voices. They provided the contours of Wordsworth's own Oedipal story by admitting the recalcitrances through which his own replotting could eventually find reflection. His imaginary insistence seeks for representation so as to arrive at a kind of closure, but by this time it is rather a work of disclosure, by which the subject comes to see itself mirrored in specific languages. The manoeuvrings entailed may be tracked through Romantic debates over different kinds of imagination, usually contrastingly associated with Shakespeare and Milton as representatives, respectively, of inclusive and exclusive practices. Wordsworth's own Preface to *Poems* (1815) distingishes between the 'human and dramatic Imagination' and the 'enthusiastic and meditative Imagination' (*Prose* III 34) of the Bible and Milton, but his poetic discourse operates intertextualities with both kinds to express its own particular interest in occupying diverse sympathies while emulating a distinctive univocalism.

The complication is registered, and differently valued, by his contemporaneous critics. Keats, for example, while he accepted Wordsworth's claim to the Shakespearean kind in his categorization of different imaginations, nevertheless elsewhere experienced contradictory impulses as to where Wordsworth should be put.[7] More slyly, Lamb discloses the un-Shakespearean nature of Wordsworth's self-consciousness when he records that '[Wordsworth] says he does not see much difficulty in writing like Shakespeare, if he had a mind to try it. It is clear then nothing is wanting but the mind' (II 274). Hazlitt especially understood that Wordsworth's interplay of subjectivities was governed by an insistent structure when he observed that 'the evident scope and tendency of Mr. Wordsworth's mind is the reverse of dramatic' (*H*, IV 113), and that it had prevented any sustained separation of characterization in *The Excursion*. But it was predictably Coleridge who was most disturbed by the compound. He thought that Wordsworth's dramatic splittings within his own voice, most formally in his 'dialogues in verse' and the 'practice of ventriloquizing through another man's mouth' (*TT*, I 307) in *The Excursion*, were symptomatic of his failure to assume the Miltonic univocalism he had unsuccessfully enjoined on him for *The Recluse*: 'a great philosophical poet ought always to teach the reader himself as from himself'. As Cynthia Chase has pointed out, Milton does help articulate Wordsworth's achieved self-representation, and he characteristically depends on Milton when his own identity is threatened,[8] though, as Geoffrey Hartman observes, Wordsworth typically mediates his confrontation with Miltonic textuality through Shakespeare.[9] But the chemistry was unstable, and Lucy Newlyn acutely adds that the kind of 'open-ended textual procedures' in *Paradise Lost* that Wordsworth was engaging with in looking beyond a public rhetoric for sublimity of language themselves offered a quality of expression that Romantics labelled 'Shakespearean' (1993, 5). Yet the Shakespearean quality of expression that becomes most serviceable when Wordsworth needs to move between different self-cohering positions, as he did in assembling the various stages of his past in *The Prelude*, is clearly 'human and dramatic'.

In the Place de Carrousel, for example, he needed to liberate himself from self-blame for what was 'Divided from (him) by a little month'. He could not, after all, absolve himself of the historicization of his oblique collusion with the mother (Gertrude) in the deposition of the king. Though his full revolutionary knowledge is only intimated at this stage, it is easy to appreciate that the hindsight of 1804 would be likely to load a greater sense of guilt on his initial encounter with revolutionary violence than he had actually experienced in 1792. The full revolutionary narrative beginning to unfold in 1792 (as Wordsworth knew for certain when he was recounting this episode, but at the time knew only in his 'prophetick soul', *Hamlet*, I v 1007) would entail the subsequent killing of the father of the *patrie*, 'le bon papa',[10] Louis XVI. Wordsworth-as-Hamlet clearly acknowledges guilt over his complicity in revolutionary bloodletting – so much so that remorse takes the self-accusatory form of a further identification with the regicide Macbeth: 'I seemed to hear a voice that cried / To the whole city, "Sleep no more!"' (76–7), picking up on the implication of his subsequent inability, like Macbeth's, to say 'Amen' to the prayers offered up for English victory in February 1793 ('I could not say, Amen, / When they did say, God bless us!', II ii 370).

In order to join in the communal responses of the nation, Wordsworth's poem required a fuller scheme of restoration that depended finally on his revised identification with the father. Despite Wordsworth's primary alliance with the mother figure, as an ambitious poet he retains a strong self-interest in coming to terms with the paternal presence, though that he remains chary of that presence may be inferred from the suggestive demonization of him in his account of the Terror, when he implicates him in the ambiguous authority of Hamlet's father's ghost: 'the crimes of few / Spread into madness of the many; blasts / From hell came sanctified like airs from heaven' (312–14). The allusion seems in a way to prejudge young Hamlet's more open-minded demand to have words with his father, whatever the complexion of his message (see Chapter 2):

> Be thou a spirit of health or goblin, damn'd,
> Bring with thee airs from heaven or blasts from hell,

Be thy intents wicked or charitable,
Thou com'st in such a questionable shape,
That I will speak to thee; I'll call thee, Hamlet,
King, father; royal Dane: O, answer me!

(I iv 1006)

But another Shakespearean echo in Wordsworth's initial vision of a disciplined revolution ('The horse is taught his manage') – of Orlando's opening complaint in *As You Like It* that he has been denied his due inheritance as a gentleman: '[My brother's] horses are bred better; for, besides that they are fair with their feeding, they are taught their manage, and to that end riders dearly hired' (I i 223), may admit the less forbidding presence of Wordsworth's own father, John. One motive for condoning the spectacle of revolutionary retribution could have been the recollection of the denial of his own birthright at the hands of his father's defaulting employer, the grasping and ruthless aristocrat, Sir James Lowther, who had similarly '[barred him] the place' of his entitlement by withholding payment of the debt of £5000 in legal and political fees due to John Wordsworth's heirs through six years of litigation. The score had only been settled by his successor in 1802.[11] It is easy to conjecture that some degree of sympathy for throwing off the subordination to that social order derived from a sense of outrage done to both his father and his heirs so as to split that altered presence from the more ferocious paternal investments that returned in revolutionary terror. Orlando's declaration that 'the spirit of my father, which I think is within me, begins to mutiny against this servitude' (20–2) fine tunes old Hamlet's summons:

HAM: Speak, I am bound to hear.
GHOST: So art thou to revenge, when thou shalt hear,
HAM: What?
GHOST: I am thy father's spirit.

(I v 1006)

Restoration Drama

The splitting away of the benevolent father, however, is taken further and into a different political register as Wordsworth's poem gets produced thanks to the largesse of his poetic father, Shakespeare himself, who helps him read in the 'tongue he cannot read' the discourse (of constitutional monarchic government) that he wants to see emerging.

Though more enigmatically, the 1804 text bears traces of a further narrative of reconciliation between a threatened awareness of revolutionary usurpation in 1792 and the later restoration of the desired paternal identification to which it had led, as the tragic Oedipalism of *Hamlet* is more explicitly revised by inner intertextualities from Shakespearean history plays.

In his evocation of the 'substantial dread' that the Parisian scenes engendered, Wordsworth writes of his reactions being 'conjured up from tragic fictions, / And mournful calendars of true history, / Remembrances and dim admonishments' (67–9). Among his lucubrations, besides the connected themes of dethronement and tyranny in Shakespearean tragedy, there is evidence that the history of regicidal deposition in Shakespeare's treatment of the English Wars of the Roses figured importantly. Schlegel was famously to stress the contemporaneity of Jack Cade's rebellion in *The Second Part of Henry VI* in his 1808 *Vorlesungen über dramatische Kunst und Literatur*, and Byron was revealingly to dismiss Wordsworth as one of 'these Jack Cades / Of sense and song' who had '[hissed]'[12] over the graves of Dryden and Pope; but for Wordsworth himself the shift of historical reference to these particular struggles for dynastic continuity in 1804 is itself deflective from the more urgently associable seventeenth-century Civil War, the other English Revolution, and its lasting stigma of regicide. The turn is from Miltonic republicanism to Shakespearean monarchism, which is available to be read as a prophetic intimation of the restored and presently victorious British Constitution. Specifically, echoes of another Shakespearean prince – not Hamlet, but Hal – help turn what looks like an act of usurpation into a story of legitimate succession.

In particular, three scenes from Acts III and IV of *The Second Part of King Henry IV* affect the language of Wordsworth's description of Paris in 1792. The first, Act III, Scene i, is set in the Palace of Westminster, where the nightgowned and ailing King Henry IV begins to revolve in his doubting mind the necessary hand-over of the crown to his son, Prince Hal:

> How many thousand of my poorest subjects
> Are at this hour asleep! – O sleep, O gentle sleep,
> Nature's soft nurse, how have I frighted thee,
> That thou no more wilt weigh my eye-lids down,
> And steep my senses in forgetfulness?
> . . .
> Uneasy lies the head that wears a crown.
>
> (487–8)

Henry fears that his predicament is effectively that of Louis XVI in October 1792, on the brink of the dispossession of his kingly power by violent forces: in Henry's case, either as the result of the rebellion taking place in the country or, as seems almost equally likely, of his son's subversion. Shakespeare follows Holinshed in evoking the king's anxieties not only over his eldest son's 'euill rule', but also his increasing political influence: 'These tales brought no small suspicion into the kings head, least his sonne would presume to usurpe the crowne, he being yet alive, through which suspicious gelousie, it was perceived that he favoured not his sonne, as in times past he had doone.'[13] The outcome of the revolt is ominous enough, but Henry's own legitimacy is itself guiltily in question.

Wordsworth, as he 'passed / The prison where the unhappy monarch lay . . . and the palace, lately stormed / With roar of cannon and a numerous host', like Henry forebodes disaster in the signs of the times. The dying king's culminating nightmare image of demoralization, as he keeps watch on his sickbed: 'O, thou wilt be a wilderness again, / Peopled with wolves, thy old inhabitants!' (IV iv 500) helps to give expression to Wordsworth's sleepless apprehension:

> When on my bed I lay, I was most moved
> And felt most deeply in what world I was;
>   . . .
> . . . at the best it seemed a place of fear,
> Unfit for the repose of night,
> Defenceless as a wood where tigers roam.
>   (X 55 ff.)

The *restoration* of his monarchy that, on the other hand, Warwick unconvincingly promises to Henry is undercut by Henry's own revolutionary knowledge of power illicitly gained, and its ceaseless instability:

> WARWICK: [The kingdom] is but as a body, yet, distemper'd;
>   Which to its former strength may be restor'd,
>   With good advice, and little medicine: –
>   . . .
> KING: O heaven! that one might read the book of fate;
>   And see the revolution of the times
>   Make mountains level, and the continent
>   (Weary of solid firmness) melt itself

Into the sea!...
...
O, if this were seen,
The happiest youth...
...
Would shut the book...
(III i 488)

Henry reads the constant danger of losing power in 'the book of fate' – the gnawing premonition expressed in his famous dictum: 'Uneasy lies the head that wears a crown'. '[T]he revolution of the times', however, is what Wordsworth is in some degree happy to be unable to fathom in his sites of violence, seen as 'a volume whose contents he knows / Are memorable but from him locked up'. The traces of an awakened engagement in the sleepless Wordsworth's more radical personal sense of transgression – in bringing literature to bear on the political situation, and so the situation to bear on literature – (as 'With unextinguished taper he kept watch' while his sense of contemporary history became interleaved with 'Reading at intervals', 61–2) can be heard in the resonances of the cautionary anecdote of Part Third of 'Peter Bell' (see Chapter 2), with its haunting revelation of 'The ghostly word' (756) 'by a taper's light' to the 'man reading in his room'(739–40):

– The light had left the lonely taper,
And formed itself upon the paper
Into large letters – bright and plain!
(748–50)

As a fundamentally unrebellious son, Wordsworth shares with the father figure, Henry, the fear of violent succession, and finds the same image as the father – of an unbroken horse – for the kind of Oedipal threat that Henry presages in his riotous son: 'his headstrong riot hath no curb' (IV iv 498). A variant manuscript version of Wordsworth's self-citation (that gives a greater emphasis to the modern French understanding of 'revolution' than the 1804 version) reads:

The Horse is taught his manage...
...
For the exhausted Hurricane the air
Calm though it be prepares a successor
Which at no distant interval shall reign

With equal power of devastation arm'd –
The waxing Moon summons the moon dismiss'd
From her *uneasy* task.[14]

Here succession to the reign depends on release from the rein, or curb, resulting in serial 'power of devastation'. The last line echoes Henry's reiterated *uneasiness*, which, critically charged with both guilt and vulnerability, associates with the king's insomnia, haunted by compunction and fear of being toppled ('tyrannic power is weak', X 167, writes Wordsworth). On the one hand, Henry as Louis merits insurrection in that he is himself an anxious usurper of power, a Macbeth, who is himself to 'Sleep no more!': 'O sleep, O gentle sleep, / Nature's soft nurse, how have I frighted thee, / That thou no more wilt weigh my eye-lids down'; but on the other, he is a father-figure, with whom ultimately the son must piously identify.

The issue of restoration is deeply conflicted: it depends not only on the succession of Henry's eldest son, but also on a legitimate succession that will cancel the king's own crime of usurpation, rather than reproduce it. In imitating the prince's fulfilment of that narrative, Wordsworth's implicit identifications slide between Henry and Prince Hal to bring about the Oedipal reconciliation of father and son, king and potential rebel, on Wordsworthian terms, achieving sovereignty by eliding the obstruction of violent opposition. The pattern had been presented by the play. In Act IV, Scene iv, Warwick offers a startling rereading of the prince's insubordination by suggesting that Hal is acquiring a new, ultimately dispensable, language in order to gain a kind of knowledge that will after all *secure* the monarchical power that his father fears losing:

The prince but studies his companions,
Like a strange tongue: wherein to gain the language,
'Tis needful, that the most immodest word
Be look'd upon, and learn'd; which once attain'd,
Your highness knows, comes to no further use,
But to be known, and hated. So, like gross terms,
The prince will, in the perfectness of time,
Cast off his followers: and their memory
Shall as a pattern or a measure live,
By which his grace must mete the lives of others;
Turning past evils to advantages.
(498)

This and the following scene (which are fraught with the issue of monarchical legitimacy, as the suppression of civil rebellion is announced) establish with reasonable credibility that Warwick's interpretation will be vindicated, and that the apparent threat of Hal's riotous behaviour will be converted into an alternative re-authorization of law and order. As Hal finds in the 'strange tongue' of his fellow-carousers the originating impetus to what will turn into a reconciling language of paternal power, so Wordsworth hears in 'a tongue he cannot read' an ambivalent 'silence', in which the initial message of bloody insurrection becomes translated as transgression, with the ultimate effect of confirming the discursive power of restoration.[15]

When, not long after the above exchange, the prince enters and, finding his father apparently dead, crowns himself, the king witnesses what he takes to be a clear act of Oedipal dispossession:

> K. HENRY: Is he so hasty, that he doth suppose
> My sleep my death?
> . . .
> PRINCE: I never thought to hear you speak again.
> K. HENRY: Thy wish was father, Harry, to that thought.
>
> (499)

The double-edged moment, a favourite one with illustrators, is actually one of Oedipal embarrassment: the composite posture of tension between guilt and rightful self-assertion that is caught in many popular depictions is split into its separate elements of conscious appropriation and self-dedication in the Boydell engravings (see Figures 8 and 9). Together, these stages mark the passage to vindicated succession in the process of paternal replacement.

The relevance of *2 Henry IV* to Wordsworth's private dilemma could have been emphasized by its established role in political debate. The satirical portrayal of the Prince of Wales, the future George IV, in the character of Hal became fixed after caricatures by William Dent and Gillray created the vogue in 1786 and 1788 respectively. Thereafter, as Jonathan Bate has elucidated in detail, 'comparisons with Henry IV became common' (1989, 78). The question of the regency precipitated by the king's 'madness' in 1788 brought the issue of succession into protracted consideration, especially in connection with the prince's notorious depravities and contraction of an illegal marriage with a Roman Catholic. Wordsworth himself had tapped into the

Figure 8 Josiah Boydell, Illustration I, *2 Henry IV* (1803)

vein in the fiercely anti-royalist imitation of Juvenal's Satire VIII, on which he collaborated with Francis Wrangham, and instalments of which Wordsworth had produced in November 1795 and February 1797:

Figure 9   Josiah Boydel, Illustration II, *2 Henry IV* (1803)

The nation's hope shall shew the present time
As rich in folly as the past in crime.
Do crimes like these a royal mind evince?
Are these the studies that beseem a prince?
Wedged in with black legs at a boxer's show

To shout with transport o'er a knock-down blow,
Mid knots of grooms the council of his state
To scheme and counter-scheme for purse and plate.
Thy ancient honours when shalt thou resume?
Oh! shame! is this thy service boastful plume?
Go, modern Prince, at Henry's tomb proclaim
Thy rival triumphs – thy Newmarket fame,
There hang thy trophies – bid the jockey's vest,
The whip, the cap, and spurs, thy praise attest.

(119–32)

But in sending George for comparison to the chantry of Henry V in Westminster Abbey, Wordsworth was effectively holding out the possibility of a virtual trajectory – whether or not it was within the prince's competence – towards legitimization by emulating Hal's career of dissoluteness abandoned for reformed majesty, represented by the splendid heraldry of Henry's shield, saddle and helmet there displayed. This was after all the thrust of the mainly anti-Foxite prints that depict the prince associating with wastrel liberals like Sheridan and Fox, the latter often in the character of Falstaff. In fact, they sometimes picture these Whigs as Jacobins or sansculottes to underline their threat to the monarchy rather than attacking the institution itself (see ibid., 76–7). Even where the reference is not laboured, the quasi-usurpation scene clearly lies behind caricatures such as Thomas Rowlandson's 'Filial Piety' (1788) (see Figure 10). Though the Prince of Wales was to become Prince Regent in 1810, in 1804 he had still sixteen years to wait for his accession to the throne, and a further year before his magnificent coronation. Instead, 1804 was the year of Napoleon's coronation. On 18 May he was proclaimed Emperor of the French, with the dignity to be hereditary in his family, and on 2 December in the cathedral of Notre Dame in Paris he took the crown which Pope Pius VII had blessed from the altar and placed it on his head with his own hands, and then proceeded to crown Josephine as Empress (Figure 11). It was a scene which for other than French eyes arrested the act of usurpation without pretending to complete the cycle of legitimization. If the Georges were hardly living up to the British counter-myth of popular monarchism, Shakespeare had nevertheless created it to be inscribed in Wordsworth's poetry. Unlike Napoleon or the Prince of Wales, Wordsworth could adopt a history – Hal's – of inherited empowerment that, without Oedipal struggle, turned out to be triumphantly legitimate, and showed him the way to both the political and literary discourses he desired.

Figure 10   Thomas Rowlandson, *Filial Piety* (1788)

Hal's restoration had a very murky pedigree which he does manage to purge by bringing dynastic and personal contests together. The pattern of serial father/son conflict in the *Henriad* (from *Richard II* to *Henry V*) has been quarried in *Richard II* (the story of a triumphant insurrection) by Harry Berger, Jr. He sees Bolingbroke, the future Henry IV's rejection of his feeble father, John of Gaunt's appeal for his son to abandon his challenge to Mowbray as an Oedipal assault on Gaunt, though addressed to Richard:

> O, heaven defend my soul from such foul sin!
> Shall I seem crest-fallen in my father's sight?
> Or with pale beggar face impeach my height
> Before this out-dar'd dastard? Ere my tongue
> Shall wound my honour with such feeble wrong,
> Or sound so base a parle, my teeth shall tear
> The slavish motive of recanting fear;
> And spit it bleeding, in his high disgrace,
> Where shame doth harbour, even in Mowbray's face.
>
> (I i 415)

Figure 11 Jacques Louis David, *Sacre de l'Empereur Napoléon Ier et Couronnement de l'Impératrice Joséphine a Notre-Dame le 2 décembre 1804*

Berger comments: 'His son's refusal to be infected with this shameful fear-bred silence challenges Gaunt's self-imposed tonguelessness: the amputated tongue symbolizes the father's "feeble wrong"... Bolingbroke is spitting his challenge to Gaunt in Mowbray's face' (218). In this exchange, the son is arrogating the word of the father while legitimizing the violence of the act in the furtherance of what he believes to be a just cause. But the justification of Bolingbroke's 'symbolic castration' (221) of his father is not sustained in his deposition of the king which exceeds it. When Hal, however, comes to take the crown, in a correction of the illegitimate self-crowning of Napoleon, the threats of castrating the father and deposition of the king are conflated, and the primary Oedipal resolution serves to legitimize the act of succession in a climactically stratified form.

Henry at first fears he sees a mirroring of his own illicit violence, though he desires to see his son realizing a rightful transmission of power that will erase his own usurpation, and so replace his own illegitimacy with a lawful reign: 'for what in me was purchas'd, / Falls upon thee in a more fairer sort, / So thou the garland wear'st successively' (*2 Henry IV*, IV iv 500). In the event, what had appeared to be an image of rebellion does offer to become one of splendid restitution, furnishing the myth of Prince Hal turning into patriot king and thereby admitting a healing hypostasizing of English constitutional tradition. The prince himself deprecates any idea of rivalry :

> If any rebel or vain spirit of mine
> Did, with the least affection of a welcome,
> Give entertainment to the might of it,
> Let heaven for ever keep it from my head!
> (ibid.)

and promises a popular re-accession of the dynasty, continuous from Henry's authority, but now made gloriously *more* legitimate by his filial piety, that is itself based on his direct inheritance of a position he had not, in his turn, needed to establish by any act of violence:

> You won it, wore it, kept it, gave it me;
> Then plain, and right, must my possession be:
> Which I, with more than with a common pain,
> 'Gainst all the world will rightfully maintain.
> (ibid.)

Immanent in Hal's claim for and from his father is the triumphalism of his future conquest over France, as Henry V, just as intrinsic to Wordsworth's identification from the late 1790s to 1804 was the national resistance to French imperialism and, beyond that, the 'inheritances... restored, and... legitimate governments... re-established, on the Continent' (*Prose* III 159) that he was to welcome following the Congress of Vienna, 1815, in his 'Address to the Freeholders of Westmorland' (1818).

Jonathan Bate has documented the politicization of *Henry V* by John Philip Kemble, from 1789, when it 'was adapted to favour English prowess and subtitled "The Conquest of France"' (1989, 63), to its revival in 1803, after the collapse of the Peace of Amiens. It played in London in 1804. Again, it is Hazlitt who provides the other face of literary politics to locate Wordsworth's emergent position. Hazlitt was to sweep aside all distinctions in his general assault on Talleyrand's pan-European doctrine of 'Legitimacy' after the Congress which underpins his essay on *Henry V* in his *Characters in Shakespeare's Plays*, published in 1817. By then, the aim of a central constitution for Europe might have been taken as the final resolution of the French Revolution which had brought it about, but for Hazlitt it entailed more than the restoration of what was to be a forty-year peace: it had heralded also the Holy Alliance of the northern sovereigns and their policy of repressing all movement towards freedom and independence. For him, the monarch in the English play could never have his spots changed:

> There he is a very amiable monster, a very splendid pageant. As we like to gaze at a panther or a young lion in their cages in the Tower, and catch a pleasing horror from their glistening eyes, their velvet paws, and dreadless roar, so we take a very romantic, heroic, patriotic, and poetical delight in the boasts and feats of our younger Harry, as they appear on the stage and are confined to lines of ten syllables. (*H* IV 286)

Hazlitt made no difference between absolutist monarchies and British representative government with its foreign policy of non-interference. Instead, Hazlitt denounced *all* 'kingly power' (ibid.) in *Henry V* as being inevitably responsible for the panorama of war it may be used to sanitize, but which, for him, is the ineradicable history lesson of scenes like the Place de Carrousel, with their 'dead men's bodies... found piled on heaps and festering the next morning' (ibid.).[16]

That Wordsworth had probably long been susceptible to a different view of the restoration and settlement of the English crown is made clear in Book VII of *The Prelude*, when, describing the sights of London, he sees the nation's prestige, represented by the parliamentary perform-ance of 'senators, tongue-favored men' (523), as continuous with Henry V's pre-Agincourt chauvinism:

> Oh, the beating heart,
> When one among the prime of these rose up,
> One of whose name from childhood we had heard
> Familiarly, a household term, like those –
> The Bedfords, Glocesters, Salisburys of old –
> Which the fifth Harry talks of.
>
> (524–9)[17]

The potency of Wordsworth's developing nationalism may be measured by the degree of its transformative effectivity. If the Norton editors are correct in identifying 'the orator with a household name' as William Pitt the younger (252, n.4), then the portrait would express an extraord-inary elision of Wordsworth's deeply embittered attitude to the prime minister and his government's original declaration and prosecution of the war with France in his later enthusiasm for the anti-Napoleonic war effort. Wordsworth has some fun at the expense of long-distance speech-makers, but such a reversal would have involved replacing the revolutionary enchantment with Pitt's rhetoric: 'Marvellous, / The enchantment spreads and rises – all are rapt / Astonished – like a hero in romance' (536–8), and investing him with the function of his repub-lican mentor, Michel Beaupuy ('He through the events / Of that great change wandered in perfect faith, / As through a book, an old romance, or tale / Of Fairy, or some dream of actions wrought / Behind the summer clouds', IX 305–9) as the more resilient representative of his ideal ego.

It is as important for the national myth as for Wordsworth that Hal's future transformation should offer more than simple post-Oedipal identification, and yet that the supplement should be self-generated, appearing out of the blue as the potential of an inner discipline, and so contributing an extra signified ('better than [his] word') to the language he has acquired:

> So, when this loose behaviour I throw off,
> And pay the debt I never promised,
> By how much better than my word I am,
> By so much shall I falsify men's hopes.
>
> (*1 Henry IV*, I ii 445)

The myth is particularly dear to Wordsworth's own radical purposes of inheriting a language that seems received rather than taken – expressed in discourses that joyfully bypass the contest for symbolic passage. As Schlegel commented, there is no opposition in *Henry V*, so that he argues it is 'not properly dramatic' (Bate (ed.) 363), and its 'subject ... was a conquest, and nothing but a conquest' (362). Hal had already represented himself as waiting to emerge into a self-realization in excess of his father's expectation of him, seeing himself as a sun/son rising above his association with the low life around him:

> Yet herein will I imitate the sun;
> Who doth permit the base contagious clouds
> To smother up his beauty from the world,
> That, when he please again to be himself
> Being wanted, he may be more wonder'd at,
> By breaking through the foul and ugly mists
> Of vapours, that did seem to strangle him.
>
> (ibid.)

The compressed narrative is in effect that of the self-generated Wordsworthian imagination, overcoming a 'struggle to break through' the cloud of mundane prosaicism, as Wordsworth was suddenly to understand in the course of revising his account of crossing the Alps for Book VI:

> Imagination! lifting up itself
> Before the eye and progress of my song
> Like an unfathered vapour, here that power,
> In all the might of its endowments, came
> Athwart me. I was lost as in a cloud
> Halted without a struggle to break through,
> And now, recovering, to my soul I say
> 'I recognise thy glory.'
>
> (525–32)

Holmes at Grasmere

Lacan has famously tracked the freeplay of the intersubjective unconscious in his seminar on Poe's *The Purloined Letter* (1956), but the Oedipal plot with which Wordsworth is peculiarly preoccupied, the originating acquisition of the phallus – the power of signification – which inaugurates the scenario that Lacan demonstrates in the Poe tale, is plainly detected – and thickened – in a different chronicle from Holinshed's, one in *The Adventures of Sherlock Holmes* that centres around discrepant interpretations of the seizing of a crown, 'The Beryl Coronet'. Both adventures – Holmes's and Wordsworth's – concern the *upbraided silence* of the site of violent textuality ('the mute leaves'), as Wordsworth had come upon it in Paris:

> upon these
> And other sights looking as doth a man
> Upon a volume whose contents he knows
> Are memorable but from him locked up,
> Being written in a tongue he cannot read,
> So that he questions the mute leaves with pain,
> And half upbraids their silence.
>
> (48–54)

In Conan Doyle's story, a banker, Alexander Holder, accepts the coronet, 'One of the most precious possessions of the Empire' (286), as surety against a large loan made to 'one of the highest, noblest, most exalted names in England' (ibid.). The *holder* of the coronet is extremely anxious over its security, which he is conscious has been put in jeopardy, and, seeing that his own good name and standing in the City depends on not losing it, decides to take it home, where he locks it in his bureau. But, sure enough, he has an only son, Arthur, who 'has been ... a grievous disappointment' (288) to him. Holder had intended that Arthur 'should succeed [him] in [his] business', but the son was 'wild, wayward' (ibid.), and, having begun to imitate the profligacy of his associates in an aristocratic club, had repeatedly amassed substantial gambling debts, so that he was not to be trusted with large sums.

The father continues with his own story:

> 'I am not a very heavy sleeper, and the anxiety in my mind tended, no doubt, to make me even less so than usual. About two in the morning, then, I was awakened by some sound in the house. It had ceased ere I was wide awake, but it had left an impression behind it as though a window had gently closed somewhere. I lay listening with all my ears. Suddenly, to my horror, there was a distinct sound of footsteps moving softly in the next room. I slipped out of bed, all palpitating with fear, and peeped round the corner of my dressing-room door.'

'"Arthur!" I screamed, "you villain! you thief! How dare you touch
that coronet?"'
'The gas was half up, as I had left it, and my unhappy boy, dressed
only in his shirt and trousers, was standing beside the light, holding
the coronet in his hands. He appeared to be wrenching at it, or bend-
ing it with all his strength. At my cry he dropped it from his grasp,
and turned as pale as death. I snatched it up and examined it. One of
the gold corners, with three of the beryls in it, was missing.'
'"You blackguard!" I shouted, beside myself with rage. "You have
destroyed it! You have dishonoured me for ever! Where are the
jewels you have stolen?"'
'"Stolen!" he cried.'
'"Yes, you thief!" I roared, shaking him by the shoulder.'
'"There are none missing. There cannot be any missing," said he.'
'"There are three missing. And you know where they are. Must I
call you a liar as well as a thief? Did I not see you trying to tear off
another piece?"'
'"You have called me names enough," said he; "I will not stand it
any longer. I shall not say another word about this business since
you have chosen to insult me. I will leave your house in the morning,
and make my own way in the world."' (293–4)

Listening to this account, Holmes immediately sees the possibility of a
misconstruction which proves to be the case:

'Was the remainder of the coronet at all injured?'
'Yes, it was twisted.'
'Do you not think, then, that he might have been trying to straighten
it?' (296)

But what maintains the quandary of the father's interpretation is the
boy's refusal to talk, his silence:

'God bless you! You are doing what you can for him and for me. But
it is too heavy a task. What was he doing there at all? If his purpose
were innocent, why did he not say so?'
'Precisely. And if he were guilty, why did he not invent a lie? *His
silence appears to me to cut both ways.*' (ibid., emphasis added)

Sidney Paget's original illustration captures the first stage of paternal
replacement as Arthur is 'caught in the act' (Figure 12). The father's

"AT MY CRY HE DROPPED IT."

Figure 12   Sidney Paget, 'At my Cry He Dropped It', illustration to 'The Beryl Coronet' by Sidney Paget (1892)

anxiety about losing his 'name' results in his fantasy of Oedipal dispossession; but though the son is actually engaged in what was intended as an act of (filial) restitution he prefers to appear guilty (since proverbially silence signifies assent) rather than speak.

The coronet is undeniably a site of violence, though seemingly not the son's. The damage is actually the result of a struggle for repossession between Arthur and the real perpetrator of the crime, his amoral crony, Sir George Burnwell, who, Arthur has just learned, has seduced and made an accomplice of Arthur's cousin, Mary, with whom Arthur is himself in love. As Holmes recounts it to Holder senior in the explication:

'You then roused his anger by calling him names at a moment when he felt that he had deserved your warmest thanks. He could not explain the true state of affairs without taking the part of one who certainly deserved little enough consideration at his hands. He took the more chivalrous view, however, and preserved her secret.' (307)

'As he loved his cousin, however, there was an excellent explanation why he should retain her secret – the more so as her secret was a disgraceful one.' (311)

Ostensibly, Arthur wished to suppress his cousin's involvement in the crime, even at the expense of his own reputation. Whereas he had seized on the coronet as an opportunity of restoring the family name (which father and son share) in the City, thereby erasing his rebellious past, his motivation is misconstrued as ruining that name.

His silence, however, not only withholds the expression of what seemed to him to be his really virtuous but unacknowledged motivation, but also leaves unspoken the complication of his own desire to have eloped with Mary, freeing her from the daughterly, and so prohibited family status that Holder senior had given her. It thereby leaves also unspoken his own 'disgraceful secret' – an identification with the real perpetrator, his closest associate and erstwhile friend, Sir George. Arthur's silence conceals the reflection of his own impiety in Sir George's crime: an overdetermining motivation that challenges the father's proprietary power, even while it desires to maintain his good name. At the point of being charged, then, he both is and is not implicated in the wish to run away with a precious object from his father's house. His silence is an act of what Lacan, in his essay 'Desire and the Interpretation of Desire in *Hamlet*', terms 'denegation', referring to the repressed identification in Hamlet's denunciation of Claudius in the closet-scene. It means that Arthur cannot *wholly* deny the charge attached to rivalrous and even patricidal instincts he partly shares, and which the unfair accusation has in fact restoked.

In the process of writing up the revolution, Wordsworth's involvement in the events of 1792 remains unresolved. For him too, 'His silence ... [cuts] both ways', in bespeaking both disabused ingenuousness and complicity. Seen through the narrative of the torn coronet, the Parisian site of royal versus revolutionary power becomes one in which a vestigial violence inevitably returns through the myth of reparation, itself borrowed from the bloody history of the Lancastrian crown. In fashioning his own political and literary discourses, Wordsworth's *half-upbraiding* ('So that he questions the mute leaves with pain, / And half upbraids their silence') becomes helplessly implicated in the full sweep of the 'mournful calendars of true history' that unfold the consequences of Bolingbroke's originating crime in the War of the Roses. Placed squarely on the carousel of a recurrent European history, the saga of the English barons helps unlock the contents not only of the textuality of the revolution, but also of the lawless English nationalism which Wordsworth would like to represent as stabilized in his own historical moment.

Confronted with the stratification of his own transgressiveness in the Place de Carrousel, however, Wordsworth only '*half* upbraids the silence' of 'the book of fate' opened to his view: he does and he does not want it to speak of 'the revolution of the times'. In that scene, he witnessed the return of a criminal subjectivity that had commenced with language acquisition, but which he does not wish to be wholly articulated, both from guilty self-knowledge *as well as* from piety (his unwillingness ever to have seized the word). He was therefore deeply interested in making the scene speak for him in a way that would continue to (only) *half* silence his originating insubordination. In sum, both then *and* later, in the telling, he wants neither language nor silence, but a kind of silent language, in which words, which are always radically signifiers of usurpation, actually turn out to signify a healing *power* of restoration.

Arising from the resolution of this inner conflict comes Wordsworth's inscription in disciplinary discourses. By penetrating the interwoven historical crises to arrive at their grounding in his own psychological narrative of restoration, Wordsworth is coming to reveal not simply his assimilation of constitutional monarchism but also his capacity to recreate it in his own poetic discourse. The key to unlock the *volume's contents* is the realization that power is always represented by the phallus, and the struggle actively to take it over never stops, even in poetry. Again, the ambiguity of both Henry's and Hal's 'upbraidings' about the metonym of power, the crown, is to the point. Henry, in *2 Henry IV*, is the object of repeated blame, as he is the subject of violent power:

> [The crown] seem'd in me,
> But as an honour snatch'd with boisterous hand;
> And I had many living, to upbraid
> My gain of it by their assistances;
> Which daily grew to quarrel, and to blood-shed
>
> (IV iv 500)

while Hal's attempt to locate that power, which he appreciates is intrinsically mobile and renders its holder constantly open to competition, leads him to shift the blame onto the signifier itself:

> I spake unto the crown, as having sense,
> And thus upbraided it: *The care on thee depending*
> *Hath fed upon the body of my father*
> ...
> *thou, most fine, most honour'd, most renown'd,*
> *Hast eat thy bearer up.*
>
> (ibid.)

The crime, in other words, inheres in the symbolization of dominion, which derives its manifest power from the fact that it will be worn by different kings, and in different ways. The only control that can be transacted is over who will wear it and how. Hal promises devoutly to restore a patrilinear order in the Lancastrian name of Henry, with the aspiration – to that extent fulfilled – of passing it on to another Henry. Most promisingly, Shakespeare's Hal does so in the revolutionary knowledge that the line of his particular rule will require constant defence and periodic redefinition, as it does eventually lead to a new dynasty in the same name of Henry (Tudor) and the reconciliation of the warring houses of Lancaster and York.[18]

Conan Doyle's father and son, however, are still unreconciled when the story ends, and, in disturbing details, the case of 'The Beryl Coronet' is never closed. Readers are left to conjecture the success of the family reunion, and of the 'very humble apology to that noble lad, your son' (305) which Holmes tells the father he owes Arthur, and which the father hurries away to deliver at the end. The coronet itself remains mutilated, even after the missing beryls are returned, and though the depositor had stated that 'Any injury to it would be almost as serious as its complete loss' (287), it remains twisted and broken with no chance at all of being repaired over the weekend before the pledge must be redeemed. The effect of this inconclusiveness is a reminder of the awkwardness, precariousness and possible *impasse* in transmitting the word. In Wordsworth's case, the deflected aggression rebounded on his revolutionary *alter ego*, as Hal had ruthlessly rejected the subversive Falstaff, turning, as Stephen Greenblatt has argued, the 'betrayal' of revolt against itself. When Wordsworth had resolved his stratified Oedipal conflicts in the discourses of restoration for the completion of *The Prelude*, the hostility that had been derived from his sympathy with popular uprising was redirected to the implacable denunciation of competing discourses that threatened the Wordsworthian scheme. For example, he mercilessly put down *his* metropolitan revolutions in Smithfield that presented themselves in the Falstaffian misrule of Bartholomew Fair: 'By nature an unmanageable sight' (*Prel* VII 709).

At the scene of crime in Paris, Wordsworth once more resolved the conundrum which had prevented composition of *The Recluse* by discovering a way of both speaking and escaping detection for the intent of parricide. The necessary casualty for Wordsworth was the forfeiture of the kind of individualized agency Coleridge was requiring, to be replaced by a highly regulated self-styling in political and poetic conventionalization. In demonstration of Franco Moretti's conclusion in his analysis of the detective story that 'Innocence is conformity; individuality, guilt' (135) – since 'crime' is, in effect, the construction of personal difference – Wordsworth simply disassembles his difference. If culprits are unmasked by the signs only they could have left behind, Wordsworth commits a perfect crime by covering his tracks and leaving no such clue, or what Moretti refers to as 'that particular element of the story in which the link between the signifier and the signified has been visibly altered' (146). Wordsworth's alterations are invisible. 'To avoid death', Moretti counsels, 'it is suggested that one conform to a stereotype; in this way, one will never be a victim or a criminal' (137), and so by admitting the camouflage of normalized and pre-existing discourses Wordsworth body-snatches the phallus without scandal.

In Book II of *The Prelude*, for example, having just described the joyfulness of his youthful apprehension of the 'one life' (430), Wordsworth seems to draw back from the claim for what might be construed as a heterodox pantheism: 'If this be error, and another faith / Find easier access to the pious mind . . . ' (435–6). But he is at the same time drawing on Shakespeare's sonnet 116, which in fact insists on its private conviction:

> Love alters not with his brief hours and weeks,
> But bears it out even to the edge of doom.

If this be error and upon me prov'd,
I never writ, nor no man ever lov'd[19]

– and, sure enough, Wordsworth goes on resolutely to uphold his 'faith / That fails not' (459) in 'A never-failing principle of joy' (465). What comes to him through Shakespeare's words is not simply a similar proposition about the unshakeability of an emotional commitment, but also a way of getting another party to speak for him. 'If this be error' then '*I* never wrote'. He can lay his self-blame elsewhere unguiltily because the intertext can be held to be completely innocent of his own intentionality, for which it is nevertheless an alibi.

On the way to the 1804 account of Paris in 1792 Wordsworth had enjoyed a significant windfall: unexpectedly he was presented with a quasi-inheritance. The letter that Wordsworth wrote to Sir George Beaumont, on 14 October 1803, was a belated thank-you to the Tory patron who had munificently presented him with a farmstead at Applethwaite at the foot of Skiddaw eight weeks previously. It was, wrote Wordsworth, 'an act which, cons[idered] in all its relations as to matter and manner . . . overpowered me' (*WL* I 406), and, with seemingly inconsequential allusions to Act III, Scene i of *2 Henry IV*, he was writing an apology for his 'silence', which had made him 'uneasy' – an anxiety that fundamentally related back to his problem in writing at all – in breaking his silence. He feels troubled whether he writes or does not:

> Owing to a set of painful and uneasy sensations which [I have] more or less at all times about my chest, from a disease which chiefly affects my nerves and digestive organs, and which makes my aversion from writing little less than madness, I deferred writing to you, being at first made still uncomfortable by travelling, and loathing to do violence to my self, in what ought to be an act of pure pleasure and enjoyment; viz the expression of my deep sense of your goodness. This feeling was indeed so strong in me, as to make me look upon the act of writing to you, not as a work of a moment, but as a business with something little less than awful in it, a task, a duty, a thing not to be done but in my best, my purest, and my happiest moments. Many of these I had, but then I had not my pen and ink, my paper before me, my conveniences, 'my appliances and means to boot' all which, the moment that I thought of them, seemed to disturb and impair the sanctity of my pleasure. (406–7)

The relevant quotation is from the end of Henry's address to sleep that resonates in Wordsworth's sleepless dread of revolutionary violence in Paris:

> Canst thou, O partial sleep! give thy repose
> To the wet sea-boy in an hour so rude;
> And, in the calmest and most stillest night,
> With all appliances and means to boot,
> Deny it to a king? Then, happy low, lie down!
> Uneasy lies the head that wears a crown.
>
> (III i 488)

The borrowed phrase originally refers to having the means to allay all discomforts which, though the king possesses them in abundance, nonetheless are inefficacious in his case. Wordsworth claims not to have the appropriate equipment (writing materials) to hand whenever he felt happily disposed to write, though he has already explained (and he continues to elaborate the point) that it is his having the means and urgent occasion to write that makes him ill and is, in fact, the cause of his extraordinary reluctance:

> the uneasiness in my chest has made [me] beat off the time when the pen was to be taken up. I do not know from what cause it is, but during the last three [y]ears I have never had a pen in my hand for five minutes, [b]efore my whole frame becomes one bundle of uneasiness, [a] perspiration starts out all over me, and my chest is [o]ppressed in a manner which I cannot describe.   (407)

How can he end his 'unease' with that which is itself producing it – the act of writing? Words have failed him, and the problem will recur under pressure for fresh poetic composition, as when he was making an effort to go on with *The Prelude* in March 1804, and he writes to De Quincey about 'a kind of derangement in my stomach and digestive organs which makes writing painful to me, and indeed almost prevents me from holding correspondence with any body: and this (I mean to say the unpleasant feelings which I have connected with the act of holding a Pen) has been the chief cause of my long silence' (*WL* I 453).

The dilemma in the letter to Beaumont traces the familiar transactions of his Oedipal plot in having to take over the property of a patron, almost a patrimony. He shares Henry's 'unease' with a power that relies on its restoration by his son, because, though he has no difficulty in accepting an unlooked-for gift from a father-figure – in fact that is exactly what he most desires – this particular acquisition has brought about a crisis of piety. It involves a self-conscious inscription in a new discourse of Tory paternalism which entails the rehearsing of his primary language trauma and which finally requires the rejection of his own rebellious youth in order to fulfil the scheme of restoration. On the one hand, Wordsworth has difficulty in entering the self-sacrificial practice of 'doing violence to [him] self, in what ought to be an act of pure pleasure and enjoyment', but on the other he acknowledges that he does owe Beaumont the expression of his indebtedness. In the upshot, Wordsworth is able to win through to the possession of his estate, even though it obviously signals a break with republican discourses, but only by finding common (Shakespearean) expression for both his own uneasy linguistic power and that of the father-figure, who consequently need not now worry that Wordsworth has not previously spoken *his* political language:

> I am sure when you are made acquainted with the circumstances...
> you will look leniently upon my silence, and rather pity than blame
> me: Though I must continue to blame myself, as I have done bitterly
> every day for these past eight weeks. One thing in particular has
> given me great uneasiness, it is, lest [i]n the extreme delicacy of your
> mind, which is well known to me, you for a moment may have been
> perplexed by a single apprehension that there might be any error,
> any thing which I might misconceive, in your kindness to me... But
> I hope that these fears are all groundless, and that you have
> ... suspended your judgement upon my silence, blaming me indeed
> but in that qualified way in which a good man blames what he
> believes will be found an act of venial infirmity, when it is fully
> explained. (407–8)

The strained deference is painfully embarrassed. Wordsworth wants Beaumont above all to realize that he really has no objection to being patronized, and that his silence should only be half-blamed because, after all, it should be construed as covering a difficult passage rather than betokening any kind of dissent.

The pause for Wordsworth to reposition himself was all the more necessary as the gift was not merely symbolic. There were strings attached to his acceptance of the patrician gift of a farmstead: his ownership gave him a vote as a Westmorland freeholder. The letter, when it did come, expressed Wordsworth's assurance of a newly formulated allegiance – something much more than backing the popular front against Napoleon. By the end of it, he showed himself willing not only loudly to proclaim his English patriotism and to renounce any traces of his former French sympathies, but also actively to assume the responsibility of a freeholder in joining the local yeomanry as a Grasmere Volunteer:

> They are sadly remiss at Keswick in putting themselves to trouble in defence of the Country; they came forward very chearfully some time ago, but were so thwarted by the orders and counter orders of the Ministry and their Servants that they have thrown up the whole in disgust. At [G]rasmere, we have turned out almost to a Man. [We] are to go to Ambleside on Sunday to be mustered, [a]nd put on, for the first time our military [ap]parel.   (409)

Wordsworth was indeed consciously changing coats. In the Intimations Ode the previous March he had been aspiring, if 'not in utter nakedness' (63), at least to remain 'Apparelled' in an ahistoricizing language of 'celestial light' (4); but now 'other gifts had followed', and he was eager to present himself in a new disciplinary uniform. As a reciprocal token of their common cause, for which Wordsworth was now willing to sacrifice himself, Wordsworth had Dorothy transcribe three sonnets which he sent to Beaumont along with the letter. The last is a sonnet, 'Anticipation', that Beaumont was to get published twice – the second time in *The Anti-Gallican* in 1804. It is a rousing fantasy of filial piety in which the enemy is executed by the violent power of nature in the form of a snow-storm, so that a patriotic British army of sons, who are spared, metaphorically, from bloodying their own hands, can embrace their fathers. The aftermath is a silence that no longer upbraids, but has triumphantly and innocuously restored the shared discourses of the unified nation:

> Shout, for a mighty victory is won!
> On British Ground the Invaders are laid low;
> The breath of Heaven has drifted them like snow
> And left them lying in the silent sun
> Never to rise again: the work is done.
> Come forth ye old men now in peaceful show
> And greet your Sons! drums beat and trumpets blow!
>
> (*WL* I 411)

5
The Shock of the Old

A voice so thrilling ne'er was heard
In spring-time from the Cuckoo-bird,

. . .

Perhaps the plaintive numbers flow
For old, unhappy, far-off things,
And battles long ago.

'The Solitary Reaper'

'Poetically electric subjects'

There is a passage in Gerard Manley Hopkins's correspondence with Canon Dixon, written on 18 October 1886 from University College, Dublin, where he tries to characterize the impact of the Wordsworthian revelation:

> There have been in all history a few, a very few men, whom common repute, even where it does not trust them, has treated as having had something happen to them that does not happen to other men, as having *seen something*, whatever that really was. Plato is the most famous of these ... human nature in these men saw something, got a shock; wavers in opinion, looking back, whether there was anything or no; but it is in a tremble ever since. Now what Wordsworthians mean is, what would seem to be the growing mind of the English speaking world and may perhaps come to be that of the world at large is that in Wordsworth when he wrote that [Immortality] ode human nature got another of those shocks, and the tremble from it is spreading. This opinion I do strongly share; I am, ever since I knew the ode, in that tremble. You know what happened to crazy Blake,

himself a most poetically electric subject both active and passive, at his first hearing: when the hearer came to 'The pansy at my feet' he fell into a hysterical excitement. Now common sense forbid we should take on like these unstrung hysterical creatures: still it was a proof of the power of the shock.   (1935, 47–8)

Hopkins was reacting to the president of the Wordsworth Society's address,[1] and beyond that to the wider influence of Arnold's scepticism about the faith of the Wordsworthian church. He was aware of the obscurities of Wordsworth's 'obstinate questionings', yet, though revolted by the excess of Blakean (nonconformist) enthusiasm, nonetheless more willing than Arnold to see in Blake's galvanized response that Wordsworth indeed 'had something to say'[2] ('had seen something') and that that 'something' ('far more deeply interfused') was not after all soothing in its predictability, but even *shocking* in its claim to ground a spiritual discourse.

It is possible that Hopkins had read De Quincey's article in *Tait's Edinburgh Magazine* (1839) in which he had viewed Wordworth's poetry as integral to the spread of the English language through America and 'through the English colonies – African, Canadian, Indian, Australian':

> In the recesses of California, in the vast solitudes of Australia, *The Churchyard amongst the Mountains*, from Wordsworth's 'Excursion,' and many a scene of his shorter poems, will be read, even as now Shakspere is read amongst the forests of Canada. All which relates to the writer of these poems will then bear a value of the same kind as that which attaches to our personal memorials (unhappily so slender) of Shakspere.   (*DeQ*, II 150)

Writing of the 'revolutionary principles' (152) of Wordsworth's composition, De Quincey also made a connection between the struggle of the Christian revelation to assert itself and the difficult effort of 'the Wordsworthian restoration of elementary power' amid 'the impulses and suspicious gleams of truth struggling with cherished error, the instincts of light conflicting with darkness':

> For there was a galvanic awakening in the shock of power, as it jarred against the ancient system of prejudices, which inevitably revealed so much of truth as made the mind jealous; enlightened it enough to descry its own wanderings, but not enough to recover the right

road ... And, universally, a transition state is a state of suffering and disquiet. (153)

By the 1830s, however, as Iwan Morus has demonstrated, the electronic telegraph had begun to wire the British imperial purpose into what in 1889 Lord Salisbury was to call its 'one single will' and 'simultaneous direction and simulataneous action' (340).

De Quincey's image stresses the check of opposition, but discourses of tradition in the nineteenth century were in effect defined and strengthened by such challenge, or became transformed into new kinds of self-expression for the continuation of the past. Geoffrey Hill, for example, has written of the resilience of the 'broken-backed' (87) Intimations Ode: the first version, written in 1802, ends with the acknowledgement of loss ('Whither is fled the visionary gleam? / Where is it now, the glory and the dream?'), which the second, written two years later, claims to have successfully soldered, both psychologically and formally:

> O joy! that in our embers
> Is something that doth live,
> That nature yet remembers
> What was so fugitive!
> (130–3)

'The break, far from being an injury sustained, is a resistance proclaimed' (ibid.), Hill writes, depending for its reinventiveness on the 'prevailing' iambic rhythm, and he construes Hopkins's letter in these terms: 'If language is more than a vehicle for the transmission of axioms and concepts, rhythm is correspondingly more than a physiological motor. It is capable of registering, mimetically, deep shocks of recognition' (ibid.). The shock of recognition which Hill sees as developing out of bringing recalcitrances into regulation is the greater not despite, but because of the threat of reversal, and marks a formal embodiment of what has discursive implications. As Hill also comments: 'If Wordsworth has indeed "seen something," he has seen, or foreseen, the developing life-crisis of the nineteenth century' (88).

Hopkins was himself reacting to the Ode's poetic language which mediates while it celebrates an extraordinary registering of a broad social experience, as Wordsworth claims that his response is both representative ('that dream-like vividness and splendour which invest objects of sight in childhood', to which he believed 'everyone ... could bear testimony') and yet in his case peculiarly insistent ('particular feelings or *experiences* of my own mind'):[3]

> those obstinate questionings
> Of sense and outward things,
> Fallings from us, vanishings;
> Blank misgivings of a Creature
> Moving about in worlds not realized,
> High instincts, before which our mortal Nature
> Did *tremble* like a guilty Thing surprised.
>
>   (142–8; emphasis added)

The claim Hopkins was making for the cultural effect of Wordsworth's poem could hardly have been stronger: the Ode's readers have been electrified, and the charge is being conducted into the language ever since throughout the English-speaking world, as Shelley had claimed in 'A Defence of Poetry', written in 1820: 'It is impossible to read the compositions of the most celebrated writers of the present day without being startled with the electric life which burns within their words' (508). On behalf of the Wordsworthians, Hopkins is telling the Arnoldians, who so mistrusted them, that far from safely '[laying] us as we lay at birth / On the cool flowery lap of earth'[4] Wordsworth had jolted his readers into a reawakening from their fall into 'a sleep and a forgetting' (58).

For Hopkins, the agitation was specifically, as he had expressed it in 'The Wreck of the Deutschland', for the reconversion of 'rare-dear Britain' to Rome: 'For my part I sh. think St.George and St Thomas of Canterbury wore roses in heaven for England's sake on the day that ode, not without their intervention, was penned' (1935, 148).[5] Hopkins's focus on the inspired and inspiring occasion of poetic composition is critical: 'when [Wordsworth] wrote that [Immortality] ode human nature got another of those shocks'. The later poet is separating the claim for some kind of imaginative experience prior to the writing from the achievement of the poem itself, and locating its composition as the moment when a quasi-religious discourse had first found memorable expression in Wordsworth's poetry. Later, Wordsworth's poetry had become far more evidently instrumental in promoting the discourse of Anglo-Catholic revivalism, a tendency that had been received in some quarters as (scandalously) shocking in its influence towards Romanism. But what Hopkins is already recognizing in the Ode is a crisis of representation through which what is in large measure a private revelation was offering itself also as what was to become a paradigm for a resurgence of Christian imperialism.

Wordsworth's own most evolved model for the national culture, which Hopkins may also have had in mind, is that of the spider's web in *The Convention of Cintra*: 'The outermost and all-embracing circle of benevolence has inward concentric circles which, like those of a spider's web, are bound together by links, and rest upon each other; making one frame, and capable of one tremor; circles narrower and narrower, closer and closer, as they lie more near to the centre of the self from which they proceeded, and which sustains the whole' (*Prose* I 340). The 'one tremor' afterwards became the Wanderer's principle of British colonization in *The Excursion*, conducting outwards a vision that depended ultimately on the resonance between the 'particular feelings or *experiences* of [Wordsworth's] own mind' and the operations of Christian civilization powered by the British industrial-military machine:

> Change wide, and deep, and silently performed,
> This Land shall witness; and as days roll on,
> Earth's universal frame shall feel the effect;
> Even until the smallest habitable rock,
> Beaten by lonely billows, hear the songs
> Of humanised society; and bloom
> With civil arts, that shall breathe forth their fragrance,
> A grateful tribute to all-ruling Heaven.
>
> . . .
>
> – Vast circumference of hope – and ye
> Are at its centre, British lawgivers.
>
> (IX 384–91, 398–9)

Even more obviously than Wordsworth, however, Hopkins laid great stress on the legislative power of poets and the effectivity of literature itself in spreading the empire. Writing from Dublin some months earlier to thank Coventry Patmore for a new edition of his works, his *trembling* had shown itself to be more disconcerting, more biblical, when he proclaimed: 'Your poems are a good deed done for the Catholic Church and another for England, for the British Empire, which now trembles in the balance held in the hand of unwisdom.' He answers his own question: 'How far can the civilisation England offers be attractive and valuable and be offered and insisted on as an attraction and a thing of value to India for instance?' by proposing 'a continual supply' of literature, 'and in quality excellent' (1956, 366–7).

Hopkins's plan prefigures George Orwell's version of Anglicist 'filtration' at the end of the Second World War, broadcasting British poetry over 'the aether-waves' at the BBC to 'a small and hostile audience' of Indian university students, who were 'unapproachable by anything that could be described as British propaganda.'[6] Orwell, of course, hated the British Empire, but he recurrently recognized the decline of Christianity, and particularly the decay of belief in personal immortality, as having 'left a big hole'.[7] As Wordsworth's faith in the French Revolution had been crushed by the rise of tyranny, so Orwell's own adherence to the Russian Revolution was destroyed by his experience of the violence and deceit of Communism in the Spanish Civil War. After spending most of the war years broadcasting to Malaya for the Indian service of the BBC, he had come to the conclusion that rather than propaganda by another name, and despite all the potential abuses, the transmission of poetic language had an immediacy that could contribute to the 'aesthetic improvement' of the 'spiritual and economic' ugliness of his times and become 'a necessary part of the general redemption of society' ('Poetry and the Microphone', 319). Wordsworth he certainly regarded as a leading sign for English civilization whose 'sonnets during the Napoleonic war might have been written during this one.'[8] For Orwell, he was a key national institution, along with parliamentary government and cricket.[9]

Some indication of the actual effectiveness of such a cultural programme is reflected in the Wordsworth Centenary Number of *The Government College Miscellany, Mangalore*, the Republic of Indian Union, 1951. There could hardly be a more convincing example of Wordsworth's poetry being received in the way invited by Hopkins and Orwell as the universalizing stimulus for British cultural values. Dedicated to the great-grandson of the poet, The Revd C. W. Wordsworth, essays on the poet of nature, solitude, humanism and joy are grouped with lectures by Bertrand Russell ('The Value of Human Individuality'), Herbert Morrison (the cautionary 'Life of [a] Russian University Student'), together with pieces entitled 'Who Is God?', 'This Cricket', and a 'Mock Session of the U.N.O. on the Declaration of Human Rights' – all in English, and followed by articles in Kannada, Malayalam, Hindi and Sanskrit. The journal represents an extraordinary effort at assimilation, reconciliation, and cultural translation still in dialogue with a poetic language that was perceived to have a special power of endorsing an elective Western discourse of human dignity and spiritual aspiration, all packed into 'Wordsworth'.

Hopkins's claims were made in answer to Canon Dixon's expression of disappointment with the caginess, or 'sense of baulk' and a pervasive

'sense of unhappiness', in Wordsworth's lyrics generally (1935, 144).
The canon's problem does not only apply to what Hopkins acknowledged as Wordsworth's automatic 'Parnassian' style, characteristic of
The Excursion itself (1956, 218), nor to his 'Castalian', when he is most
assured of his own individual voice, but even to what Hopkins regarded
as 'the language of inspiration' (216), the 'Great Ode' itself. Dixon was
by no means alone in finding that Hopkins's reception of Faraday's
'line of electric force' had short-circuited as far as he was concerned.
Even Ruskin, who had originally been energized by Wordsworth's
poetry, came to judge Wordsworth's endorsement of prestigious registers as bathetic and narrow-minded. In the papers entitled 'Fiction –
Fair and Foul' (1881), he writes witheringly:

> Wordsworth's rank and scale among the poets were determined by
> himself in a single exclamation:
>
> 'What was the great Parnassus' self to thee,
> Mount Skiddaw?'
>
> Answer this question faithfully, and you have the relation between
> the great masters of the Muse's teaching and the pleasant fingerer of
> his pastoral flute among the reeds of Rydal.[10]

In particular, Ruskin engaged in a protracted intertextual refutation of
the compensatory scheme of the Intimations Ode.[11] Yet Hopkins held
to his own experience of the effect of Wordsworth's '*charisma*, as the
theologians say' (1935, 141) which somehow carried over both the sense
of loss *and* gain. The anecdote about Blake that Hopkins cites from Henry
Crabb Robinson's *Reminiscences* leads him to explore the metaphor for
influence – of an electric shock – that was developing through the passage. '[A] most poetically electric subject' turns out to be 'both active
and passive'. Hopkins suggests that Blake's response to the poem was
produced by both positively and negatively charged particles, attraction
and repulsion – a *wavering* and *trembling* in which opposite forces generate a flow of energy, and that the passivity and activity *within* the influential charge might bring about conduction from one body to another,
first receiving and then relaying it. The sequence through which the
electric field is spread becomes 'unstrung' when the reaction is unrestrained (Blake's case), but may continue when poetic language effects a
passage into reflective religious or political discourses (Hopkins's).
    There can be no doubt that Wordsworth himself had increasingly
come to see his works as deliberately furthering national religious ends,

as he spelled out to Haydon in 1820: 'I am sending to the press a collection of poems, that conclude the third and *last* Vol: of my miscellaneous pieces. – In more than one passage their publication will evince my wish to uphold the cause of Christianity' (*WL* II 593–4). It is equally clear that he based his expectation of eventual fame on the assumption of his representativeness, believing that his readers would indeed see themselves in a radically timeless imaginary relation to his poetic language, as he stated to another correspondent in 1823: 'The ground upon which I am disposed to meet your anticipation of the spread of my poetry is, that I have endeavoured to dwell with truth upon those points of human nature in which all men resemble each other, rather than on those accidents of manners and character produced by times and circumstances' (*LY* I 127). But, though he evidently wished to represent his increasingly specific Christian message as one that spoke a universal language with particular power, the question remained as to what extent his works *did* recharge the discourses in which his later poetry became securely inscribed. In the case of Hopkins, for example, who was definitely a 'poetically electric subject', Wordsworth's discovery of something that could remotivate a spiritual register that was in turn able to empower Christian imperialism did serve to reflect his own historical needs and convictions, whereas some contemporaries and later Victorians 'wavered' and 'trembled' with half-recognitions, only to feel finally cheated by a current gone dead.

The shared evocation of both historical jarring *and* the discursive representation of a quasi ahistorical condition regained in consequence is required for the full transmission of the thrill of the poetry. The shocks that created Wordsworth's poetic language had been less immediately pleasurable – they contained a much higher voltage – than the tremulous excitement that Hopkins derives from the Ode. Nonetheless, Hopkins's reception does replicate the passage from painful jolting to reconfirmation that characterizes the original Wordsworthian experience rather than simply inheriting its after-effect. Wordsworth's traumatic past included, for example, the 'bitter shock' ('The Vale of Esthwaite', 423) with which he absorbed the news of his father's death; the impact of the English declaration of war on revolutionary France in 1793: 'No shock / Given to my moral nature had I known / Down to that very moment / ... / ... that might be named / A revolution, save at this one time' (*Prel* X 233–7); and the convulsions that found vent in the 'powers' emitted from the Girondist press, which were 'Like earthquakes, shocks repeated day by day, / And felt through every nook of town and field' (IX 178–83). But Wordsworth was gradually able to *compose* all these shock waves, eventually as the inspiration for counter-revolutionary discourses. His own *trembling*, as the *Hamlet* reference in the Ode suggests ('high instincts before which our mortal Nature / Did tremble like a guilty Thing surprised'), is always bound up Oedipally with guilty fear that results in the fulfilment of his demand for linguistic or discursive empowerment. One example comes in the childhood episode of the stolen boat, when the 'huge peak . . . Upreared its head' (*Prelude* I 378–80): 'With trembling oars I turned, / And through the silent water stole my way / Back to the covert of the willow tree' (385–7). Again, Wordsworth feels a mixture of apprehension and exhiliration in contemplating a (future) state when mediation will be unnecessary: 'Tremblings of the heart / It gives, to think that the immortal being / No more shall need such garments . . . '(V 22–4). As the reflected image of Piel Castle in the summer of 1794, described in *Elegiac Stanzas*, had supported an imaginary sense of well-being through the crisis of revolutionary knowledge: 'It trembled, but it never passed away' (8), so the subsequent 'shock' of 'the loss of the Earl of Abergavenny East Indiaman', together with Wordsworth's 'most beloved Brother' (*WL* I 541), John, was after all 'welcomed' through the mediation of art in Beaumont's picture as serving to confirm the 'fortitude, and patient chear' (157) of a 'mind serene' (40). So Hopkins intuits an enormous power inflected within the language, and he welcomes a contact with Wordsworth's poetry that he believes may be sufficiently potent to convert his 'trembling' fear about the fate of the empire expressed in the letter to Patmore into a national crusade.

'Poetically electric subjects', those, that is, who receive the Wordsworthian influence most directly, are therefore likely to be those who find their own history reflected in Wordsworth's poetic language – a history more than usually interested in the deflection of trauma, personal and / or historical. The French Revolution was the crucial shock, without which the Ode's pattern of imaginative restoration, making its peace with elective registers, would not have come about. In 1886, when Hopkins's letters were written, the alternative stimulus of imperialism was being called on once more to absorb what Hopkins saw as the shock of a possible new revolution. When Gladstone dissolved Parliament in July over the first Home Rule for Ireland bill, and a new House was returned, there ended what has been called 'the most dramatic thirteen months in English party history'.[12] As a diehard conservative imperialist Hopkins only reluctantly supported Home Rule in order to relieve England of what he saw as 'the task of attempting to govern a people who own no principle of civil allegiance' (*Letters* III 281–2). 'The hand of unwisdom' which held 'the balance', in which the British Empire was held in June, was that of Gladstone, but Hopkins had a greater contempt for Gladstone's 'dissolution of the empire' than for the Tories' policy of anti-Home Rule, though he feared it would produce further civil rebellion.[13] His Irish apprehensions merged with those that had been aroused by the rise of a popular radical movement driven by the distresses of the unemployed, and commandeered by the Social Democratic Federation, headed by H. M. Hyndman, John Burns, and H. H. Champion. London got a taste of revolution on 7 February when a meeting in Trafalgar Square led to windows being broken in Pall Mall, and a huge gathering in Hyde Park later that month was broken up by the police. In that context, it is the reactive shock that converts threatened destruction into the empowerment of a counter-discourse that is topically re-experienced by Hopkins from the spreading tremble of Wordsworth's poetry.

In Dublin in 1886, Hopkins found himself in the right place at the right time to feel the shock of Wordsworth's post-revolutionary literary discourse as that of Christian imperialism, a discourse that for Hopkins was represented by the signifier 'Rome', the capital of nineteenth-century reaction.

Shock Therapy

At the beginning of 1804 Wordsworth registered what he called 'the severest shock...I think, I have ever received' (*WL* I 464), when he feared that Coleridge might die without imparting to him the philosophical base for *The Recluse*, only to discover, as a result of this desertion (Coleridge left for Malta in May), the source of his own alternative imaginative strength by ignoring his symbolic father-figure in completing *The Prelude*. The second part of the double-barrelled Intimations Ode written in 1804 asserts the scheme of a continuing 'primal sympathy' (184), and makes claims for a loss-surviving 'habitual sway' (194) that Wordsworth was to take as the template some months later for the Cave of Yordas simile in Book VIII of *The Prelude*. The associated passages in Book VI describe Wordsworth's analysis of the experience of the shock of sudden dejection and its aftermath, when his youthful reaction of disappointment in having inadvertently 'crossed the Alps' suddenly emerges as an expression of a mental power that preceded the blocking experience and now, self-reflexively, survives it: 'I was lost as in a cloud, / Halted without a struggle to break through, / And now, recovering, to my soul I say / "I recognise thy glory"' (529–32).

The same reversal occurs in the cave. Wordsworth's description of the adjustment of internal vision within the cave turns on a reduction to literalism: 'Till, every effort, every motion gone, / The scene before him stands in perfect view / Exposed, and lifeless as a written book! –' (1850, VIII 574–6).[14] There is an explicit opposition between the initial exhilaration of unopposing indeterminacy and its termination in linguistic representation that is then resolved by the operation of the creative imagination: 'But let him pause awhile, and look again, / And a new quickening shall succeed' (577–8). The sights that Wordsworth's inspired eye creates within the cave are not arbitrary, but are in fact allusions to figures that had processed through his own Gothic poetry, so that his analysis of the process is recuperating the effects of his own past work as well as seeing it as exemplary for that to come. (The gigantic mailed warrior, the ghostly hooded monk, the veiled mists, and the pilgrim on his staff had all appeared in his juvenile and earlier poetry.) The shock has after all become one of recognition, confirmatory of something that has persisted through the challenge to expectation and that, after all, can be perceived to go marching on: a register that had once before enabled the negotiation of his Oedipal revision. It is, in effect, *the shock of the old*, which had resulted in successful re-expression despite checking. As the Gothic had been already there to serve his former purposes, it exemplifies the way in which linguistic self-representation can deflect violent confrontation with the letter. As with the associatively loaded expression, 'crossing the Alps', the same language may be re-registered to sustain the imaginary position it had represented in the past. So the language Wordsworth is seeking for his great poem can be seen after all to take the shape of the established epic and biblical registers in the representation of the Simplon Pass that immediately follows, with its allusions to Milton and the scriptures: 'Characters of the great apocalypse, / The types and symbols of eternity, / Of first, and last, and midst, and without end' (VI 570–2). Fittingly, in his 'Essay, Supplementary to the Preface' (1815), Wordsworth revisits this terrain to figure the tension between established languages and innovation: 'The predecessors of an original Genius of a high order will have smoothed the way for that which he has in common with them; – and much he will have in common; but, for what is peculiarly his own, he will be called upon to clear and often to shape his own road: – he will be in the condition of Hannibal among the Alps' (*Prose* III 80).

The pattern of re-entry into the self-fulfilling discourse of poetry was to continue throughout Wordsworth's works, though the shock-effect of inner challenge leading to a revived inscription in pre-established discursive registers became much fainter with time. The 1830s, however, were dogged by events, both personal and national, that badly tried Wordsworth's reclosures in the political and religious discourses that had come to represent his version of English nationalism. While his literary reputation had become solidly established (sales and reprints were at their height, and academic honours were accorded), with the deaths and declines of family and friends, he again urgently needed the support of the powerful securities he had painstakingly prepared to withstand such shocks. But the tide of political change, with a privately desperate irony, was at the same time threatening precisely those personal investments. In 1832 he was moved deeply by the death of Scott, in 1834 'the mortal power of Coleridge was frozen at its marvellous source' (*'Extempore Effusion Upon the Death of James Hogg'*, 16) and Lamb died, and during 1834–5 five friends followed: James Losh, John Fleming, Robert Jones, Felicia Hemans and James Hogg. From 1829, Dorothy's health had deteriorated worryingly, and by 1835 she had become one of three domestic invalids at Rydal Mount, including his daughter Dora and Sara Hutchinson. Sara died that year, and shortly after Dorothy became irreversibly impaired in mind. Most of all, it was just during these years, when he was also beset by problems affecting his own health, that that series of reforms was being promoted that radically disturbed the nation as he had imagined it. Amid these events, the institution on which his sense of confidence had most depended was, of course, the established Church of England.

Wordsworth feared that the whole fabric of the British establishment – most particularly the Anglican tradition – was in danger of failing to live up to its privilege over alternative versions of the nation. His Anglicanism was by then firmly High Church and deeply opposed to the current tradition of Erastianism 'which made the church a department of the state, an *imperium in imperio*'.[15] He was clearly opposed to the subjugation of church to state advocated in Thomas Arnold's Broad Church and reverenced an authority that professed a divine foundation. The consequence of the rupture of expectation was the usual replay of symbolic alienation: England had become a state which was in danger of no longer representing the Wordsworthian constitution. It is hardly surprising that in 1831, after making the last attempt to write *The Recluse* by returning to work on the fragments he had started – 'Home at Grasmere' and 'The Tuft of Primroses' – Wordsworth had attempted to regain some equanimity in switching his attention to revising *The Prelude* in the MS D version by making it speak for a more orthodox Anglicanism which was to be consolidated in his revisions for the collected poems of 1845. Wordsworth's bishop nephew, Christopher, comments in 1851 that the poet was 'predisposed to sympathize with a form of religion which appears to afford some exercise for the imaginative faculty' (*Memoirs* II 151).[16]

By the reformist 1830s the great wave of Evangelicalism was swelling. Wordsworth was privately outspoken in his rejection of key Evangelical doctrines such as eternal punishment and personal salvation: he told Crabb Robinson, for example, that he 'felt no need of a personal redeemer' (*HCRBW*, I 158). The Church of England was itself under reform as a Royal Commission was appointed to enquire into its financial position just three weeks after the passing of the Reform Bill in 1832, and again with new official investigations during the brief Tory government of Sir Robert Peel in 1835, and subsequently under that of Lord Melbourne. An Ecclesiastical Commission, advocated by the Bishop of London, C. J. Blomfield, sat to defend its interest and ensure its survival as the established church by putting its house in order, reorganizing revenues, pluralism and non-residence, sinecures and nepotism. In the words of one Church historian: 'in the 1830s the most serious question about the Church of England was: "Can these dry bones live?"' (Vidler, 48) In 1834 Wordsworth was driven to the extravagant declaration that he would 'lay down [his] LIFE for the church!',[17] yet, as he had corresponded despairingly with his aristocratic acquaintances, political and ecclesiastical reforms *were* introduced, and he recurrently feared that 'nothing can prevent an explosion and the entire overthrow of the Institutions of the Country' (*WL* V 601).

His disappointment with Anglicanism required the imaginative re-empowerment of his religious discourse, and his trajectory towards the rediscovery of a universalist religious tradition within his own church was developing along the lines of the 'Anglican revival' of spiritual values which was moving in the direction of the Oxford Movement. In the 1830s and 1840s, the Wordsworth circle, which already included his Catholic son-in-law, Edward Quillinan, was joined by a group of Anglo-Catholics, both anti-Roman and those who converted, with whom he became intimate. One of them was one of the closest friends of his old age, Isabella Fenwick (to whom he dictated the autobiographical commentary on his poems), and a younger generation of poets who became zealous acolytes, including Frederick Faber, Sara Coleridge and Aubrey de Vere. An early example of Wordsworth's effect on Catholic literature was a book Wordsworth particularly admired, Kenelm Digby's *The Broadstone of Honour: or, Rules for the Gentlemen of England* (1822), a rambling compendium of historical evocations (laced with scholarly and literary quotations, among which Wordsworth features liberally), of what its subsequent secondary titles describe as 'The Origin, Spirit, and Institutions of Christian Chivalry', or 'The True Sense and Practice of Chivalry'. Stephen Gill's recent account of Wordsworth's Catholic affinities and especially his relations with Faber does not, I think, give enough weight to Wordsworth's personally evolved position on church reform, nor to the broader circle of Catholic friendships (especially that with de Vere), rather than 'Father Faber's' single-handed machinations.[18] Even Faber was a partner in a two-way dialogue through which his own predispositions were strengthened by Wordsworth's writings. When Faber printed Wordsworth's poem, 'Stanzas Suggested in a Steamboat Off St Bees' Heads', with his *Life of St Bega* in *Lives of the English Saints* (1844), edited by John Henry Newman, he pointed out in a prefatory note that it was 'written . . . as long ago as 1833' (*PW* IV 403), several years before they met. In the key *Tract XC* (1841), Newman himself was to salute the religious influence of Wordsworth and other Romantics on the Catholic cause:

> In truth there is at this moment a great progress of the religious mind of our Church to something deeper and truer than satisfied the last century . . . The poets and philosophers of the age have borne witness to it for many years. Those great names in our literature, Sir Walter Scott, Mr. Wordsworth, Mr. Coleridge, though in different ways and with essential differences one from another, and perhaps from any Church system, all bear witness to it.   (xlviii)

In 1835 Mary Wordsworth invited Crabb Robinson to come and help relieve her husband, and the plan to go to Rome which resulted was no mere diversion, but a journey that by then Wordsworth was being drawn to undertake, in part to reconstitute his relation to the Anglican discourse of nationalism that was under stress at home. In his later sixties, when Wordsworth did eventually travel to Rome, he repeatedly confessed to his companion on the journey, Crabb Robinson, that 'It [was] too late' (*Memoirs* II 329). His identity had become so firmly circumscribed within the field of family, local and national relations that, as Crabb Robinson reports, 'It often happened that objects of universal attraction seemed chiefly to bring back to his mind absent objects dear to him' (ibid.). Nevertheless, while Wordsworth's responses to the immediate objects of his admiration were fondly limited by familiar pacts which still carried his major self-investment, he was also in search of fuller self-representation on other cultural ground.

In order to encounter 'Rome', as the sign of his success, Wordsworth would need to re-enact the paradigm of imaginative re-creation as it had been established centrally in the *Prelude* account of crossing the Alps. Predictably, after he reached Rome, the initial result was a sense of let-down, as he acknowledged in the sonnet 'At Rome':

> Is this, ye Gods, the Capitolian Hill?
> Yon petty Steep in truth the fearful Rock,
> Tarpeian named of yore, and keeping still
> That name, a local Phantom proud to mock
> The Traveller's expectation? – Could our Will
> Destroy the ideal Power within, 'twere done
> Thro' what men see and touch.
>
> (1–7)

He felt much the same about the Parthenon. As in the Cave of Yordas simile, the expectation of the 'curious traveller' raised by the phantasmal content of an illustrious place-name is 'mocked' by the actual experience, only to be reconfirmed by the insistence of the interrupted structure claiming to find a new discursive envelope:

> Full oft, our wish obtained, deeply we sigh;
> Yet not unrecompensed are they who learn,
> From that depresssion raised, to mount on high
> With stronger wing, more clearly to discern
> Eternal things; and, if need be, defy
> Change, with a brow not insolent, though stern.
>
> (9–14)

The promise of the 'eternal' city admits an access of meaning that can only be measured by seeing it as an inflection of a major shift in the English religious culture of the time. In the note attached to the poem, Wordsworth attempted to spell out the way historical imagination might be restored:

> *Sight* is at first a sad enemy to imagination and to those pleasures belonging to old times with which some exertions of the power will always mingle; nothing perhaps brings this truth home to the feelings more than the city of Rome; not so much in respect to the impression made at the moment when it is first seen and looked at as a whole, for then the imagination may be reinvigorated and the mind's eye

quickened; but when particular spots or objects are sought out, disappointment is I believe invariably felt. Ability to recover from this disappointment will exist in proportion to knowledge, and the power of mind to reconstruct out of fragments and parts, and to make details in the present subservient to more adequate comprehension of the past.   (*PW* III 494)

The returning sense of fulfilment depends on the mind's power to restore what preceded fragmentation. But what Wordsworth is seeking to describe as a 'more adequate comprehension of the past' that can irradiate 'details in the present' is not so much a discourse that specifically prevailed in the past as a re-empowered discourse of the present which, connecting past and present, reaffirms an unbroken structure of identity and so healingly represses the trace of division and loss.

That the signified of 'Rome' was inevitably in some ways bound up with the institution of Catholicism for Wordsworth is clear from the recurrent appreciative encounter with Catholic history and customs which the series of *Memorials of a Tour in Italy, 1837* records, following the opening poem, 'Musings Near Aquapendente', with its wide gaze over a panorama of convent, cathedral and the prospect of Roman 'Christian Traditions' (291). This and two other pieces from the series were published in a pamphlet entitled *Contributions of William Wordsworth to the Revival of Catholic Truths* in 1842. The companion sonnet to 'At Rome' is 'At Rome. – Regrets. – In Allusion to Niebuhr, and Other – Modern Historians', which insists on sustaining the fabulous content of 'Rome' (largely derived from Livy's *History*) in the face of Niebuhr's methods of historical source-criticism in his *History of Rome* (1811–12):

> What is it we hear?
> The glory of Infant Rome must disappear,
> Her morning splendours vanish, and their place
> Know them no more? If Truth, who veiled her face
> With those bright beams yet hid it not, must steer
> Henceforth a humbler course perplexed and slow;
> One solace yet remains for us who came
> Into this world in days when story lacked
> Severe research, that in our hearts we know
> How, for exciting youth's heroic flame,
> Assent is power, belief the soul of fact.
>
> (4–14)

The empowering 'assent' to fabulous registers restores the lost 'glory' of Rome, replaying in terms of Roman historiography the structure of loss ('The glory of infant Rome must disappear, / Her morning splendours... With those bright beams') and recompense ('One solace yet remains') centrally fixed in the Immortality Ode. What was called for, however, at this later stage in Wordsworth's life, could not simply be a regression to former registers of nature or nation, but rather the reinstatement of his threatened imaginary position within the originating and now, Wordsworth finds, non-factious discourse of a continuing tradition, partly represented by the religious diction of 'Rome' ('Assent... belief the soul of fact').

Hopkins may be seen to have been calling on the discourse of religious reaction represented by 'Rome' as a powerful counter to the reappearance of revolution. Typically, the Wordsworthian experience of shock is doubled, so that an unpleasant jolt develops into an animating stimulus. The charge Hopkins inherits comes from the transformation of the original language-shock into the discourse of reaction so as unexpectedly to find – and this is the lasting thrill of receiving the revelation – one's own self-representation not simply reflected but also empowered. But the reason so many of Wordsworth's readers were to feel well insulated from the after-effect may be explained in terms of another capital, which is the signifier of those discourses which 'Rome' rises up against in order to occlude, but which was becoming the site of the representatively modern cultural experience – the revolutionary city of Paris, where, in the Place de Carrousel, Wordsworth had been terrified to decipher the signs of the popular power of modern urban democracy that would become increasingly represented by the crowd.

In his essay, 'On Some Motifs in Baudelaire', Walter Benjamin elaborates on some of Marx's ideas on revolutionary power, which in *The Class Struggles in France* (1850) the latter had seen in terms of electricity: 'the bloody uprising of the people of Palermo worked like an electric shock on the paralyzed masses of people' (98). Benjamin also pursues Marx's evocation of London from *Contribution to a Critique of Political Economy* (1859) and his description of the phantasmagoria of capitalist commodity exchange in *Capital* in writing of 'the close connection... between the figure of shock and contact with the metropolitan masses' of Paris, and in discussing the 'hidden figure' of the crowd that is 'imprinted on [Baudelaire's] creativity' (162): 'it is the phantom crowd of the words, the fragments, the beginnings of lines from which the poet, in the deserted streets, wrests the poetic booty' (ibid.). Baudelaire, he argues, derived his creative energy from the new form of social experience: 'Moving through this traffic involves the individual in a series of shocks and collisions. At dangerous intersections, nervous impulses flow through him in rapid succession, like the energy from a battery. Baudelaire speaks of a man who plunges into the crowd as into a reservoir of electric energy' (171). 'The shock experience' which Benjamin finds 'at the very centre' of Baudelaire's work, and which is the effect most immediately of industrial revolution, is seen as imparting to poetic language a dynamic of separation from the matrix of 'experience' when people become 'increasingly unable to assimilate the data of the world around [them])', a response as automatic as the rhythms of industrial production. It was a novel aesthetic, most significantly opposed to the integrating shock effects of the Burkean sublime, which depend on a 'common observation, that objects which in reality would shock, are in tragical, and such like representations, the source of a very high species of pleasure' (44). Baudelaire was on the cusp of this alienation and fragmentation which becomes the impetus behind a new kind of poetic expression of an unprecedented kind of social encounter that set in around 'roughly...the middle of the last century' (153): 'Les Fleurs du Mal was the last lyric work that had a European repercussion; no later work penetrated beyond a more or less limited linguistic area' (188).

Baudelaire's transitional status is described as having not yet wholly lost contact with the sensibility that seeks to deflect shock. Benjamin describes an aggressiveness about Baudelaire's *traumatophilia* as he 'wrests the poetic booty', but he also sees the self-defensiveness behind Baudelaire's bravado image of the duel which he recovers as a kind of creative *parrying*: 'it is easy to trace in his works his defensive reaction to [the masses'] attraction and allure' (164). There is an ambivalence about Benjamin's account of the Baudelairean shock which both wards off disturbance and is dynamized by it. With recourse to Freud's view in *On the Pleasure Principle* that traumatic neurosis can be countered by bringing the origins of a shock to consciousness, Benjamin concludes that, though the experience of shock can be 'cushioned' by consciousness, that 'would sterilize this incident for poetic experience' and make it subject to 'a plan [that] was at work in . . . composition' (158). His argument proceeds that such planning did begin to characterize lyrical poetry in response to constant retraumatizations, and he refers to the alienation effect in 'the interstices between image and idea, word and thing, which are the real site of Baudelaire's excitation' (160–1). Both Baudelaire's and Wordsworth's writings somehow contain revolutionary trauma by the production of poetic language, but while Wordsworth's attempt to restore the 'aura' ('the associations which, at home in the

[Proustian] *mémoire involuntaire*, tend to cluster around the object of perception', 182), Benjamin's Baudelaire actively seeks to minister to its decline. The assault on the aura is the 'shock experience' that Baudelaire places 'at the centre of his work', effectively repeating the alienating moment of resubjectification.

Benjamin's notion of this modernist aesthetic remains conflicted in failing completely to reject the aural for the mechanical. Though he claims categorically that Baudelaire 'indicated the price for which the sensation of the modern age may be had: the disintegration of the aura in the experience of the shock' (190), his own criticism cannot renounce, for example, the magic of the industrial cinema, and even famously laments the introduction of the sound track. Baudelaire's constantly focusing on the switch to subjectification recapitulates entry into the social domain while it highlights the loss of personal control involved. Yet while Baudelaire's form of individualism only serves to produce the recognition of alienation, he is still demanding an *original* kind of impersonality, so that Benjamin notes that 'he went so far as to proclaim as his goal "the creation of a cliché"' (188). In this way, Baudelaire succeeds in representing the new social reality in the jostling for expression in Second Empire France – of increased alienation – at the same time as seeking to protect himself from it by reiterating the act of subjectification. It is this preoccupation with origination and differentiation that places Baudelaire at a moment of historical change for Benjamin, and he quotes from an essay by Valéry to define Baudelaire's related predicament within poetic tradition: 'The problem for Baudelaire was bound to be this: to become a great poet, yet neither Lamartine nor Hugo nor Musset. I do not claim that this ambition was a conscious one in Baudelaire; but it was bound to be present in him, it was his reason of state' (159). Benjamin had strenuously to resist, while still emulating a pre-established poetic tradition in a way that no longer came unconsciously: 'He envisioned blank spaces which he filled in with his poems' (ibid.).

Standing at the same cross-ways, Wordsworth's response to shock was different. Confronted with the parallel dilemma over his succession as the pre-eminent national poet: how to become a great poet, yet not Milton, he involuntarily found himself still spoken and controlled by the language of his great progenitors: 'We must be free or die, who speak the tongue / That Shakespeare spake; the faith and morals hold / Which Milton held' ('It is not to be thought of that the flood', 11–12). His earlier encounter with the same industrialized society was one which coupled the revolutionary society in France with that resulting from the British manufacturing system, and he responds by calling on the memory of what is being displaced to reaffirm its privileged operations. This effect, however, is not to be confused with the attempt simply to deny the actual historical experience of shock as a distinctly new source of power – camouflaging it, in the age of mechanical reproduction, by presenting it in the same, familiar and unbroken style, as David Nye describes the domestication of electrification in the designing of light fixtures

> to look like crystal chandeliers, candles, or gas jets. Electric coffee pots often looked like parts of a typical Victorian silver table service. The same tendency to emphasize traditional design recurred in the earliest electrical advertising. Advertisments for the light bulb placed it in traditional settings such as Persian throne rooms and Chinese villages, suggesting that there was no disjuncture between the premodern world and that antimodernists longed for and new technology.   (145–6)

Instead, all Wordsworth's reactivations depend on the continuingly live transmission of aural power. 'To perceive the aura of an object we look at', writes Benjamin, 'means to invest it with the ability to look at us in return' (184). It represents, that is, the imaginary position of self-reflection, and it is just that delightfully creative shock of self-recognition that Wordsworth's eye solicits in every scene it visits, just as he describes its presentation in some unpublished lines he wrote for 'Michael':

> For me,
> When it has chanced that I have wandered long
> Among the mountains, I have waked at last
> From dream of motion in some spot like this,
> Shut out from man, some region – one of those
> That hold by an inalienable right
> An independent Life, and seem the whole
> Of nature and unrecorded time;
> If, looking round, I have perchance perceived
> Some vestiges of human hands, some stir
> Of human passion, they to me are sweet
> As lightest sunbreak, or the sudden sound
> Of music to a blind man's ear . . .
>
> . . .
> They are as a creation in my heart.
> (*PW* II 479–80)

As the recollection of inchoate language in 'the voice of inland waters' had come to the boy hooting at owls in *The Prelude*, 'with a gentle shock of mild surprize' (IV 407), so a stone 'Couched on the bald top of an eminence' causes him 'a flash of mild surprize', when it begins to speak in a register he could himself own, 'with something of a lofty utterance drest' ('Resolution and Independence', 58, 90, 94).

Within English Romanticism, the text that is most premonitory of the threat of modernism is *Frankenstein* (1818), which narrates horrifically the fear of a new 'unmanageable' creativity that entails losing the aural shock of recognition. Written after the career of the French Revolution had been finally halted at Waterloo, it foresees the repetition of related cultural dislocations. The Creature stands for the new realization of the contingency of *man* – that the category of 'the human' was still being invented. As Foucault explains, 'Before the end of the eighteenth century, *man* did not exist . . . He is quite a recent creature, which the demiurge of knowledge fabricated with its own hands less than two hundred years ago' (1971, 308). The burden on the liberal version of the imagination – whose modern poets, in Percy Shelley's phrase, were (through the 'electric life' burning in their words) to become 'the unacknowledged legislators of the World'[19] – was to give birth to a new and improved humanity. The critique that runs through the book is of a Promethean enterprise that comes to recognize itself as a perversion of Romantic creativity as it had been conceived by Wordsworth and Coleridge, and a series of intertextualities serves to 'parry' the rise of mechanical reproduction.

Frankenstein relates that the object of his quest was to discover 'the principle of life' (51), recalling the 'one life'[20] that the youthful Coleridge and Wordsworth had pursued, and that in 'The Ancient Mariner' Coleridge had linked to galvanism and electricity. Coleridge's culminating definition of the 'secondary' (creative) imagination in *Biographia Literaria* also rests on the breathing of new life into the inanimate: 'It dissolves, diffuses, dissipates, in order to re-create; or where this process is rendered impossible, yet still at all events it struggles to idealize and unify. It is essentially *vital*, even as all objects (*as* objects) are essentially fixed and dead' (*BL* I 304). That vitality is informed by aural coherence, and once its supply is cut off what is left is merely the literal life of an automaton – a reductive view which is, of course, that of Frankenstein's own project: 'After days and nights of incredible labour and fatigue, I succeeded in discovering the cause of generation and life; nay, more, I became myself capable of bestowing animation upon lifeless matter' (52), while the Creature in fact embodies the cross-currents of both kinds of creativity. It was the principle of life that Byron and the Shelleys had been discussing at Geneva when the book was formulated, but when it finds expression in echoes of the poetic language of the earlier Romantics, something has gone wrong. The language has become aborted.

One of the doubles who enact the splitting involved in the Frankensteinian project is his childhood friend, Henry Clerval, to whom he refers as 'the very image of my former self' (158), and who is depicted in terms highly reminiscent of the young Wordsworth:

> He was a being framed in the 'very poetry of nature.' His wild and enthusiastic imagination was chastened by the sensibility of his heart. His soul overflowed with ardent affections, and his friendship was of that devoted and wondrous nature that the worldly-minded teach us to look for only in the imagination...The scenery of external nature, which others regard only with admiration, he loved with ardour...   (156)

Then Frankenstein actually bursts into a lengthy quotation from 'Tintern Abbey':

> The sounding cataract
> Haunted him like a passion: the tall rock,
> The mountain, and deep and gloomy wood,
> Their colours and their forms, were then to him
> An appetite; a feeling, and a love,
> That had no need of a remoter charm,
> By thought supplied, or any interest
> Unborrow'd from the eye.

But at the University of Ingolstadt, Frankenstein hears the 'panegyric upon modern chemistry' delivered by Professor Waldman which inspires him to believe that modern science can achieve wonders that exceed those promised in the works of the ancient pseudo-scientists on which Frankenstein had fed his youth:

> these philosophers, whose hands seem only made to dabble in dirt, and their eyes to pore over the microscope or crucible, have indeed performed miracles. They penetrate into the recesses of nature, and show how she works *in her hiding places. They ascend into the heavens*: they have discovered how the blood circulates, and the nature of the air we breathe. They have acquired new and almost unlimited powers;

they can command the thunders of heaven, mimic the earthquake, and even mock the invisible world with its own shadows.

Frankenstein refers to these words as 'the words of fate, enounced to destroy me':

> As he went on, I felt as if my soul were grappling with a palpable enemy; one by one the various keys were touched which formed the mechanism of my being: chord after chord was sounded, and soon my mind was filled with one thought, one conception, one purpose. So much has been done, exclaimed the soul of Frankenstein, – more, far more, will I achieve: *treading in the steps already marked, I will pioneer a new way*, explore unknown powers, and unfold to the world the deepest mysteries of creation. (47–8; emphases added)

Waldman's lecture and Frankenstein's response contain a tissue of echoes of Wordsworth's Prospectus to the *Recluse* (which had been published in 1814 in the prefatory materials to his poem, *The Excursion*) where Wordsworth invokes the muse of astronomy for his great philosophical work to come:

> Urania, I shall need
> Thy guidance, or a greater Muse, if such
> Descend to earth or dwell in highest heaven!
> For I must tread on shadowy ground, must sink
> Deep – and, aloft ascending, breathe in worlds
> To which the heaven of heavens is but a veil.
> All strength – all terror, single or in bands,
> That ever was put forth in personal form –
> Jehovah – with his thunder, and the choir
> Of shouting Angels, and the empyreal thrones –
> I pass them unalarmed . . .
>
> . . .
> – Beauty – a living presence of the earth,
> Surpassing the most fair ideal Forms
> Which craft of delicate Spirits hath composed
> From earth's materials – waits upon my steps.
> (25–45)

The scheme that Frankenstein devised turns into a parody of Wordsworth's for the superhuman work of the age. 'The creation of a human being' (53) 'had taken an irresistible hold of [Frankenstein's] imagination' (55), and he 'pursued nature to her hiding-places' (54). Though Mary Shelley could not have also known the lines Wordsworth had written for *The Prelude*: 'the hiding-places of man's power / Open; I would approach them, but they close' (XII 279–80), Wordsworth was expressing in them his difficulty, despite the initial 'experiments' he had engineered for *Lyrical Ballads*, in imagining the new community in terms radically other than those of the old, and in fulfilling the vaunt of the Prospectus to create the advertised work.

Wordsworth had already, and foundationally, discriminated his kind of creativity from that which he had confronted in Godwinian rationalism. In Book X of *The Prelude*, Wordsworth describes his own period of driven experimentation:

> I took the knife in hand
> And stopping not at parts less sensitive,
> Endeavoured with my best of skill to probe
> The living body of society
> Even to the heart; I pushed without remorse
> My speculations forward; yea, set foot
> On Nature's holiest places.
>
> (278–82)

Significantly, it is here, when Wordsworth is describing the influence of Mary Shelley's father (a major presence in Frankenstein's characterization), that his anatomizing of the body politic pre-echoes Frankenstein's deranged dismemberings: 'I seemed to have lost all soul or sensation but for this one pursuit ... I ... disturbed, with profane fingers, the tremulous secrets of the human frame' (54–5). But by the time he had counselled the young Hazlitt about the dangers of abstract ethics, Wordsworth had learned the lesson for himself of giving precedence to the involuntary memory :

> Sweet is the lore which Nature brings;
> Our meddling intellect
> Mis-shapes the beauteous forms of things: –
> We murder to dissect.
>
> ('The Tables Turned', 25–8)

The Wordsworthian passage into aural restoration is pivotally recorded in the disciplining of his shocked perception of the crowd by which 'London' was able to absorb his experiences of both industrialized Britain and revolutionary Paris. His description in *The Prelude* of Bartholomew Fair, 'that lays, / If any spectacle on earth can do, / The whole creative powers of man asleep' (VII 653–5), has often been acknowledged as a prescient apprehension of the phenomenon that Benjamin describes with the help of an array of European writers from later in the century. Engels's *The Condition of the Working Class in England* (first published in Germany in 1845) broaches some features of the seeming uncontrollability of the northern metropolis of industrial revolution, Manchester. His reaction that 'There is something distasteful about the very bustle of the streets, something that is abhorrent to human nature itself' (quoted by Benjamin, 163) is a paler echo of Wordsworth's

> What a hell
> For eyes and ears, what anarchy and din
> Barbarian and infernal – 'tis a dream
> Monstrous in colour, motion, shape, sight, sound.
> (659–62)

Engels's unending displacement in the modern city, 'where one can roam about for hours without reaching the beginning of an end' (quoted by Benjamin, 162–3), chimes in with Wordsworth's desolating alarm at what Poe, in his story 'The Man in the Crowd', terms an 'absurd kind of uniformity' (172) in the crowd: 'Living amid the same perpetual flow / Of trivial objects, melted and reduced / To one identity by differences / That have no law, no meaning, and no end' (702–5). The relating of the pedestrians' 'uniformly constant movements of an automaton' to the processes of mechanical production which Benjamin finds in Poe, 'as if they had adapted themselves to the machines and could express themselves only automatically' (172), develops an insight also prefigured by Wordsworth:

> Tents and booths
> Meanwhile – as if the whole were one vast mill –
> Are vomiting, receiving, on all sides,
> Men, women, three-years' children, babes in arms.
> (692–5)

Radically, the fair images the modern crisis in representation: it is a blank space from which all coherence and possibility of intelligible redefinition has been lost:

> O, blank confusion, and a type not false
> Of what the mighty city is itself
> To all, except a straggler here and there –
> To the whole swarm of its inhabitants –
> An undistinguishable world to men.
>
> (696–700)

Book VII, 'Residence in London', is impelled by a stream of spectacles, pageants, and processions that evoke in bursts an increasingly ambivalent attitude to the great capital, from his 'living chearfully abroad' during his student years, when 'life . . . was new' (440), to living hell in Bartholomew Fair by the book's end. At first the riot is animating, but it is punctuated by gasping retreats from 'the thickening hubbub' (227) to 'aery lodges' in inns of court, 'privileged regions and inviolate' (202), or 'Some half-frequented scene, where wider streets / Bring straggling breezes of suburban air' (207–8). The manifold becomes progressively difficult to comprehend as Wordsworth looks in vain for the shock of recognition:

> How often in the overflowing streets
> Have I gone forwards with the crowd, and said
> Unto myself, 'The face of every one
> That passes by me is a mystery.'
>
> (595–8)

Instead, he resorts to the hold of fantasy to view it as 'A second-sight procession' (602), choreographing its unpredictable dynamism into a 'moving pageant' (610). When in this frame of mind Wordsworth is 'abruptly smitten with the view' (611) of the blind beggar ('upon his chest / Wearing a written paper, to explain / The story of the man, and who he was', 613–15), the language-shock is replayed ('My mind did at this spectacle turn round / As with the might of waters', 616–17). Wordsworth finds this alternative subjectivity – of linguistic reductionism – no more satisfactorily representative than the chaotic unconscious unleashed in the modern city. This jostling into self-consciousness ('in this label was a type / Or emblem of the utmost that we know / Both of ourselves and of the universe', 618–20) also runs against the grain of Wordsworth's imaginary self-recognition, and the extraordinariness of the effect on Wordsworth results from the discontinuity between his apprehension of the imperturbable depth of the man's interiority ('this unmoving man, / His fixed face and sightless eyes', 621–2), and the minimalism of his representation ('a written paper . . . the utmost that we know').

When it comes to regulating the experience of Bartholomew Fair, natural forms and outlines recall the 'comprehensiveness and memory' (718) that helps group the crowd into more stable and familiar masses, and its variegations are brought into the slower rhythm of atmospheric effects among the mountains so as to allow the scenes to subside into a discourse of 'Composure and ennobling harmony' (741):

> nor less
> The changeful language of their countenances
> Gives movement to the thoughts, and multitude,
> With order and relation.
>
> (727–30)

In this way the revolutionary crowd can be marginalized by a greater whole, and the 'under-sense of greatest' (735) brings back the reassurance of the socially co-ordinated nation. The discursive transformation replays that which emerges in the 'Strange congregation' (1850, 588) that Wordsworth's traveller eventually comes to behold in the Cave of Yordas, which is the key Wordsworthian version of the disciplined crowd as 'moving pageant':

> the senseless mass,
> In its projections, wrinkles, cavities,
> Through all its surface, with all colours streaming,
> Like a magician's airy pageant, parts,
> Unites, embodying everywhere some pressure
> Or image, recognised or new, some type
> Or picture of the world – forests and lakes,
> Ships, rivers, towers, the warrior clad in mail,
> The prancing steed, the pilgrim with his staff,
> The mitred bishop and the thronèd king –
> A spectacle to which there is no end.
>
> (VIII 731–41)

The 'Ships, rivers, towers' echo the panorama of 'Composed Upon Westminster Bridge' which serves as a familiar hieroglyph for British imperialism: 'Ships, towers, domes, theatres, and temples lie / Open unto the fields, and to the sky' (6–7), while the representational restraint of that dawn city-scape develops into a procession of the feudal state of monarchy, aristocracy and church that re-emerges by controlling the *pressures* of *the senseless masses*.

Wild Grasses

Yet Wordsworth never could write his modern epic, *The Recluse*. His peculiar relation to language left him as the privileged apologist for a reactionary poetics – one that parried the shock of the new by attempting to translate it into the milder shock of recognizing himself again in the old. A pre-established register – of chivalry, for instance – did mean something new *after* the shock of revolution. It had become part of a new intervention of nationalism and tradition, and Wordsworth could greet it on the other side of the Alp-like border as the profession of a counter-revolutionary presence that had preceded, co-existed with, and survived an enormous historical rift: it had never not been there in some form, and now it had emerged as a prevalent register of Britishness. It was also possible for minority readers, like Hopkins, to discover an imaginary intersubjectivity represented in Wordsworth's poetry and to read in it the re-empowerment of a threatened reactionary discourse and an endorsement of 'Rome'. Many of Wordsworth's readers, however, who resisted the democratic elbowing and competitive thrusting of Victorian England, were unable assuredly to confront the rise of modernism with the literary discourse of Wordsworth's later poetry, which, in effect, had not been powerful enough to produce his own great work.

George Eliot is representative of a broad positioning in Victorian culture – somewhere between Hopkins's imaginary relation to an expanding national tradition and Baudelaire's invigorating disconnections from it – which still relied on Wordsworth's poetic language to stand for a dispersion of more or less resilient religious and political beliefs. Gill, who has illuminatingly examined the uses to which the Victorians put Wordsworth's reputation, points out that the relative absence of doctrinal specificity, especially before his later work, enabled the poetry to be adopted by representatives of different faiths as well as non-believers. In a detailed and sympathetic account of Wordsworth's influence on Eliot, particularly on *Adam Bede*, *Mill on the Floss* and *Silas Marner*, he describes the narrative shape of the last of these novels in terms that would characterize the aspiration – whether realized or not – in all her work: 'The trajectory from trauma and alienation to recovery and integration into domestic and community life parallels *The Prelude* and it is embodied throughout in Wordsworthian language' (1998,

162). Though Gill maintains that 'there is no strong case for arguing that Wordsworth's poetry was an active, shaping agent in the later direction of George Eliot's art as it was in the earlier' (165), I believe that the way in which Wordsworth's poetic language helps both to constitute and to qualify her critique of the visionary, which goes back to her treatment of clairvoyance in *The Painted Veil* (1859), in order to sustain her later 'humanist vision' (167) may be recovered, (though less obviously and under greater strain), by attending closely to her treatment of trauma and reintegration in two of her later works.

Some of the observations she made after the appearance of *Middlemarch* (1872) in what was posthumously named her *Essays and Leaves from a Note-book* (1884) help pithily to characterize her shrewd balancing of old and new forms of expression. In her note on 'Value in Originality', for example, her opinion that 'The supremacy given in European cultures to the literatures of Greece and Rome has had an effect almost equal to that of a common religion in binding Western nations together' leads her on to stress the value of a common tradition: 'It would be foolish to be for ever complaining of the consequent uniformity, as if there were an endless power of originality in the human mind' (303). Originality can only be registered by proceeding from a prior inscription in established languages of cultural power: '[masters of language] use words which are already a familiar medium of understanding and sympathy. Originality of this order changes the wild grasses into world-feeding grain' (ibid.). On the other hand, as her note on 'Historical Imagination' makes clear, the participation of later generations in the aura of historical forms of expression is not automatic. The recreation of aura depends on differences as well as similarities: 'A false kind of idealisation dulls our perception of the meaning in words when they relate to past events which have had a glorious issue: for lack of comparison no warning image rises to check scorn of the very phrases which in other associations are consecrated' (302). The complexity of expression demonstrates the complicated manoeuvring within words that is being described: prestigious clichés have to be challenged into re-expression. Some understanding of the actualities of Hannibal's and Napoleon's Alpine campaigns, for example, would have to be brought to bear imaginatively on consideration of later events, such as a Swiss walking trip, for a phrase like 'crossing the Alps' to be admitted to new and effective representation (which might indeed then be seen to have correspondences with the glorious past). For Eliot, in her revision of Wordsworth's symbolic passage ('Imagination! – lifting up itself / Before the eye and progress of my song . . . here that power / In all the might of its endowments, came / Athwart me'), it is the creation of the 'veracious imagination' which 'lifts itself up' (301) to challenge both the fetishizing of the past and the debunking of literalistic reductionism in order to effect the restoration of historical aura.

It may be generalized that Eliot's novels are characteristically structured around the articulation and accommodation of the related split between past and present, and its assuaging. *Felix Holt: The Radical* (1866) directly addresses the political discourses of reform that in England contained those of revolution for two generations, and depicts the resultant dilemma between old and new. Centred on the elections following the First Reform Act of 1832, it examines the penumbral claims to inherited property of a cast of characters embroiled in the convoluted law of entail. The book analyses the legitimate inheritance of the new social and political powers that reform had produced and that could no longer be located simply in party or family. Instead, a series of painful but enlightening shocks leads to a complication of interests in the alliance between Esther, a self-dispossessing half-French heiress, and Felix, the would-be pattern of an educated working man as natural aristocrat, whose idealism discredits the sordid actuality of Radical politics.

Agitation, in its several senses, is the keynote, and an attentive recuperation of the novel's related lexicon, which is extraordinarily pervasive, unfolds the deliberate moderation of its perils into wholesome zeal. The *grande dame*, Mrs Transome, 'trembles' throughout with her guilty secret as to the bastardy of her son, the Radical candidate, Harold, which is the hint for a more truly radical exposé of political legitimacy in the England of the 1830s. The victorious Tory family, the Debarrys, and in particular the idealized future heir, Philip (who was to die at Rome fifteen years after the novel ended, 'a convert to Catholicism', 157), retain an instinctive decency, at least as far as it is probed, that chimes more with that of Esther and Felix, the labourers-to-be, than with the rashness of the deracinated Harry and his unpredictably savage heir, born of a slave-girl from Smyrna. The domestic virtues that prevail over all the book's heady conflicts are expressed in the epigraph to Chapter XVIII taken from 'Tintern Abbey': 'The little, nameless, unremembered acts / Of kindness and of love', which are the manifestation of an implicit but diffuse intertextual support throughout. The Debarrys approvingly superintend the climactic church wedding of the leading duo.

The first major shock comes as the fulfilment of Mrs Transome's sense of alienation from her son after his arrival back at the family estate:

'But I shall not be a Tory candidate.'

Mrs Transome felt something like an electric shock.

'What then?' she said, almost sharply, 'You will not call yourself a Whig?'

'God forbid! I'm a Radical.'   (18)

Thereafter, the whole town of Treby Magna seems to be connected to the shock waves produced by this spasm, as the social web relays it individually and communally. Esther's dissenting minister stepfather, for example, becomes roused to a state of perturbation by disputes over church governance, 'and his small body was jarred from head to foot by the concussion of an argument to which he saw no answer. In fact, the only moments when he could be said to be really conscious of his body, were when he trembled under the pressure of some agitating thought' (53). As his challenge to the Debarry rector to engage in public debate is meant to demonstrate, the consequence of these marginal considerations 'had a wider bearing, and might tell on the welfare of England at large' (169). In fact, *all* disputation and debate does bear on the political and social struggles of the moment, and the 'thriving tradesmen' of Treby are right in their instinct that 'there was a nemesis in things which made objection unsafe, and even the Reform Bill was a sort of electric eel which [they] had better leave alone' (266). The rector himself manages to avoid all such unpleasantness by '[associating] only with county people': 'a clergyman who would have taken tea with the townspeople would have given a dangerous shock to the mind of a Treby Churchman' (46).

Felix Holt – massive, Gothic and outlandish – creates a huge stir wherever he goes, and most particularly in the affections of Esther. The minister's parish is scandalized by the 'shock' (238) of his political assertiveness and of his aspiring to friendship with Esther, and the 'slight shock' (60) at his uncouthness, which first impressed the minister himself, becomes unpleasantly animating to new feelings in his stepdaughter when Felix seems indifferent: 'a pang swift as an electric shock darted through her' (223). But her 'long-continued agitation' (255) finds no outlet in the perverted Radicalism of the Treby election revolt, which Felix finds himself unable to control, bringing 'with a terrible shock the sense that his plan might turn out to be as mad as all bold projects are seen to be when they have failed' (318–19). Instead, he is swept along by the destructive animus of a (revolutionary) crowd that brings his individual powerlessness into crisis – 'It was that mixture of pushing forward and being pushed forward, which is a brief history of most human things' (317) – and that after all represents social impulses which he cannot share: 'As he was pressed along with the multitude into Treby park, his very movement seemed to him only an image of the day's fatalities, in which the multitudinous small wickednesses of small selfish ends, really undirected towards any larger result, had issued in widely shared mischief that might yet be hideous' (319–20).

The revelation about the legitimate succession to the Transome estate comes in a series of convulsions to the consciousness of Esther and Harold. Harold's real father, the hated lawyer Jermyn, broaches it in such a way as to give 'an unpleasant shock to Harold's sense of mastery' (331). When a former friend of Esther's own real father tells Harold who the lawful claimant is, his release from Jermyn's control of the situation makes his response more ambivalent: 'He was electrified by surprise at the quarter from which this information was coming. Any fresh alarm was counteracted by the flashing thought that he might be enabled to act independently of Jermyn' (341). Esther first receives the intelligence about her altered situation from her stepfather, when 'The possibility ... that her real father might still be living, was a new shock' (254). But the news that Felix had been arrested for his presumed part in the election riot is a further blow that becomes part of a series of unanticipated complications in which ostensibly enhanced expectations were puzzlingly involved in apparent defeats: 'In the interval since Esther parted with Felix Holt on the day of the riot, she had gone through such emotions, and had already had so strong a shock of surprise, that she was prepared to receive any new incident of an unwonted kind with comparative equanimity' (350). The 'great shock of surprise' (357) eventually arrives for Esther with a lawyer's letter announcing *her* inheritance.

After this, the dreadful realization of Mrs Transome's long-standing fear of exposure (when Jermyn indicates that he will establish his relation to Harold to save himself from ruin) almost completes the sequence of eruptions around which the novel is structured: 'As Jermyn, sitting down and leaning forward with an elbow on his knee, uttered his last words – "if he knew the whole truth" – a slight shock seemed to pass through Mrs Transome's hitherto motionless body, followed by a light in her eyes, as in an animal's about to spring' (400). This culminating 'terrible blow' (458) to Harold arrives with Jermyn's public declaration.

The final shock, however, happens off-stage: again Harold is the subject, as he learns that Esther prefers to share her life with Felix and wishes to renounce her inheritance in Harold's favour. It comes as the fulfilment of Esther's presentiment that 'it would come on [him] as a shock, if he suspected that there had been any love-passages between her and this young man' (406) when Harold had first begun to make love to her.

But the whole flow of shocks to the established social order throughout result in the political representation of Felix's amply redefined kind of Radicalism: 'The words of Felix at last seemed strangely to fit [Esther's] own experience' (435), and they call for no fundamental upsetting of social order, but rather a rediscovery of its present potential for co-operation and dignity:

> 'I don't mean to be illustrious, you know, and make a new era, else it would be kind of you to get a raven and teach it to croak "failure" in my ears. Where great things can't happen, I care for very small things, such as will never be known beyond a few garrets and workshops. And then, as to one thing I believe in, I don't think I can altogether fail. If there's anything our people want convincing of, it is, that there's some dignity and happiness for a man other than changing his situation.' (435)

The issue of the 'something short of an inward revolution' (464) that Esther had undergone was this hard-won continuity. Her meeting with Felix before his trial prepares for her greatest test: resisting disillusionment with what had been becoming her own deepest convictions:

> It seemed to her as if he too would look altered after her new life – as if even the past would change for her and be no longer a steadfast remembrance, but something she had been mistaken about, as she had been about the new life...The dread concentrated in those moments seemed worse than anything she had known before. It was what the dread of a pilgrim might be who has it whispered to him that the holy places are a delusion, or that he will see them with a soul unstirred and unbelieving. (433)

'The revolutionary struggle' (464), occasioned by the different shocks she experiences, had threatened her world with the overthrow of established values that could no longer be simply reinscribed. As she changes tack in her culminating interview with Harold from her sympathy with his kind of power under threat to her stronger preoccupation with the chance of Felix's release, (albeit partly through the influence of that power), and so with a possible future with Felix, the positive doubling of the shock begins to take effect: 'Harold did not gather that this was what Esther had waited for...the introduction of a new subject after very momentous words have passed, and are still dwelling on the mind, is necessarily a sort of concussion, shaking us into a new adjustment of ourselves' (463). The renegotiation of traditional values rather than the shift of political support from the governing classes to an untried and unpredictable dispensation is what is winning out. Esther's chiastic choice of a new *old* future with Felix over an old *new* one with Harold emerges from the hint of sustained pieties within her confusions throughout. When that choice of her 'tranquil restoration' first starts presenting itself, again it is significantly articulated in the language of 'Tintern Abbey' that had historically addressed the lesion of revolutionary knowledge, and that is perhaps also echoed in Esther's modest vision of 'very small things, such as will never be known beyond a few garrets and workshops' (260):

> But oft, in lonely rooms, and 'mid the din
> Of towns and cities, I have owed to them
> In hours of weariness, sensations sweet,
> Felt in the blood, and felt along the heart;
> . . .
> Nor less, I trust,
> To them I may have owed another gift,
> Of aspect more sublime; that blessed mood
> In which the burthen of the mystery,
> In which the heavy and the weary weight
> Of all this unintelligible world,
> Is lightened: – that serene and blessed mood,
> In which the affections gently lead us on.
>   (25–42)

When Harold had enquired about her 'deep wishes and secrets', she finds her desire to return home to Malthouse Lane with the 'unremembered pleasure' of 'Wordsworth': '"I could not possibly tell you one at this moment – I think I shall never find them out again. O yes," she said, abruptly, struggling to relieve herself from the oppression of unintelligible feelings – "I do know one wish distinctly. I want to go and see my father"' (387).

The novel, however, has mostly disappointed readers because it in effect lacks what Geoffrey Hill, borrowing a phrase of Coleridge's, refers to as 'the drama of reason' (90). Felix's pamphlet, *Address to Working Men*, for example, he accuses of 'rhythmic gerrymandering', deficient in the 'cross-rhythms and counterpointings' (ibid.) that should motivate such activating political interventions. But that is not where Eliot's own sympathies completely lie, while her finer verbal energies are reserved for the laborious subtleties that go into preserving a middle ground. *Middlemarch*, the novel about necessarily coming to acceptable terms with disillusionment set in the age of reform, is partly produced as her most substantial critique of the Wordsworthian imagination. Both *Middlemarch* and *Felix Holt*, especially in the opening pages of the latter, looked back to the 1830s as the pastoral past when 'the glory had not yet departed from the old coach-roads' (1), hinting at the structure implied in 'the glory and the dream' of the Intimations Ode, and *Middlemarch* is suffused by regrets for the fallings off of aural tradition. In particular, the strain on the modern imagination in revising stultifying literalism into cultural self-enlargement can be seen in its arduous refashioning of the Wordsworthian passage to 'Rome' in Chapter XX of Book Two, 'Old and Young', concerning the Roman honeymoon, which David Carroll has written of as the crisis of Dorothea's 'religious disposition' (24).[21] As a whole, the experience presents the intersection of two related defeats: the anticlimax of Dorothea's rite of passage into wifehood and of her husband's pretension to be producing a great life-work.

Secretly weeping in the 'boudoir of a handsome appartment in the Via Sistina' (157), after six weeks of marriage and five weeks in Rome, Dorothea is registering a series of let-downs that have been exposed by the confrontation with Rome as *the* symbol of cultural fulfilment: 'after the brief narrow experience of her childhood she was beholding Rome, the city of visible history, where the past of a whole hemisphere seems moving in funeral procession with strange ancestral images and trophies gathered from afar' (158). The echo of the Intimations Ode ('The Soul that rises with us, our life's Star, / Hath had elsewhere its setting, / And cometh from afar', 59–61) places 'Rome' immediately next to some precultural plenitude from which it is still 'trailing clouds of glory' (64), but also at the point of origin for the fall into the symbolic order – the *setting*, that makes the triumph funereal. Like Wordsworth's cisalpine imagination, her mind is not invasive, it 'Thinks not of spoils or trophies' (VI 544), yet she cannot enter into otherness as she prefers driving out to the Campagna to get away from the urgency of alien historical and cultural texts – 'the oppressive masquerade of ages' – to which she has no key, and so is unable to play any appropriate part in their related religious and artistic practices: 'her own life too seemed to become a masque with enigmatic costumes' (158). Her experience amounts to a failure of the kind of entry into the social domain of language and culture that is celebrated in Wordsworth's entrance into London in

Book VIII of *The Prelude*, and by extension his entry into 'The human nature unto which [he] felt / That [he] belonged' (761–2) for which the Cave of Yordas is the simile:

> A weight of ages did at once descend
> Upon my heart – no thought embodied, no
> Distinct remembrances, but weight and power,
> Power growing with the weight.
>
> (703–6)

Not yet successfully alienated in the cultural Other, Dorothea's deferral of her anticipated inscription in 'Rome' has begun to disturb signifieds that might offer to represent her: 'Dorothea had no distinctly shapen grievance that she could state even to herself' (158). A series of echoes from the Ode help reveal her experience of 'Rome' as a replay of culture-shock with its challenge to the effort of the imagination to persist in finding adequate self-representation. Incapable of the Wordsworthian imaginative reconstruction of 'Rome', creating an 'adequate comprehension of the past . . . out of fragments and parts' (see section II), the 'stupendous fragmentariness [that] heightened the dream-like strangeness of her bridal life' (158) in effect recalls as it disturbs that lost but longed-for state which, in the Fenwick note to the Intimations Ode, Wordsworth wrote precedes the fall into social passage: 'that dream-like vividness and splendour which invest objects of sight in childhood' (*PW* IV463–4). She is precisely in the position of the Wordsworthian infant rudely left to discover for itself the need of imaginative redemption – one of the 'souls [who] in their young nudity are tumbled out among incongruities and led to "find their feet" among them' (159). As a virgin bride and cultural handmaiden, she stands confusingly at the threshhold, and her crisis dramatizes the painful evolution of Eliot's 'veracious imagination' itself, with its demand for the acknowledgement of differences between past and present, ghosted by the promised antidote recorded in the passages related to crossing the Alps in Books VI and VIII of *The Prelude*.

Dorothea's inability to comprehend the city is complicated by the absence of her husband's sexual and cultural initiations on which, unconsciously and consciously, she had been relying. Her chances of finding fulfilment in 'Rome' were doubled: as an expression of her own untutored fantasy and of her relation to Casaubon's great life-work, *The Key to All Mythologies*. Despite its awakening an ancient sense of loss, 'Rome' had promised also to restore childhood intimations that

Dorothea now experiences as non-compensatory and debarring, yet because her self-realization in 'Rome' is invested in its mediation by Casaubon she feels defeated by his literalism, 'the matter-of-course statement and tone of dismissal with which he treated what to her were the most stirring thoughts' (161). She is repelled by his guide-book idiom, 'as of a clergyman reading according to the rubric' (162), which, in drawing attention to the emptying power of language, excites a sensation of disgust rather than trembling receptivity: 'her husband's way of commenting on the strangely impressive objects around them had begun to affect her with a sort of mental shiver' (161). Neil Hertz has written of Casaubon as 'the personification of the dead letter' (78), and certainly the exhibition of 'a mind in which years full of knowledge seem to have issued in a blank absence of interest or sympathy' (162) records a similar stultification to that which initially jolted Wordsworth's traveller in the Cave of Yordas, when a content quite beyond hackneyed reception ('Substance, and shadow, light and darkness, all / Commingled, making up a canopy / Of shapes and forms and tendencies to shape / That shift and vanish, change and interchange / Like spectres, – ferment silent and sublime!', VIII 568–72) suddenly becomes 'Exposed, and lifeless as a written book!' (VIII 576) Dorothea had struggled to interpret Casaubon's limitations as representing his greater knowledge and insight: 'She filled up all the blanks with unmanifested perfections, intrepreting him as she interpreted the works of Providence, and accounting for seeming discords by her own deafness to the higher harmonies' (61). Nevertheless, Dorothea's experience of Rome retains something of its former excess of Casaubon's prosaic closure, a qualified sense of aura, and her passionate release in tears keeps this demand alive, as their traces register the gap between desire and disappointment which Ladislaw waits ready to address in the following chapter: 'However, Dorothea was crying, and if she had been required to state the cause, she could only have done so in . . . general words . . . to have been driven to be more particular would have been like trying to give a history of the light and shadows' (159).

The enlargement of her own sense of 'Rome' would amount to a radical rejection of what Dorothea now sees her husband standing for. She is faced with the discrepancy between the marital piety of having to support her husband's claim to be engaged in heroic intellectual struggle, (prickly in its discouraging attitude to a kind of 'presumption . . . which sees vaguely a great many fine ends, and has not the least notion what it costs to reach them', 164–5), and the awareness that her own conception, which might perhaps all along have been the more powerful, was

being 'scattered in fits of agitation, of struggle, of despondency, and
. . . visions of more complete renunciation, transforming all hard conditions into duty' (163). The studied revisions to the novel's penultimate
paragraph revolve around the definition of a predicament which in the
first edition is described precisely as Dorothea's 'struggling under
prosaic conditions' (707, n.682). Her criticism of Casaubon's 'Rome', in
short, was undergoing an anxiety of influence, as she still feels irksomely
obliged to subdue her divergent reading to his narrow-mindedness: 'in
the midst of her confused thought and passion, the mental act that was
struggling forth into clearness was a self-accusing cry that her feeling of
desolation was the fault of her own spiritual poverty' (ibid.).

   Since Casaubon was certainly failing to measure up to her anticipa-
tions, the question remained whether her disappointment related only
to her husband, or whether the possibilities of 'Rome' as a reflection of
her own separate aspirations were also to be totally undermined, or,
again, whether they might not still be restored in response to the shock
of recognizing her mistake about her husband. At this point in the
novel, Dorothea is undergoing a psychomachia between what 'Rome'
has been reduced to in Casaubon's case, and what she is uneasily
becoming conscious that it has been signifying for herself:

> But now, since they had been in Rome, with all the depths of their
> emotion roused to tumultuous activity, and with life made a new
> problem by new elements, she had been becoming more and more
> aware, with a certain terror, that her mind was continually sliding
> into inward fits of anger and repulsion, or else into forlorn
> weariness . . . What was fresh to her mind was worn out to his; and
> such capacity of thought and feeling as had ever been stimulated in
> him by the general life of mankind had long shrunk to a sort of dried
> preparation, a lifeless embalmment of knowledge.   (161)

What was changing, of course, were not Casaubon's 'forms of expression', but the primacy of *his* reading over the rival interpretations that
Dorothea's own attempt to grasp the aura of 'Rome' were producing:
'But was not Mr Casaubon just as learned as before? Had his forms of
expression changed, or his sentiments become less laudable? . . . And
was not Rome the place in all the world to give free play to such accomplishments?' (160) Overall, the revised reading of 'Rome' which she is
negotiating in this scene may be viewed as the working of the 'veracious imagination', scrutinizing the disjuncture between her anticipation of an idealized fulfilment and her own actual destiny: 'Some

discouragement, some faintness of heart at the new real future which replaces the imaginary, is not unusual' (159). Dorothea's disappointment becomes a process of graduated transformation: 'for that new real future which was replacing the imaginary drew its material from the endless minutiae by which her view of Mr Casaubon and her wifely relation, now that she was married to him, was gradually changing with the secret motion of a watch-hand from what it had been in her maiden dream' (159–60).

Dorothea was anticipating the insight that would come from the shock of the old: the sudden illuminating of interior meaning within pre-established forms of expression. But Eliot's brilliant picture of Dorothea's 'electric shock' from the 'alien world' of the city of Rome does *not* issue in the instant switch to an alternatively fulfilling discourse:

To those who have looked at Rome with the quickening power of a knowledge which breathes a growing soul into all historic shapes, and traces out the suppressed transitions which unite all contrasts, Rome may still be the spiritual centre and interpreter of the world. But let them conceive one more historical contrast: the gigantic broken revelations of that Imperial and Papal city thrust abruptly on the notions of a girl who had been brought up in English and Swiss Puritanism, fed on meagre Protestant histories and on art chiefly of the hand-screen sort ... The weight of unintelligible Rome might lie easily on bright nymphs to whom it formed a background for the brilliant picnic of Anglo-foreign society; but Dorothea had no such defense against deep impressions. Ruins and basilicas, palaces and colossi, set in the midst of a sordid present, where all that was living and warm-blooded seem sunk in the deep degeneracy of a superstition divorced from reverence; the dimmer but yet eager Titanic life gazing on walls and ceilings; the long vistas of white forms whose marble eyes seemed to hold the monotonous light of an alien world: all this vast wreck of ambitious ideals, sensuous and spiritual, mixed confusedly with the breathing forgetfulness and degradation, at first jarred her as with an electric shock, and then urged themselves on her with that ache belonging to a glut of confused ideas which check the flow of emotion ... Our moods are apt to bring with them images which succeed each one like the magic-lantern pictures of a doze; and in certain states of dull forlornness Dorothea all her life continued to see the vastness of St Peter's, the huge bronze canopy, the excited intention in the attitudes and garments of the prophets and evangelists in the mosaics above, and the red drapery which was being hung for Christmas spreading itself everywhere like a disease of the retina.   (158–9)

Dorothea simply has no discourse into which *veraciously* to translate her new experience of the old in 'Rome'. In fact, she is undergoing the impact of two linked shocks: that of Casaubon's desiccating literalism, which challenges the recovery of a lost plenitude, and that of Dorothea's own experience of the disjointed manifold of the great city which so oppressively impairs any coherent apprehension of its aura through which to restore what had preceded the primary fall. For Dorothea, the traumatic passage into the city both rehearses and falls short of restoration by the Wordsworthian imagination. The allusion ('The weight of unintelligible Rome') to the restorative power of Wordsworthian memory in 'Tintern Abbey':

> that blessed mood,
> In which the burden of the mystery,
> In which the heavy and the weary weight
> Of all this unintelligible world
> Is lightened
>
> (37–41)

ruefully denies it to her predicament, though it still calls upon it enough to preclude her admission into the stimulated modernism of her second husband. Two chapters later, Ladislaw is shown to have enjoyed a 'new sense of history' in the 'very miscellaneousness of Rome', 'which made the mind flexible with constant comparison, and saved you from seeing the world's ages as a set of box-like partitions without vital connexion' (174).

When she had encountered Wordsworth in her own youth, Eliot had found him adequately self-reflective: 'I never before met with so many of my own feelings, expressed just as I could like them', but by this point Dorothea's response completely misses the poet's capacity to re-establish his familiar subject-formation in its encounters with the Other. The opening sentence of Eliot's passage above deprecates any emulation of Wordsworth's imaginary passage into London, the 'centre and interpreter of [*his*] world', as described in Book VIII of *The Prelude*:

> London, to thee I willingly return.
>   . . .
> A weight of ages did at once descend
> Upon my heart; no thought embodied, no

Distinct remembrancess, but weight and power, –
Power growing under weight . . .
(532–5, 552–5)

Instead, the *confusion* of her Rome is reminiscent of the 'blank confusion' (722) in 'the picture' (731) of Bartholomew Fair, Wordsworth's image of a disorientating exposure to the 'unmanageable sight' (732) of London, that, like Dorothea's Roman gaze, '[wearies] out the eye' (708) in Book VII of *The Prelude*, with the 'oppression' of its 'perpetual flow' (702).

Throughout the passage, the remotivated impression of Wordsworth's Bartholomew Fair is superimposed on the spectacle created by the restored Wordsworthian imagination that is brought to crucial definition in the Cave of Yordas simile. Whereas Wordsworth's fantasy pageant promises that 'a new quickening shall succeed' (VIII 578), Eliot specifically lays no claim to a 'quickening power' for Dorothea, whose perception of the phantasmagoria is of 'images which succeed each other like the magic-lantern pictures of a doze . . . the vastness of St Peter's, the huge bronze canopy, the excited intention in the attitudes and garments of the prophets and evangelists in the mosaics above'. Though her encounter brings back that cave interior, with its 'canopy / Of shapes and forms and tendencies to shape / That shift and vanish . . . there the shape / Of some gigantic warrior clad in mail, / The ghostly semblance of a hooded monk, / Veiled nun, or pilgrim resting on his staff' (VIII 569–71, 584–7), it only succeeds finally in mirroring the 'vast wreck of ambitious ideals, sensuous and spiritual'. In sum, she can discover no religious or cultural discourse in which to recreate the structure of her expectation, so that the shock of a new domain of experience with its uncoordinated contrasts instead of being revivified by her husband's example is answered only by the continuing reverberation of his literalism. Yet she cannot concede defeat to her expectation, and her changing relation to Casaubon is responsible for the re-insistence of her Wordsworthian expectation as well as the reality of her auraless modern apprehension of Rome. 'Wordsworth' is still at play in the confusion between rebellion and regained reverence in their relationship:

It was too early yet for her fully to recognise or at least admit the change, still more for her to have readjusted that devotedness which was so necessary a part of her mental life that she was almost sure sooner or later to recover it. Permanent rebellion, the disorder of a life without some loving reverent resolve, was not possible to her;

but she was now in an interval when the very force of her nature heightened its confusion.   (160)

Nevertheless, her own subjectivity is being helplessly challenged. The city's rousing dynamics and shameless exhibitionism, as 'the gigantic broken revelations . . . thrust abruptly on [her] notions', and its forms 'took possession of her young sense', offer a rude awakening of consciousness to her linguistic and sexual identity, bringing her to 'strange associations'. In this climax of Book II, 'Old and Young', Dorothea's inner eye, disappointed in its prediction of the Wordsworthian shock of the old that had failed to replace the shock of literalism, has become irreversibly contaminated by the shock of the new.

Unlike Wordsworth in *The Prelude*, Eliot can make no claim for epic equivalence. In the confrontation between puritanical English provincialism and 'Rome', Dorothea becomes just one 'later-born' St Teresa of Avila, who found 'no epic life wherein there was a constant unfolding of far-resonant action' (3). In reality, no plenitudinous discourse was available in middle England around the time of the Great Reform, in circles that were 'still discussing Mr Peel's late conduct on the Catholic question' and unconsciously heading towards 'future gold-fields, and . . . that gorgeous plutocracy which has so nobly exalted the necessities of genteel life' (8). *Middlemarch* imagines such a critical predicament of transition from old to new in which the aura of the past and the shock of the new are suspended with a *veracity* that represents the psycho-social reality rather than feeling it must itself effect an intervention by offering to rediscover that 'epic life':

> With dim lights and tangled circumstance [these later-born Theresas] tried to shape their thought and deed in noble agreement; but after all, to common eyes their struggles seemed mere inconsistency and formlessness; for [they] were helped by no coherent social faith and order which could perform the function of knowledge for the ardently willing soul.   (3)

Robert Kiely has argued that Eliot fell under the influence of Feuerbach's stress on 'the psychological and social power of language' in his 'demysticizing' of 'the Johannine conception of Logos' while at the same time she appreciated that, according to Herbert Spencer, 'certain structures and uses [of language] – especially those having to do with religion – retain elementary links to the past and appear almost exempt from the usual flow' (107). Wordsworth's poetry surely was a case in point. She had been able to recover from her own sudden traumatic loss of faith by rediscovering continuing values in another form of imaginative self-extension, the humanistic religion that allowed her in this way to complete her *magnum opus* as a Victorian 'realist' novel, though similar projects had proved impossible for both Casaubon and Wordsworth. As Eliot implies in *her* 'Prelude' to her great work – a continuing involvement in Dorothea's imagination – 'the incalculably diffusive . . . effect of her being' requires a recognition of inevitable frustrations and limitation as well as continuing longing: 'Here and there is born a Saint Theresa, foundress of nothing, whose loving heart-beats and sobs after an unattained goodness tremble off and are dispersed among hindrances, instead of centering in some long-recognised deed' (4). The various fates of such beings may or may not be deplorable, but that there are such beings remains the most heartening awareness in her own social imagination.

Dorothea's embarrassment is intimately involved in her dawning appreciation that her husband's great work, *The Key to All Mythologies*, (a project of such intellectual hubris that the Eternal City had seemed an appropriate venue in which to consummate their dedication to its composition), is in effect being exposed as odd and recessively pedantic. What impedes Casaubon from entering into the sublime excess of meaning in 'Rome' is something he has in common with Wordsworth: 'a mind weighted with unpublished matter' (163). Weighing most heavily on Wordsworth's mind, of course, was *his* impracticable life-work, *The Recluse*. His feeling of oppressiveness, which Dorothea shares, is radically that of 'unintelligibility', gloriously alleviated on those occasions when a self-reflective register is identified in the Other, so that 'weight' becomes 'power', 'Power growing under weight'. Dorothea's aspiration was to lift that burden, but it could only be lightened by appreciating its impossibility, and simply supporting, believing in, her husband's endeavour effectively added to his load: 'Besides, had not Dorothea's enthusiasm especially dwelt on the prospect of relieving the weight and perhaps the sadness with which great tasks lie on him who has to achieve them? – And that such weight pressed upon Mr Casaubon was only plainer than before' (160).

Like Casaubon, in whose mind Dorothea had found only 'antechambers and winding passages which seemed to lead nowhither' (ibid.), Wordsworth had been capable only of the 'ante-chapel' (*The Prelude*) to his barely commenced 'gothic church' (*PW* V 2). In 1824, Dorothy Wordsworth wrote to Henry Crabb Robinson of the situation throughout the 1820s: 'My brother has not yet looked at the Recluse; he seems

to feel the task so weighty that he shrinks from beginning with it'
(*WL* IV 292). For some time, Mary Wordsworth, shrinking from the
inevitable conclusion about her husband's 'great work', had been
urging Wordsworth to make the final effort, and she saw the Italian
journey of 1837 as a possible stimulus towards that end. In September
1836 she wrote to Crabb Robinson: 'the Poet may leave home with a
perfect holiday before him – &, but, I dare not say so – return to *the
Recluse*; – & let me charge you, not to encourage the Muse to *vagrant*
subjects – but gently recur, upon such indications should they arise, to
Rogers' hint that "jingling *rhyme* does not become a certain age." entre
nous' (*Correspondence of Crabb Robinson*, I 318). Mary's frustration, though
longer seasoned, is in origin not far from Dorothea's unwilling apprehension that the grand ambition is incapable of realization:

> 'And all your notes,' said Dorothea, whose heart had already burned
> within her on this subject, so that now she could not help speaking
> with her tongue. 'All those rows of volumes – will you now not do
> what you used to speak of? – will you not make up your mind what
> part of them you will use, and begin to write the book which will
> make your vast knowledge useful to the world?' (164)

But his tour effectively brought the recognition of defeat home to
Wordsworth himself. By this stage, the philosophical and religious
endeavour of his great poem had begun to appeal to a Catholic cultural
tradition that would have entailed nothing less than the full imaginary
endorsement of 'Rome' which he, unlike Hopkins, barely glimpsed. The
huge recalcitrance of the materials – the weight of the dead letter that
had been repeatedly lifted in the past by such answering registers as
pantheism or nationalism – is easily sensed. Inevitably, it would have
turned out 'lifeless as a written book'.

If Wordsworth had gone to Rome with an implicit agenda for '[mak-
ing] details in the present subservient to more adequate comprehension
of the past', he lacked, as he saw, the discursive energy to translate his
disappointments into a revivifying aura. In the course of the journey,
according to Crabb Robinson, '"I have matter for volumes" he said
once, "Had I but youth to work it up"', and he wrote to his family on
leaving Italy:

> I have, however, to regret that this journey was not made some years
> ago, – to regret it, I mean, as a Poet; for though we have had a great
> disappointment in not seeing Naples, etc., [due to cholera] and more

of the country among the Appenines not far from Rome, Horace's country for instance, and Cicero's Tusculum, my mind has been enriched by innumerable images, which I could have turned to account in verse, and vivified by feelings which earlier in my life would have answered noble purposes, in a way they now are little likely to do. (*LY* II 876)

What had been increasingly wanting for over twenty years had been not the personal ratification of a reactionary poetics: *that* he had fixed on with conviction – but a cultural discourse in which what he remembered could find contemporaneous expression. Only so equipped could he produce a work powerful enough the subdue the shock of industrialized democracy which had re-opened the suture of organic nationalism that he had successfully stitched over the wound of the revolution. In May 1838, in the course of composing the poems that made up the Italian *Memorials*, he turned 'very decidedly' to George Ticknor, the Harvard professor whom Mary had also commissioned to urge the poem's completion, and said: 'Why did not Gray finish the long poem he began on a similar subject? because he found he had undertaken something beyond his powers to accomplish. And that is my case.'[22]

Notes

Notes to the Introduction

1. 'The Old Cumberland Beggar', 153. Unless otherwise noted (when individual volumes from the so far incompete *Cornell Wordsworth*, general editor Stephen Parrish, are cited by editor), all quotations from Wordsworth's poetry other than *The Prelude* are taken from the complete standard edition, *PW*. Further references parenthetically in the text give titles and line numbers only, and other materials from that edition are given with volume and page numbers.
2. *The Monthly Review*, 29 (June 1799). Quoted in Elsie Smith, 37.
3. 'The Pedlar', MS. E, *The Ruined Cottage and The Pedlar*, ed. Butler, 410: 328–9. See T. S. Eliot, 54.
4. X, 870–78. All references to *The Prelude* are to the 1805 version in *Prel*, unless other versions from the same edition are indicated as *1799* or *1850*. Further references parenthetically in the text are to book and line numbers only, and additional materials from that edition are given with page numbers.
5. *Specimens of the Table Talk of the Late Samuel Taylor Coleridge* (2 vols, London, 1835), II 71–2.
6. Barron Field's *Memoirs*, quoted by de Selincourt, *PW* V, 412–13.
7. 'Of the Pathetic Fallacy', *Works* V 210.
8. See Chapter 5, n. 11, below for Ruskin's comments in 'Fiction, Fair and Foul'. For an account of Ruskin's increasing exasperation with Wordsworthian consolations, see my 'In Wordsworth's Shadow: Ruskin and Neo-Romantic Ecologies'.
9. The contours of Coleridge's blueprint for triumph out of destruction are those reflected in the American tradition of *Prelude* criticism founded in M. H. Abrams's application of Hegelian dialectic, deriving consciousness from negation. This philosophical transformation of 'internalization' and the related crisis-recovery paradigm promoted by Harold Bloom and Geoffrey Hartman are neatly summarized by Geraldine Friedman, 66. Unlike Friedman, however, I see this scheme as homologized in the workings of Wordsworthian language and history rather than subverted by them.
10. 'Stanzas in Memory of the Author of "Obermann"', 53–4. All parenthetical Arnold quotations are from *Matthew Arnold*, 1986.
11. Reprinted from the *North British Review*, August 1850.
12. 'Frost at Midnight', 74. All parenthetical references to Coleridge's poetry in the text are from *PSTC* II.
13. See my essay, 'Crossings Out: The Problem of Textual Passage in *The Prelude*', for a detailed expansion of this reading.
14. *The Unremarkable Wordsworth*, xxvi.
15. Preface to *Lyrical Ballads*, *Prose* I 138. All quotations from Wordsworth's prose are taken from the complete standard edition, *Prose*. Further references parenthetically in the text give volume and page numbers.

16. Rieder has recently emphasized this growing primacy of Wordsworth's translation of a fantasy of community into literature.
17. De Selincourt's word. See *PW* I vi.
18. R. P. Graves in his *Recollections*, quoted by Batho, 38.
19. For an extensive positioning of my argument in relation to ideology and New Historicist approaches, see my discussion of Jerome McGann, David Simpson, Marjorie Levinson and Alan Liu in 'Wordsworth's Revolution in Poetic Language'.
20. My own application of Lacan to Wordsworth has benefited from contrasting it with those of Robert Young and Jonathan Culler.
21. It is suggestive to speculate about the complicating effect of Dorothy Wordsworth's birth on her brother's relation to his mother when he was twenty months old and may be supposed to be just emerging from the mirror stage.
22. See Leavy, 10. Principal Lacanian terms that are used throughout appear in inverted commas on first use in the text.
23. See Heffernan on water-reflections, 205–6.
24. See Lacan's *Seminar I*, discussed by Roudinesco, 284.
25. Seminar X, 5 December 1962, ibid., 53.
26. Indeed, Beer (1989) argues that 'while Coleridge is drawn to images of reflection, Wordsworth distrusts it' (26).
27. See Bakhtin's *The Dialogic Imagination* and Bialostosky's comprehensive application to Wordsworth's poetry and its reception.
28. 'Discipline' is used in the Foucauldian sense throughout. 'Discourse' is similarly intended throughout in its Foucauldian application as a definable system of material activities, though it is part of my argument that Wordsworth's poetic language is purposefully engaged in the attempt to represent itself as culturally materialist, which may occasionally give rise to what is a thematic ambiguity between language and discourse. The term 'register' refers to a distinct genre or category of writing.
29. Jameson, 187.
30. See Bruce Fink, 49–51, for a lucid explanation of the relationship between alienation and separation in Lacan's thought.
31. Fenwick note in *The Prose Works*, ed. Grosart, III 16–17.
32. For this trajectory, see Chandler, 1984.
33. Raymond Williams's term, 48.
34. See Fulford and Kitson (eds), for the by then manifestly 'sinister undercurrent' of Wordsworth's vision of Albion in *The Excursion* (4).

Notes to Chapter 1: The Spectral Mother

1. Saturday, 15 December, No. 267; quoted by Legg, 259.
2. *The White Doe of Rylstone, or, The Fate of the Nortons*, ed. Dugas, 5.
3. Ed. Johnson and Grant, 32: 2, 5–6.
4. For an extended discussion of this painting in relation to Wordsworth's revolutionary aesthetics, see the section on 'The Beauty of the Revolution' in Liu, 366–73. If it is true, as Liu argues, that Wordsworth in 1791 misread the revolution in the sentimental beauty of this painting, it nevertheless

remained there, in the past, to support the structure by which Wordsworth would eventually come to view the containment of *his own* revolutionary involvement.

5. I am quoting, until indicated in the text, from the first version of 1803 taken from Page's reconstruction (based on Curtis's notes in *Poems, in Two Volumes*, 68). I am generally indebted to Page's discussion of this poem.

6. *Hamlet*, III.i.1017. All quotations from Shakespeare, unless otherwise indicated, are taken from *S* throughout, and referred by page. The copy referred to is kept at the Wordsworth Library, Grasmere, and is probably that listed by Chester L. and Alice C. Shaver as included in Dora Wordsworth's catalogue of books at Rydal Mount (232). It belonged to three of Wordsworth's grandsons by his son John. An inscription at the front states, following their names:

given
by their Grandfather
William Wordsworth
Rydal Mount
25th Janry 1846

Later in the book another inscription reads : 'This copy of Shakespeare's plays belonged to the poet Wordsworth when a schoolboy at Hawkshead. He gave it to me when I first went to school in 1846. W[illiam] Wordsworth [grandson], Elphinstone Coll., Bombay. 1883.' Though the date of publication precludes its use during Wordsworth's schooldays, it does seem to be the only substantial edition of Shakespeare that Wordsworth may have consistently known early, and for that reason, though the text is occasionally censored to avoid blasphemous expressions, I quote from it throughout as a possible source of this key intertextuality.

7. *Peter Bell the Third*, Pt IV, 51–5; *Works*, III 271.

8. But see Haigwood, who argues otherwise.

9. A suggestion made by Hartman in 1967, and developed by Weiskel when he describes the confrontation with literalism: 'The dynamic ends in a limited zone between image and signifier, with images that seem to portend a meaning that they withhold. In other words, they appear as signifiers without signifieds' (174–5).

10. See Burke's 'reverence' for the British 'world of reason, and order, and peace, and virtue' opposed to 'those . . . who are prompt rashly to hack [their] aged parent to pieces', in *Reflections*, 195 and 194.

11. See the account in the *Town and Country Magazine*, December 1772; quoted by Owen, 293–4.

12. In his letter to Edward Quillinan, quoted by Battiscombe, 204.

13. Barrell makes a detailed examination of the classical precedents and textual variants. His argument that the poem reveals an early Victorian insecurity behind the kind of masculinity ostensibly portrayed provides a contextual extension of what I am here viewing rather as a personalized technique of self-disciplining.

14. To John Wordsworth, within a letter to his brother Christopher (*WL* V 215–16). Barrell repeats the Cornell editor's error that this letter was addressed to Wordworth's 'son', John: see *Shorter Poems*, ed. Ketcham, 530.

15. That Wordsworth was alive to the association of the oracle's commands for the sacifices of both Protesilaus and Iphigenia is evident from his letter to De Quincey, *c.* 5 Feb. 1815, where he explains a temporary alteration as designed to distinguish between the two conditions (*WL* III 194).
16. *Euripides*, I 145:1552–6.
17. From his *Diary*, quoted in *Shorter Poems*, ed. Ketcham, 530.

Notes to Chapter 2: The Elided Father

1. IV 52; *Poetical Works*, ed. Carey and Fowler, 611.
2. The explanatory note in *S* reads: 'ie in a shape or form capable of being conversed with. *To question*, certainly, in our author's time signified "to converse".'
3. Preface to *The Excursion*; *PW* V 1.
4. See Freud's 'Group Psychology and the Analysis of the Ego' (1921), in 1955, 134–43. Among many interpreters of Kristeva's work I have found Oliver particularly helpful, and I am specifically indebted to her exploration of the idea of the imaginary father.
5. The story is told by Wordsworth's brother, Christopher, in his notebook which also includes entries by William himself. See Z. S. Fink, 88–9.
6. MS E, 172–5; *The Ruined Cottage and the Pedlar*, ed. Butler, 396.
7. Though Beattie never fulfilled his early promise, he enjoyed a considerable reputation at the time he influenced Wordsworth, and was 'the leading poet and philosopher' in the Scottish Age of Improvement movement: see King, 124.
8. This phrase is used by a critical commentator in the 1819 edition, 5.
9. Several features which are dispersed throughout 'The Vale' are drawn together in a sonnet Wordsworth wrote *c.* October 1787 as a farewell to the Lakes when he was about to leave for Cambridge. The poem, 'What is it tells my soul the Sun is setting?', addresses a governing female presence as 'Spirit of these / Mountains ... throned on Helvellyn'; describes her as 'wrapped in mist' and emitting light from a 'taper that twinkling in the / cottage casts a wan shadow over the [lake?]'; and adjures her to 'nod / me thrice farewell, farewell[,] farewell':

> [For?] no more shall the ghosts leaning from
> The [?] from the [howling of the wind?]
> listen while thou instructed me in [thy?] law
> Of [Nature?].
> (*Poems* I, ed. Hayden, 67)

Landon also quotes early MS verses where the painful and violent effects of 'the various Lyre' of nature are resolved in harmony. She refers to passages in John Dyer's and William Gilpin's *Lake District Observations*, where the 'terrific harmony' of the lyre of nature is evoked (370).

10. *Salisbury Plain, The Salisbury Plain Poems*, ed. Gill, 24: 91–5.
11. See Oliver, 41.
12. See Bronfen, 1992 and 1995.
13. See Homans's chapter, 'Eliot, Wordsworth, and the Scenes of the Sisters' Instruction', in 1986.

14. A similar kind of argument extends through the three chapters (by Alan Richardson, Marlon B. Ross and Kurt Heinzelman) in the 'Silencing the Female' section of Mellor's 1988 essay collection.
15. Significantly, as Page has argued, it was in the Preface to *Lyrical Ballads* (1800), and against the grain of his previous poetry, that Wordsworth first 'distanced himself from the feminine and from the women writers who may have influenced him' (54).
16. Women readers in particular have responded variously to this construction. Elizabeth Barrett Browning's sonnet 'On a Portrait of Wordsworth by R. B. Haydon', despite hinted ambiguities, fixes admiringly on an image of powerful solipsism: '*He*, with forehead bowed / And humble-lidded eyes, as one inclined / Before the sovran thought of his own mind, / And very meek with inspirations proud – / Takes here his rightful place as poet-priest / By the high-altar, singing prayer and prayer / To the higher Heavens' (418).
17. Page suggest that Wordsworth's sensitivity to the charge of unmanliness, especially by Jeffrey, contributed to his reluctance to publish *The White Doe*; see 102.
18. For the debate over whether androgyny is necessarily sexist, see the bibliography in Hoeveler's *Romantic Androgyny*, xix, n. 7. The position I am applying to Wordsworth is broadly that developed from Virginia Woolf by Toril Moi in her introduction to 1985, 14–15.
19. See Oliver: 'The identification with the imaginary father allows an identification with the paternal function as it already exists in the mother. This identification allows the child to abject its mother's body and separate from her. The separation is not tragic, because it is supported by the imaginary father, which is the mother's love itself' (79). Toril Moi explains that he is 'understood as the mother's desire of the phallus, who intervenes crucially at the fourth month of the child's life in order to effectuate the first, preliminary split within the void of primary narcissism' (1986, 12).
20. Nancy A. Jones has mounted a related argument about the male 'pastourelle' poet of 'A Solitary Reaper' who 'cannot fully disguise the fact that his poetic tribute to a solitary peasant songstress originates in a displaced but nonetheless intense desire to assert his power over her, and this remains a form of violation' (274). The issue is one about the nature of the 'violence' that Wordsworth uses to bring the reaper into imaginary relation with himself. I am suggesting that Wordsworth, from the developed position of his ideal ego, is attempting rather to bring himself into relation with a reciprocal positioning, reawakened in himself by the semiotic call of her singing in a Gaelic language that is unintelligible on a literal level, yet that still speaks to and for him.
21. From Wordsworth's modernized extract from his *Poems and Extracts* (1905), 10–11: 33–42; emphasis added.

Notes to Chapter 3: Describing the Revolution

1. In 'Was ist Aufklärung?', quoted in Paulson, 9.
2. Quoted by Small in Crossley and Small, xi.

3. The editors of *Prel* suggest these probably included the best-known responses to Burke's *Reflections*: Paine's *Rights of Man*, Part I, and Mackintosh's *Vindiciae Gallicae*, both 1791.
4. This was, of course, the general mood in which British radicals greeted the Revolution. Even Pitt himself hoped that the 'present convulsions' would end in 'general harmony and regular order' (Quoted by Woodcock, 6).
5. See Richardson, 112–27, for the conservative status of fairy-tales in the literary debate.
6. See Arthur Young's entry for 30 May 1787, 15.
7. See 'the chivalry of England', 2 *Henry IV*, II.iii.483. Compare also Burke: 'But the age of chivalry is gone ... and the glory of Europe is extinguished for ever' (*Reflections*, 170).
8. See Moorman, I 174–5.
9. See *Prel*, 334, n. 7, which points out that Beaupuy in fact 'lived to play a part in the wars of conquest which turned the Republic into an imperialist power'.
10. See Schama, 584.
11. Geraldine Friedman notes that the French 'carrousel' 'names the square after the rounds of military exercises regularly held on it' and that it is also another French word for 'manage' (75). The passage also appeals to a pre-established rhetoric of checked political authority. Schama writes that

> Since the days of the great riding instructor Pluvinel in the reign of Henri IV, the mastery of equitation had been both metaphor and a literal preparation for the exercise of public power. From Richelieu onwards a succession of rulers had learned through the didactic parallel between horsemanship and statesmanship the importance of self-control, the breaking of spirit and the display of authority. (27)

12. W. H. White was the first seriously to question that reading. Cobban's is the classic account of Wordsworth's political trajectory.
13. Certainly Wordsworth's remarks on an enlightened tyranny, as he saw its role in the aftermath of the September massacres, reveal his desire for highly centralized government, when required, to guide the moderate populist Revolution amid the tide of anarchy:

> not doubting at that time
> . . .
> But that the virtue of one paramount mind
> Would have abashed those impious crests, have quelled
> Outrage and bloody power, and . . .
> . . .
> Have cleared a passage for just government.
>   (X 178–85)

14. See Johnston's so far exhaustive investigation in his Chapter 15, 'A Return to France?'
15. I am indebted generally to Roe's analysis of the same passages in his Chapter 6, and particularly to his consideration of Robespierre's execution.

Roe argues that this identification with Robespierre resulted in Wordsworth's 'own ineluctable responsibility for the Terror' (41).

16. See Kershaw, 115.
17. Loustalot, *Révolutions de Paris*, quoted in Schama, 446.
18. For a later conservative diagnosis of the revolution in similar terms, see Scruton: 'Like the doctrine of "full communism", it had no other meaning than to license destruction of existing things: it was not so much a system of belief as a system of unbelief, a means to the delegitimization of rival powers, and to the undoing of true commitments' (194).
19. These expressions militate against Johnston's suspicions that Wordsworth was himself up to the neck in those operations.
20. Godwin saw this danger just as clearly as Burke, who wrote in his 'Preface to the Address of M. Brissot' (1794): 'Things are never called by their proper names. Massacre is sometimes *agitation*, sometimes *effervescence*, sometimes *excess*; sometimes too continued an exercise of *revolutionary power*' (quoted by Paulson, 15). It was, after all, Godwin whom Coleridge, wondering 'Is *thinking* impossible without arbitrary signs?', wished 'to write a book on the power of words, and the processes by which human feelings form affinities with them'. He believed they both were interested in '(destroying) the old antithesis of *Words & Things*, elevating, as it were, words into Things, & living Things too' (*LSTC*, I 352, 625–6).
21. *The Borderers*, ed. Osborne, 216.; early version, 1797–9: III v 81–4.
22. '*The Ruined Cottage' and 'The Pedlar'*, ed. Butler, 75: 521–2.
23. See Woodcock, 12.

Notes to Chapter 4: Changing Spots

1. Hazlitt was to quote Shenstone's opinion that 'poets are Tories by nature, supposing them to be by nature poets' as the epigraph to a later essay for *The Liberal*, 'On the Spirit of Monarchy', January 1823 (*H* IX 255).
2. During 1810 or 1811. For De Quincey's access to *The Prelude* and his full-length quotations from it, see Lindop, 187. Lindop speculates persuasively that De Quincey may have made 'his own secret copy, recognizing the work as a masterpeice and seeing no prospect of its early publication' (ibid.).
3. See Ernest Jones and Lacan's 'Desire and Interpretation of Desire in *Hamlet*'.
4. In the 'Essay, Supplementary to the Preface' (1815), Wordsworth had made the sweeping, and to Coleridge ungenerous, generalization that 'The Germans only, of foreign nations, are approaching towards a knowledge and feeling of what [Shakespeare] is. In some respects they have acquired a superiority over the fellow-countrymen of the Poet' in – and here Wordsworth's meaning is imprecise – appreciating his judgement and unifying art, though he does not state that such an appreciation is unprecedented in England, only that he hopes the German view will become 'universally acknowledged' (*Prose* III 69).
5. For a clarification of this issue from Coleridge's viewpoint, see Foakes (ed.), *Lectures, 1808–1819*, lix–lxiv.
6. See Kucich, 21–3.
7. See particularly his letter to J. H. Reynolds, ed. Rollins I 223–5.

8. Chase (ed.). See Jacobus's account of the use of *Samson Agonistes* here introduced: 122–7.
9. See his discussion of '*A LITTLE onward lend thy guiding hand*' in 1987, 125–8.
10. A phrase from a contemporary *poissarde* quoted in Schama, 461.
11. See Owen, 297–8.
12. *Don Juan*, III 893–4; McGann (ed.), 516.
13. Holinshed, 95.
14. de Selincourt and Darbishire (eds), 370: 70–82n; emphasis added.
15. My approach to Wordsworth's poetic discourse parallels that of Stephen Greenblatt's reading of *1 Henry IV* in his essay 'Invisible Bullets', pp. 21–65. In telling the story of *his* revolution as that of Hal's reformation, Wordsworth can represent his own revolutionary phase as part of a programme that allowed him to incorporate and control another discourse by giving it vent.
16. For an account of Wordsworth's critical opinions on the European settlements and the Alliance, see Batho, 134–49.
17. Ostensibly the picture of famous parliamentarians is taken from Wordsworth's early stay in London in the 1790s, but many details of the London panorama belong to subsequent visits, particularly that made with Charles Lamb in 1802 shortly before Dorothy probably read *Henry V* to Wordsworth in the orchard at Grasmere. See Dorothy Wordsworth's *Journals*, 8 May 1802; I 145.
18. The history of the 'Shepherd-lord' (170), Henry Lord Clifford, recounted in 'Song at the Feast of Brougham Castle', 1806, and Wordsworth's long note of 1807, offers a consummate historical version of Wordsworthian restoration set at the end of the Wars of the Roses. Henry expiates his father's crime of killing the youthful son of the Duke of York and comes into his estate to forego violence and rebuild the family's castles.
19. Dodsworth (ed.), 118.

Notes to Chapter 5: The Shock of the Old

1. Gill points out that Hopkins must have gained his knowledge of Lord Selbourne's address of 9 July 1886 from newspaper reports: 1998, 6.
2. Arnold, 'Address to the Wordsworth Society', ed. Super, 133.
3. Fenwick note, *PW* IV 463.
4. 'Memorial Verses', 39: 48–9.
5. The word 'conversion' recurs throughout this book in relation to the effect that the poetry had, particularly on such diverse Victorian readers as 'Mark Rutherford', John Stuart Mill and William Charles Macready, who all used it to express their reactions to Wordsworth. See Gill, 1998, 40–80. The spiritual conversion narrated in 'Peter Bell' clearly prefigured a narrower evangelical reception.
6. 'Poetry and the Microphone', *Collected Essays*, II 332.
7. 'As I Please', ibid., III 103. See also 'Arthur Koestler', III 243–4.
8. See 'The English People', ibid., III 7.
9. See Orwell's review of Edmund Blunden's *Cricket Country*, ibid., III 47.
10. XXXIV 318.
11. See my 'In Wordsworth's Shadow', 204, 222–3.
12. Ensor, 99.

13. See Norman White, 431.
14. *1850* is quoted throughout this chapter, as the edition read by the English writers discussed in this chapter.
15. Peek, 103.
16. After his Italian tour, Wordsworth returned to this process of revision in the final transcription, MS E of 1838 / 9.
17. See Sara Coleridge, I 117.
18. See Gill, 1998, 70–80.
19. 'Defense of Poetry', 508.
20. 'The Pedlar', ed. Jonathan Wordsworth, 1969, 179: 218.
21. See 1992, 242–6.
22. Hillard, II 167. Gray's reason for leaving his philosophical poem, 'The Alliance of Education and Government', in a fragmentary state resonates with Wordsworth's family's fears that their poet had become habituated to polishing short lyrical poems. See Ketton-Cremer, 91.

Works Cited

Ariès, Philippe, *The Hour of Our Death*, trans. Helen Weaver (London, 1981).

Armistead, Wilson, *Tales and Legends of the English Lakes* (London and Glasgow, 1891).

Arnold, Matthew, *Matthew Arnold: Philistinism in England and America*, ed. R. H. Super (Ann Arbor, 1974).

——, *Matthew Arnold*, Oxford Authors, ed. Miriam Allott and Robert H. Super (Oxford, 1986).

Ashby, Godfrey, *Sacrifice, Its Nature and Purpose* (London, 1988).

Bakhtin, Mikhail M., *The Dialogic Imagination: Four Essays*, ed. Michael Holquist, trans. Caryl Emerson and Michael Holquist (Austin, TX, 1981).

Barrell, John, '"Laodamia" and the Moaning of Mary', *Textual Practice*, 10: 3 (Winter 1966).

Bate, Jonathan, *Shakespeare and the English Romantic Imagination* (Oxford, 1989).

——, *Shakespearean Constitutions: Politics, Theatre, Criticism, 1720–1830* (Oxford, 1989).

—— (ed.), *Romantics on Shakespeare* (Harmondsworth, 1992).

Bateson, F. W., *Wordsworth: A Reinterpretation*, 2nd edn (London, 1956).

Batho, Edith, *The Later Wordsworth* (Cambridge, 1933).

Battiscombe, Georgina, *Reluctant Pioneer: The Life of Elizabeth Wordsworth* (London, 1978).

Beattie, James, *The Minstrel; or the Progress of Genius and Other Poems* (London, 1819).

Beer, John, 'Coleridge and Wordsworth on Reflection', *The Wordsworth Circle*, 20: 1 (Winter 1989).

Benjamin, Walter, *Illuminations*, ed. Hannah Arendt, trans. Harry Zohn (London, 1992).

Berger, Harry, Jr, *Making Trifles of Terrors: Redistributing Complicities in Shakespeare* (Stanford, CA, 1997).

Bialostosky, Don H., *Wordsworth, Dialogics and the Practice of Criticism* (Cambridge, 1992).

Blake, William, *Blake's Poetry and Designs*, ed. Mary Lynn Johnson and John E. Grant (New York and London, 1979).

Blakemore, Steven, *Burke and the Fall of Language: The French Revolution as Linguistic Event* (Hanover, NH, 1988).

Blanshard, Francis, *Portraits of Wordsworth* (London, 1959).

Bloom, Harold, *The Anxiety of Influence: A Theory of Poetry* (New York, 1973).

Boose, Lynda, 'The Father's House and the Daughter in It: the Structures of Western Culture's Daughter–Father Relationship', in *Daughters and Fathers*, ed. Betty Flowers and Lynda Boose (Baltimore, MD, 1989).

Bromwich, David, *Disowned by Memory: Wordsworth's Poetry of the 1790s* (Chicago and London, 1998).

Bronfen, Elisabeth, *Over Her Dead Body: Death, Femininity and the Aesthetic* (Manchester, 1992).

——, '"Jerusalem was the omphalos of mortality": Gender and Thomas De Quincey's Hysteric Phantasies', in *Romanticism, Theory, Gender, News from Nowhere: Theory and Politics of Romanticism*, ed. Tony Pinkney, Keith Hanley and Fred Botting (Keele, 1995).

Browning, Elizabeth Barrett, *The Poems of Elizabeth Barrett Browning* (London, 1893).

Bulmer, T. F., *History, Topography and Directory of East Cumberland* (Manchester, 1884).

Burke, Edmund, *Speeches and Letters on American Affairs* (London, 1961).

——, *Reflections on the Revolution in France*, ed. Conor Cruise O'Brien (London, 1988).

Burn, Richard, *The Ecclesiastical Law*, 4 vols (London, 1842).

Byatt, A. S., *Wordsworth and Coleridge in Their Time* (London, 1970).

Byron, George Gordon, *Byron*, Oxford Authors, ed. Jerome J. McGann (Oxford, 1986).

Carlyle, Thomas, *The French Revolution*, ed. K. J. Fielding and David Sorensen, 2 vols (Oxford and New York, 1989).

——, *Reminiscences*, ed. James Anthony Froude, 2 vols (London, 1881).

Carroll, David, *George Eliot and the Conflict of Interpretations: A Reading of the Novels* (Cambridge, 1992).

Castle, Terry, 'The Spectralization of the Other in *The Mysteries of Udolpho*', in *The New Eighteenth Century: Theory, Politics, English Literature*, ed. Felicity Nussbaum and Laura Brown (New York and London, 1987).

Chandler, James K., *Wordsworth's Second Nature: A Study of the Poetry and Politics* (Chicago and London, 1984).

——, *England in 1819: The Politics of Literary Culture and the Case of Romantic Historicism* (Chicago and London, 1998).

Chase, Cynthia, *Romanticism* (Harlow, 1993).

Cobban, Alfred, 'Wordsworth and Nationality', in his *Edmund Burke and the Revolt against the Eighteenth Century: A Study of the Political and Social Thinking of Burke, Wordsworth, Coleridge and Southey* (London, 1929).

Coleridge, Samuel Taylor, *Specimens of the Table Talk of the Late Samuel Taylor Coleridge*, 2 vols (London, 1835).

——, *The Complete Poetical Works of Samuel Taylor Coleridge*, ed. Ernest Hartley Coleridge, 2 vols (Oxford, 1912).

——, *Collected Letters of Samuel Taylor Coleridge*, ed. Earl Leslie Griggs, 6 vols (Oxford and New York, 1956–71).

——, *Biographia Literaria*, ed. James Englell and W. Jackson Bate (Princeton, NJ, 1984); vol. 7 of *The Collected Works of Samuel Taylor Coleridge*, gen. ed. Kathleen Coburn, Bollingen Series LXXV (London and Princeton, 1969–).

——, *Lectures 1808–1819 On Literature*, ed. R. A. Foakes, 2 vols (London and Princeton, 1987); vol. 5 of *The Collected Works*.

——, *Table Talk*, ed. Carl Woodring, 2 vols (London and Princeton, 1990); vol. 14 of *The Collected Works*.

Coleridge, Sara, *Sara Coleridge, Memoirs and Letters*, ed. Edith Coleridge, 2 vols (London, 1873).

Cowper, Henry Swainson, *Hawkshead (the Northernmost Parish of Lancashire): Its History, Archaeology, Industries, Folklore, Dialect, Etc., Etc.* (London, 1899).

Crossley, Ceri and Ian Small (eds), *The French Revolution and British Culture* (Oxford, 1989).

Culler, Jonathan, 'The Mirror Stage', *High Romantic Argument*, ed. L. Lipking (Cornell, NY, 1981).

De Quincey, Thomas, *The Complete Works of Thomas De Quincey*, 3rd edn, ed. David Masson, 16 vols (Edinburgh, 1862–71).

Digby, Kenelm, *The Broadstone of Honour: or, Rules for the Gentlemen of England* (London, 1822).

Doyle, Arthur Conan, *The Adventures of Sherlock Holmes* (London, 1895).

Dryden, John, *The Works of Virgil in English*, ed. William Frost (1987); vol. 5 of *The Works of John Dryden*, ed. Alan Roper and H. T. Swedenberg (Berkeley, CA, 1956–).

Easthope, Antony, *Wordsworth Now and Then* (Buckingham and Philadelphia, 1993).

Eliot, George, *Essays and Leaves from a Note-book of George Eliot* (Edinburgh and London, 1884).

——, *The George Eliot Letters*, ed. Gordon S. Haight, 9 vols (Oxford, 1954–78).

——, *Middlemarch*, World's Classics, ed. David Carroll (Oxford, 1988).

——, *Felix Holt, the Radical*, ed. Linda Mugglestone (Harmondsworth, 1995).

Eliot, T. S., 'Tradition and the Individual Talent', in *The Sacred Wood: Essays on Poetry and Criticism* (London, 1960).

Engels, Friedrich, *Condition of the Working Class in England: from Personal Observation and Authentic Sources* (Moscow, 1973).

Ensor, R. C. K., *England, 1870–1914* (Oxford, 1936).

Euripides, *Works*, Loeb Classics Library, trans. Arthur S. Way, 4 vols (London, 1916).

Fink, Bruce, *The Lacanian Subject: Between Language and Jouissance* (Princeton, NJ, 1995).

Fink, Z. S., *The Early Wordsworthian Milieu* (Oxford, 1958).

Fletcher, Pauline and Murphy, John (eds), *Wordsworth in Context* (Lewisburg, PA, 1992).

Foucault, Michel, *The Order of Things: An Archaeology of the Human Sciences* (New York, 1971).

——, *Discipline and Punish*, trans. Alan Sheridan (New York, 1979).

——, 'Nietzsche, Genealogy, History', in *The Foucault Reader*, ed. P. Rabinow (Harmondsworth, 1984).

Ffrench, Yvonne, *News from the Past* (London, n.d.).

Freud, Sigmund, *Beyond the Pleasure Principle: Group Psychology and Other Works* (London, 1955); vol. 18 of *The Complete Psychological Works*, trans. James Strachey, 24 vols (London, 1953–74).

——, *Psychopathic Characters on the Stage* (London, 1960).

——, *On the Pleasure Principle* (London, 1961).

Friedman, Geraldine, *The Insistence of History: Revolution in Burke, Wordsworth, Keats, and Baudelaire* (Stanford, CA, 1996).

Friedman, Michael, *The Making of a Tory Humanist: William Wordsworth and the Idea of Community* (New York, 1979).

Fulford, Tim and Peter J. Kitson (eds), *Romanticism and Empire, 1780–1830* (Cambridge, 1998).

Furet, François, *Penser la Révolution française* (Paris, 1978).

Garber, Marjorie, *Shakespeare's Ghost Writers: Literature as Uncanny Causality* (London, 1987).

Gill, Stephen, *William Wordsworth: A Life* (Oxford, 1989).

——, *Wordsworth and the Victorians* (Oxford, 1998).

Godwin, William, *Enquiry Concerning Political Justice* (Harmondsworth, 1985).

Greenblatt, Stephen, *Shakespearean Negotiations: The Circulation of Social Energy in Renaissance England* (Berkeley, CA, 1988).

Greer, Germaine, 'Wordsworth and Winchelsea: the Progress of an Error', in *The Nature of Identity: Essays Presented to Donald E. Hayden by the Graduate Faculty of Modern Letters* (Tulsa, 1981).

Haigwood, Laura, 'Oedipal Revolution in *Lyrical Ballads*' in *Wordsworth and the Modern World*, ed. A. C. Goodson, *Centennial Review*, Special Issue, 33: 4 (Fall 1989).

Hanley, Keith, 'Crossings Out: the Problem of Textual Passage in *The Prelude*', in *Romantic Revisions*, ed. Robert Brinkley and Keith Hanley (Cambridge, 1991).

——, 'In Wordsworth's Shadow: Ruskin and Neo-Romantic Ecologies', in *Influence and Resistance in Nineteenth-Century English Poetry*, ed. G. Kim Blank and Margot K. Louis (Basingstoke, 1993).

——, *An Annotated Critical Bibliography of William Wordsworth* (Hemel Hempstead, 1995).

——, 'Wordsworth's Revolution in Poetic Language', *Romanticism on the Net*, 9 (Feb. 1998), ed. Nicola Trott and Seamus Perry.

Hare, Augustus J. C., *Memorials of a Quiet Life*, 2 vols (London, 1873).

Harper, G. M., *Wordsworth's French Daughter* (Princeton, NJ, 1921).

Harris, R. W., *Romanticism and the Social Order, 1780–1830* (London, 1969).

Hartman, Geoffrey, 'Wordsworth, Inscriptions, and Romantic Nature Poetry', in *From Sensibility to Romanticism: Essays Presented to Frederick A. Pottle*, ed. Frederick W. Hilles and Harold Bloom (New York, 1965).

——, *The Unremarkable Wordsworth* (London, 1987).

Hazlitt, William, *The Works of William Hazlitt*, ed. P. P. Howe, 21 vols (1930–4).

Heffernan, James, *The Re-Creation of the Landscape: A Study of Wordsworth, Coleridge, Constable, and Turner* (Hanover, NH, and London, 1984).

Herz, Neil, 'Recognizing Casaubon', in *The End of the Line: Essays on Psychoanalysis and the Sublime* (New York, 1985).

Hill, Geoffrey, *The Lords of Limit: Essays on Literature and Ideas* (London, 1984).

Hillard, G. S. (ed.), *Life, Letters, and Journals of George Ticknor*, 2 vols (Boston and New York, 1909).

Hoeveler, Diane Long, *Romantic Androgyny: The Women Within* (University Park and London, 1990).

Holinshed, Ralph, *Holinshed's Chronicles*, ed. R. S. Wallace and Alma Hansen (Oxford, 1917).

Homans, Margaret, *Bearing the Word: Language and Female Experience in Nineteenth-Century Women's Writing* (Chicago, IL, 1980).

Hopkins, G. M., *The Correspondence of G. M. Hopkins and R. W. Dixon*, ed. Claude Colleer Abbott (London, 1935).

——, *Further Letters of Gerard Manley Hopkins*, ed. C. C. Abbott, rev. and enlarged (London, 1956).

Hunt, Lynn, *Politics, Culture, and Class in the French Revolution* (London, 1986).

Jacobus, Mary, *Romanticism, Writing and Sexual Difference: Essays on 'The Prelude'* (Oxford, 1989).

Jameson, Frederic, *Postmodernism, or, The Cultural Logic of Late Capitalism* (London, 1991).

Johnston, Kenneth R., *The Hidden Wordsworth: Poet, Lover, Rebel, Spy* (New York and London, 1998).

Jones, Ernest, *Hamlet and Oedipus* (London, 1949).

Jones, Nancy A., 'The Rape of the Rural Muse: Wordsworth's "The Solitary Reaper" as a Version of Pastourelle', in *Rape and Representation*, ed. Lynn A. Higgins and Brenda R. Silver (New York, 1991).

Keats, John, *The Letters of John Keats*, ed. Hyder Edward Rollins, 2 vols (Cambridge, 1958).

Kershaw, Alister, *A History of the Guillotine* (London, 1958).

Ketton-Cremer, R. W., *Thomas Gray: A Biography* (Cambridge, 1955).

Kiely, Robert, 'The Limits of Dialogue in *Middlemarch*', in *The Worlds of Victorian Fiction*, ed. Jerome H. Buckley (Cambridge, MA, and London, 1975).

King, Everard H., 'James Beattie, William Wordsworth, and the Evolution of Romantcism', *REAL: The Yearbook of Research in English and American Literature*, 3 (1985).

Kristeva, Julia, *Powers of Horror: An Essay on Abjection* (New York, 1982).

——, *The Revolution of Poetic Language*, trans. Margaret Waller (New York, 1984).

——, *In the Beginning Was Love: Psychoanalysis and Faith*, trans. Arthur Goldhammer (New York, 1988).

——, 'Women's Time', in *The Feminist Reader: Essays in Gender and the Politics of Literary Criticism*, ed. Catherine Belsey and Jane Moore (Basingstoke, 1989).

Kucich, Greg, 'Gendering the Canons of Romanticism: Past and Present', in *Romantic Masculinities*, ed. Tony Pinkney, Keith Hanley and Fred Botting, *News from Nowhere: Theory and Politics of Romanticism*, 2 (Keele, 1997).

Lacan, Jacques, 'Seminar on "The Purloined Letter"', *Yale French Studies*, 48 (1972).

——, 'Desire and the Interpretation of Desire in *Hamlet*', in *Yale French Studies*, 55/6 (1977).

——, *Ecrits: A Selection*, trans. Alan Sheridan (London, 1977).

——, *The Four Fundamental Concepts of Psycho-analysis*, ed. Jacques-Alain Miller, trans. Alan Sheridan (London, 1977).

Lamb, Charles and Mary, *The Letters of Charles and Mary Anne Lamb*, ed. Edwin W. Marrs, Jr, 3 vols (Ithaca and London, 1975–8).

Landon, Carol, 'Some Sidelights on *The Prelude*', in *Bicentenary Wordsworth Studies in Memory of John Alban Finch*, ed. Jonathan Wordsworth and Beth Darlington (Ithaca, NY, 1970).

Leavy, Stanley A., 'The Image and the Word: Further Reflections on Jacques Lacan', in *Interpreting Lacan*, ed. Joseph H. Smith and William Kerrigan (London and New Haven, CT, 1983).

Legg, J. Wickham, *English Church Life: From the Restoration to the Tractarian Movement, Considered in some of its Neglected or Forgotten Features* (London, 1914).

Legouis, Emile, *The Early Life of Wordsworth*, trans. J. W. Matthews (London, 1921).

——, *William Wordsworth and Annette Vallon* (London, 1922).

Lindop, Grevel, *The Opium-Eater: A Life of Thomas De Quincey* (London, 1981).

Liu, Alan, *Wordsworth: The Sense of History* (Stanford, CA, 1989).

Macaulay, Thomas Babington, ed. G. O. Trevelyan, *The Life and Letters of Lord Macaulay* (London, 1880).

——, *The History of England*, 8 vols (London, 1882).

Marx, Karl, *Class Struggles in France, 1848 to 1850* (Moscow, 1968).

Masson, David, *Essays Chiefly on the English Poets* (Cambridge, 1856).

Mellor, Anne K., 'Teaching Wordsworth and Women', in *Approaches to Teaching Wordsworth's Poetry*, ed. Spencer Hall with Jonathan Ramsey (New York, 1986).

——, ed., *Romanticism and Feminism* (Bloomington, IN, 1988).

——, *Romanticism and Gender* (London, 1993).

Milton, John, *The Poems of John Milton*, ed. John Carey and Alastair Fowler (London, 1968).

Moi, Toril, *Sexual / Textual Politics: Feminist Literary Theory* (London, 1985).

——, *The Kristeva Reader* (Oxford, 1986).

Moorman, Mary, *William Wordsworth: A Biography*, 2 vols (Oxford, 1967).

Moretti, Franco, *Signs Taken for Wonders: The Sociology of Literary Forms*, trans. Susan Fischer, David Forgacs and David Miller (London, 1983).

Morley, Henry, *Memoirs of Bartholomew Fair* (London, 1859).

Morus, Iwan Rhys, 'The Electric Ariel: Telegraphy and Commercial Culture in Early Victorian England', *Victorian Studies*, 39: 3 (Spring 1996).

Newey, Vincent and Philip Shaw (eds), *Mortal Pages, Literary Lives: Studies Nineteenth-Century Autobiography* (Aldershot, 1996).

Newlyn, Lucy, *Coleridge, Wordsworth and the Language of Allusion* (Oxford, 1986).

——, *'Paradise Lost' and the Romantic Reader* (Oxford, 1993).

Newman, J. H. (ed.), *Lives of the English Saints* (London, 1844).

——, *Tract Ninety, or, Remarks on Certain Passages in the Thirty-Nine Articles*, ed. A. W. Evans (London, 1933).

Nye, David, *Electrifying America: Social Meanings of a New Technology* (Cambridge, MA, 1990).

Oliver, Kelly, *Reading Kristeva: Unraveling the Double-bind* (Bloomington, IN, 1993).

Onorato, Richard, *The Character of the Poet: Wordsworth in* 'The Prelude' (Princeton, NJ, 1971).

Orwell, George, *The Collected Essays, Journalism and Letters of George Orwell*, ed. Sonia Orwell and Ian Angus, 4 vols (London, 1968).

Overton, John Henry and Elizabeth Wordsworth, *Christopher Wordsworth, Bishop of Lincoln, 1807–1885* (London, 1888).

Ozouf, Mona, *La Fête revolutionnaire, 1789–1799* (Paris, 1976).

Owen, Hugh, *The Lowther Family* (Chichester, 1990).

Page, Judith, *Wordsworth and the Cultivation of Women* (Berkeley, CA, 1994).

Paine, Thomas, *The Rights of Man*, ed. H. Collins (Harmondsworth, 1969).

Parker, Noel, *Portrayals of Revolution: Images, Debates and Patterns of Thought on the French Revolution* (Hemel Hempstead, 1990).

Paulson, Ronald, *Representations of Revolution, 1789–1820* (New Haven, CT, and London, 1983).

Paxton, John, *Companion to the French Revolution* (New York and Oxford, 1988).

Peek, Katherine Mary, *Wordsworth in England: Studies in Honour of His Fame* (New York, 1969).

Percy, Thomas, *Reliques of Ancient English Poetry* (London, 1765).

Phillimore, Robert, *The Ecclesiastical Law of the Church of England*, 2 vols (London, 1873).

Pinkney, Tony, Keith Hanley and Fred Botting (eds), *News from Nowhere: Theory and Politics of Romanticism* (Keele, 1995).

Reed, Mark L., *The Chronology of the Early Years, 1770–1799* (Cambridge, MA., 1967).

Richardson, Alan, *Literature, Education, and Romanticism: Reading as Social Practice, 1780–1832* (Cambridge, 1994).

Rieder, John, *Wordsworth's Counterrevolutionary Turn: Community, Virtue and Vision in the 1790s* (Newark and London, 1997).

Robinson, Henry Crabb, *Henry Crabb Robinson's Diary*, ed. T. Sadler, 3 vols (London, 1872).

——, *Correspondence of Crabb Robinson with the Wordsworth Circle*, ed. Edith J. Morley, 2 vols (Oxford, 1927).

——, *Henry Crabb Robinson on Books and their Writers*, ed. Edith J. Morley, 3 vols (London, 1938).

Roe, Nicholas, *Wordsworth and Coleridge: The Radical Years* (Oxford, 1988).

Ross, Marlon B., *The Contours of Masculine Desire: Romanticism and the Rise of Women's Poetry* (New York, 1989).

Roudinesco, Elisabeth, *Jacques Lacan*, trans. Barbara Bray (New York, 1997).

Ruskin, John, *The Works of John Ruskin*, ed. E. T. Cook and A. Wedderburn, 39 vols (London, 1903–12).

Schama, Simon, *Citizens: A Chronicle of the French Revolution* (Harmondsworth, 1989).

Schapiro, Barbara, *The Romantic Mother: Narcissistic Patterns in Romantic Poetry* (Baltimore, MD, 1983).

Scruton, Roger 'Man's Second Disobedience: a Vindication of Burke', in *The French Revolution and British Culture*, ed. Ceri Crossley and Ian Small (Oxford 1989).

Shakespeare, William, *Shakespeare's Dramatic Works, with Explanatory Notes: A new edition . . . by the Rev. S. Ayscough*, 3 vols (Dublin, 1790).

——, *'The Sonnets' and 'A Lover's Complaint'*, ed. Martin Dodsworth (London, 1995).

Shaver, Chester L. and Alice C. Shaver, *Wordsworth's Library: A Catalogue Including a List of Books Housed by Wordsworth for Coleridge from c. 1810 to c. 1830* (New York and London, 1979).

Shelley, Mary, *Frankenstein, or The Modern Prometheus*, ed. M. K. Joseph (Oxford, 1980).

Shelley, Percy Bysshe, *Shelley's Poetry and Prose*, ed. Ronald H. Reiman and Sharon B. Powers (New York, 1977).

Sieyès, Emmanuel Joseph, *What is the Third Estate?*, trans. M. Blondel, ed. S. E. Finer (London, 1963).

Simmons, Jack, *Southey* (London, 1945).

Simpson, David, *Irony and Authority in Romantic Poetry* (London, 1979).

Smith, Elsie, *An Estimate of William Wordsworth by his Contemporaries* (Oxford, 1932).

Smith, Olivia, *The Politics of Language, 1791–1819* (Oxford, 1984).

Spivak, Gayatri Chakravorty, 'Sex and History in *The Prelude* (1805), Book Nine to Thirteen', *Texas Studies in Literature and Language*, 23: 3 (Fall 1981).

Stephen, Leslie, *Hours in a Library*, 3 vols (London, 1892).

Taylor, A. J. P., *Revolutions and Revolutionaries* (Oxford and New York, 1981).

Trevelyan, G. M., *British History in the Nineteenth Century, 1782–1901* (London, 1928).

Vidler, Alec R., *The Church in an Age of Revolution: 1798 to the Present Day* (Harmondsworth, 1978).

Viswanathan, Gauri, *Masks of Conquest: Literary Study and British Rule in India* (London, 1989).

Weiskel, Thomas, *The Romantic Sublime: Studies in the Structure and Psychology of Transcendence* (Baltimore, MD, 1986).

West, Thomas, *A Guide to the Lakes in Cumberland, Westmorland and Lancashire*, 3rd edn (London, 1784).

Whitaker, Thomas Dunham *History and Antiquities of the Deanery of Craven* (London, 1805).

White, Norman, *Hopkins: A Literary Biography* (Oxford, 1992).

White, W. H., *An Examination of the Charge of Apostasy Against Wordsworth* (London and New York, 1898).

Williams, Raymond, *The Long Revolution* (London, 1961).

Woodcock, George, 'The Meaning of Revolution in Britain', *The French Revolution and British Culture*, ed. Ceri Crossley and Ian Small (Oxford, 1989).

Wordsworth, Christopher, *Memoirs of William Wordsworth*, 2 vols (London, 1851).

Wordsworth, Dorothy, *Journals of Dorothy Wordsworth: The Alfoxden Journal 1798; The Grasmere Journal 1800–1803*, 2nd edn, ed. Helen Darbishire, rev. Mary Moorman, 2 vols (London, 1971).

Wordsworth, Jonathan, *The Music of Humanity* (London, 1969).

——, *The Borders of Vision* (Oxford, 1982).

——, and Beth Darlington (eds), *Bicentenary Wordsworth Studies* (Ithaca, NY and London, 1970).

Wordsworth, William

Collected and historical editions:

The Poems of William Wordsworth, D. C. L., Poet Laureate (London, 1845).

Prose Works of William Wordsworth, ed. A. B. Grosart, 3 vols (London, 1876).

The Poetical Works of William Wordsworth, ed. William Knight, 8 vols (London, 1896).

Wordsworth: Poetical Works, ed. Thomas Hutchinson (London, 1904).

Poems and Extracts Chosen by William Wordsworth for an Album Presented to Lady Mary Lowther, Christmas, 1819 (London, 1905).

The Poetical Works of William Wordsworth, rev. edn, ed. Ernest de Selincourt and Helen Darbishire, 5 vols (Oxford, 1952–9).

The Prose Works of William Wordsworth, ed. W. J. B. Owen and Jane Worthington, 3 vols (Oxford, 1974).

William Wordsworth: The Poems, ed. John O. Hayden, 2 vols (Harmondsworth, 1977).

The Prelude:

The Prelude, ed. Ernest de Selincourt (Oxford, 1927, rev. edn, by Helen Darbishire, 1959).

The Prelude 1799, 1805, 1850, ed. Jonathan Wordsworth, M. H. Abrams and Stephen Gill (New York and London, 1979).

The Prelude: The Four Texts (1798, 1799, 1805, 1850), ed. Jonathan Wordsworth (Harmondsworth, 1995).

The Five-book Prelude, ed. Duncan Wu (Oxford, 1997).

From The Cornell Wordsworth, gen. ed. Stephen Parrish (Ithaca, NY, 1975–):
The Salisbury Plain Poems, ed. Stephen Gill (Ithaca, NY, and Hassocks, Sussex, 1975).
'The Ruined Cottage' and 'The Pedlar', ed. James Butler (Ithaca, NY, 1979).
Poems, in Two Volumes, and Other Poems, 1800–1807, ed. Jared Curtis (Ithaca, NY, 1983).
Descriptive Sketches, ed. Eric Birdsall, with the assistance of Paul M. Zall (Ithaca, NY, and London, 1984).
The White Doe of Rylstone, or, The Fate of the Nortons, ed. Kristine Dugas (Ithaca, NY, 1988).
Shorter Poems, 1807–1820, ed. Carl H. Ketcham (Ithaca, NY, and London, 1989).

Letters:

The *Letters of William and Dorothy Wordsworth*, gen. ed. Alan G. Hill, 8 vols (1967–93); vol. 1: rev. Chester L. Shaver (1967); vol. 2: rev. Mary Moorman (1969); vol. 3: rev. Mary Moorman and Alan G. Hill (1970); vol. 4: rev. Alan G. Hill (1978); vol. 5: rev. Alan G. Hill (1979); vol. 6: rev. Alan G. Hill (1982); vol. 7: rev. Alan G. Hill (1988); vol. 8: rev. Alan G. Hill (1993).

Young, Arthur, *Travels in France during the Years 1787, 1788 and 1789*, ed. Constantia Maxwell (Cambridge, 1950).
Young, Robert, 'The Eye and Progress of his Song: a Lacanian Reading of *The Prelude*', in *William Wordsworth's 'The Prelude'*, ed. Harold Bloom (New York, 1986).

Index

Works by Wordsworth are indexed under their titles.